LADIES FOR LIBERTY

LADIES FOR LIBERTY

Women Who Made a Difference
in American History

SECOND, EXPANDED EDITION

JOHN BLUNDELL

Algora Publishing
New York

Library of Congress Cataloging-in-Publication Data —

Blundell, John, 1952-
    Ladies for liberty: women who made a difference in American history / John Blundell.
        p. cm.
    Includes bibliographical references and index.
    ISBN 978-0-87586-864-6 (soft cover: alk. paper) — ISBN 978-0-87586-865-3 (hard
cover: alk. paper) — ISBN 978-0-87586-866-0 (ebook) 1. Women—United States—
Biography. 2. United States—Biography. 3. Women—United States—History. 4. United
States—History. I. Title.
    CT3260.B615 2011
    920.72—dc22
                                    2011014287

Front Cover: Popular image of Lady Liberty in the 1910s. Courtesy of Old Picture.

Printed in the United States

For Christine Violet Blundell (née Lowry, aka "Lucky")

TABLE OF CONTENTS

It should come as no surprise that throughout the United States' history, women have played an intrinsic (albeit, under appreciated) role in the movement for liberty. Women are caregivers; it is to be expected that they would be sensitive both to the needs of others as well as the effects of government policies on the most vulnerable. Yet all too frequently, the expansion of government services has been justified because such programs are for the "benefit of women."

As such, *Ladies for Liberty* serves an important role in combating the myth that women want, and benefit from, big government. Although their actions may have varied, the underlying motivation of these many women was the same — that self-determination is a virtue, and that individuals should be allowed to pursue their own ends, free from the coercion of others. How different the nation would be today if these women did not stand up for what they believed in!

The grassroots activism of 2009 and 2010 demonstrate that individual liberty and personal responsibility are still values that resonate with American women. From Sarah Palin's "mama grizzlies" to Tea Party organizers like Jenny Beth Martin, it has become abundantly clear that millions of American women have come to recognize that there are serious costs to a too big, intrusive, wasteful government.

They understand that government is strangling private business with costly mandates, high taxes, and uncertainty about what rules businesses can expect to operate under in the future.

But how many of these women know that today's political culture is only possible thanks to the groundwork lain by the *Ladies for Liberty* many years ago?

Modern-day Tea Party activists are following in the footsteps of activists like the Grimké sisters, Elizabeth Cady Stanton, and Sojourner Truth, who bravely organized social movements in the face of tremendous odds. Political pundits are translating ideas to the people in the same way as Mercy Otis Warren, Rose Wilder Lane, and Clare Boothe Luce, who gave voice to the truth. And academics are standing upon the shoulders of intellectual giants like Rose Director Friedman, Isabel Paterson, and Jane Jacobs, who challenged conventional wisdom through their scholarship.

Women today do not face the same challenges that these brave ladies did, but they still must combat cultural pressures that highlight women's weaknesses and encourage dependency. Affording women special treatment in order to be able to "compete" — although well intentioned — is itself an insult, as it implies that women are not capable of doing so on their merits alone. At the end of the day, the true essence of feminism is to not be dependent on anyone else — not a husband, not a father, and not the government — because women are just as adept, clever, and skilled as their male counterparts.

Today, women have opportunities that previous generations could never have dreamed of; they are graduating from colleges in record numbers, opening businesses, and achieving positions of power from the Cabinet to the boardroom. Through technological advances, women are able to more easily balance work and home life — opening up additional possibilities for employment, activism, and education. Consider the options that Abigail Adams or Harriet Tubman faced, versus how a woman can live her life today. Our foremothers would be pleased to see how easily a modern woman can empower herself!

Accordingly, it becomes all the more imperative that we use the tools available to us to continue pressing for reforms that will truly benefit future generations — promoting personal responsibility, individual liberty, and free markets. Only a robust, dynamic economy will be able to provide women with the continued opportunities to choose their own path — be it as an entrepreneur, a writer, an activist, or something else. Women themselves should be allowed to make those decisions, however — not government bureaucrats.

John Blundell's *Ladies for Liberty* serves as an important reminder of the struggles of our predecessors. The best way to honor their sacrifices is to carry on their work, and to teach our daughters that they, too, can make a difference in the lives of others.

Nicole Neily

Nicole Neily is the former executive director of the Independent Women's Forum, a Washington DC-based think tank that focuses on educating the public about the benefits of economic liberty and limited government.

In 2006 and 2007, I gave speeches on the achievements of Lady Thatcher in Colorado Springs and in Washington, DC (for The Heritage Foundation) and Dallas (for the Texas Public Policy Foundation). The reaction to those speeches was so overwhelmingly positive that I wrote the book *Margaret Thatcher: A Portrait of the Iron Lady* (Algora, 2008) to explain "Thatcherism" to America. This in turn led to many more speaking engagements on Lady Thatcher.

Inevitably discussion at these events turned to American equivalents to Lady T. Names would be bandied around such as Martha Washington, Abigail Adams and Ayn Rand, and everyone in the audience would nod their heads in agreement. But it was quite striking that once I moved beyond those three, audience recognition just plummeted. Many conservative- and libertarian-inclined women and men *au fait* with US current affairs simply did not seem to be aware of many of their foremothers who fought for liberty. That directly led me to write this book.

How did I select my ladies for liberty?

First, they had to be dead — no open-ended stories; their contribution had to be complete. Second, they had to have had an inner core of principles that could clearly be seen to be pro-liberty, pro individual responsibility, free markets, private property rights and the rule of law. Third, there had to be some jaw-dropping achievement in their stories. Fourth, I wanted to present a range of brilliant successes by century, geography, and area of expertise. And finally there should be as little overlap as possible — women have made outstanding achievements in so many fields, I felt there was no room to include both Elizabeth Cady Stanton *and* Susan B. Anthony (whose lives were so intertwined), for instance. Likewise, the tsunami of frontier novelists, however good they all were, could only be represented by one exemplar.

I strove for 20 unique stories that would inspire women of every stripe to take up the cudgels for liberty. Why? Because the crusade for limited government, for liberty, perhaps with the exception of the mid to late 1940s — see Chapters 13, 15, and 18 through 20 — has been male-dominated, yet women have ever so much to offer.

Thus, this book is a set of twenty stories that I hope will not only educate both men and women but also inspire more women to join the cause of liberty.

NOTE TO THE SECOND, EXPANDED EDITION

Responses to the first edition were so positive that in the summer of 2012, I added five more of what I consider to be the best stories in US Women's History, namely Anne Hutchinson, Clara Barton, Alice Paul, Rosa Parks, and Mildred Loving. Should you feel I have overlooked somebody worthy of inclusion in a third edition, please e-mail me with relevant details at johnblundell100@gmail.com; but do remember my criteria for inclusion as outlined in paragraph four above.

CHAPTER 1. ANNE HUTCHINSON

"A courageous exponent of civil liberty and religious toleration" — Inscription on Anne Hutchinson's State House monument in Boston, Massachusetts.

Dissident
July 1591–August 1643

BOSTON, MASSACHUSETTS

If America has a Founding Mother, then ANNE MARBURY HUTCHINSON has foremost claim to the title. In just nine years (1634–1643), she fought for religious liberty, faced down the State, became an astonishing exemplar to other women both professionally as a midwife and philosophically as a religious lecturer, and co-founded the state of Rhode Island. She defended Native Americans but was finally butchered by them.

She was born to Francis Marbury and Bridget Dryden (an antecedent of playwright John Dryden) in Alford, a small town in the English east coast county of Lincolnshire. (Coincidentally, Lincolnshire was also the birthplace of Margaret Thatcher, more than 300 years later, and there are interesting parallels with the life of Britain's only woman prime minister to date.)

Francis Marbury was a Puritan minister imprisoned twice in London for his attacks on the leadership of the Anglican Church, especially what he perceived to be poor leadership by the bishops and the poor training of ministers.

On his release, he was sent 140 miles northeast to Alford to become curate at its church and schoolmaster at its grade school. Among his pupils was John Smith, who was to become Captain John Smith, founder of the colony of Jamestown, Virginia, and the man who charted the New England coast.

Francis Marbury had three children with his first wife before she died. Within a year, he married Bridget, who gave birth to 15 children, including Anne. Twelve of them survived.

Anne's father was soon in trouble again for criticizing the church hierarchy and was sentenced to house arrest. This gave him the time to devote to educating his children — five girls at that point, including Anne. Educating women was a very rare occurrence in 1590s England.

Francis Marbury was thus an enormous influence on his fourth daughter, Anne, just as Alf Roberts would be on Margaret Thatcher (née Roberts). While Alf Roberts the grocer instilled Methodism, individual responsibility and personal morality in his daughter, Anne had her father to thank for opening her eyes to a Puritan ethic, and a radical non-conformist Presbyterianism in which leaders of the church would be chosen by the congregation and not the monarch.

Eventually Francis was reinstated and in 1605 when Anne was 14, he was called to lead the church of St. Martin's in the Vintry, the wine district of the City of London, England's bustling trading and financial district. At that time London was the largest city and port in the world. For Anne, this represented a huge change from the rural tranquility of Lincolnshire. She moved from a town of fewer than 1,000 people to one with a population of close to 250,000.

Francis died suddenly, aged 55, when Anne was not quite 20. She had, however, maintained a link with Alford and a childhood friend called William Hutchinson, the son of a prosperous cloth merchant and sheep farmer, who was a few years older than her. They married in London in 1612 and together moved back to Alford.

Over the next two decades, Anne had 15 children. Her husband's business prospered and they would have enjoyed financial security and high social status.

They were pious, too, and began visiting different churches in Lincolnshire. In doing so, they heard of a young Puritan minister the Rev John Cotton (1584–1652) who was preaching in Boston, another Lincolnshire town some six hours' ride from Alford. But they went — six hours there, six hours back, in all weathers, with the often pregnant Anne riding pillion on her husband's horse. The couple was riveted by Cotton's four-hour services. He preached about the "covenant of grace," the central tenet of which was that all those who have faith in God can go to heaven. For Anne, this was a refreshing departure from the traditional Anglican — Church of England — view that in order to reach heaven you had to meet a covenant of works; in other words, you had to obey a set of biblical rules interpreted by and enforced by ministers. This approach heavily empowered and favored men, who exercised a significant degree of control over their wives and daughters, while the covenant of grace opened up the possibility for women of a personal relationship with God. It was a highly individualist philosophy — everything was between you and God and nothing to do with your husband, your father or the State.

Cotton's covenant of grace, shutting out as it did men and a male-run state machinery from any interaction with God, was enormously appealing to Anne, whose own maverick father had equipped her with the skills to think for herself. She wanted nothing more to do with the collectivist approach of the covenant of works.

But such thinking undermined the fabric of society and was nothing if not revolutionary for the time. In fact, it was so revolutionary that these principles would eventually inform the separation in the US of Church and State, enshrined in the Constitution 150 years later. But it was not there at the founding of America. Anne Hutchinson, who would soon move to Massachusetts to join a Puritan community led by John Cotton, was to have a palpable influence on the shaping of the US.

Near to Alford lay Bilsby, where the Rev John Wheelwright preached. He was Anne's husband's brother-in-law and very much in tune with Cotton. At that time, without the mass media we have today, church attendance took on a significance we probably cannot appreciate in the twenty-first century.

Most homes had a Bible but maybe as few as only three or four other books. The weekly, often twice-weekly, sermon or lecture by the minister, lasting up to two hours, was the big show in town. People wanted to talk about it and ruminate over it. So Anne began to host pioneering "conventicles" where women could debate and discuss matters. The authorities in England were not amused — women were banned from holding and leading such meetings unless they were for the benefit of their children and servants.

By 1633, Cotton's doctrine was considered so inflammatory that he was forced into hiding. He fled to Massachusetts, accompanied by Anne's eldest child Edward. In 1634, the 43-year-old Anne, her 48-year-old husband William, and all their remaining children followed, together with William's elderly mother Susanna.

The trip across the Atlantic took two months and the ship, the *Griffin*, was the very same one Cotton and Edward had taken a year earlier. There was on board a minister, the Rev. Zechariah Symmes, who preached often. Anne organized meetings for female passengers as they sailed, heavily criticizing Symmes for his pro-works views.

On landing in Boston Symmes promptly reported her to the authorities as a heretic. The "covenant of grace" approach espoused by Anne Hutchinson threatened to loosen the stranglehold the Church and state — effectively the same entity — had on individuals and society. Fortunately for Anne, the Governor of the Massachusetts Bay Colony, Sir Henry Vane, was a supporter and no action was taken against her.

The Hutchinsons at first fit seamlessly into Boston, its ways, and its society. They built a substantial house and purchased hundreds of acres. William set up in the cloth trade and Anne practiced as a midwife, a respected profession. John Wheelwright had also migrated so Anne had her two favorite ministers close to hand. She restarted her "conventicles," where she would reiterate and interpret the main points in Cotton's latest sermon. They became so popular that her large house could not accommodate all the attendees at one sitting and she was forced to hold two meetings a week. At first these prayer meetings were for women only, but soon men started to accompany their wives. Even Governor Vane would attend during his sole one-year term and sit at her right hand. Her followers were soon known as Hutchinsonians. Some 60 to 80 came to every meeting. Self-confident and combative, she proved a magnetic speaker with listeners preferring to hear her views than the sermons delivered from the pulpit. Hutchinsonians tended not to be first-wave immigrants such as military men or ministers or aristocrats. Rather they came in following waves and were traders and entrepreneurs, individualists as opposed to members of the establishment.

By 1636, Anne had trodden on so many priests' toes and offended so many senior political and religious leaders, in particular John Winthrop, the newly re-elected Governor, that trouble was inevitable. He wrote of her that she was "a woman of haughty and fierce carriage, a nimble wit and active spirit, and a very voluble tongue." She had denounced all the ministers except for Cotton and Wheelwright; she and her followers had walked out of church before or during sermons; and in early 1637, she opposed the military expedition that became known as the Pequot War, during which 700 members of that Native American tribe were burned alive and the survivors enslaved.

The Massachusetts Bay Colony was an astonishingly centralized society governed under a royal charter from the British monarch. There was no real separation of church and state and all three branches of government — executive, legislative, and judicial — were gathered together in one body, the General Court. This was headed by the annually elected Governor and all the Church ministers sat there.

Anne challenged the authority of the ministers, all of them male; by her example she exposed and challenged the subordination of women generally; and by rejecting the authority of the government over religion paved the way for separation of Church and state. If religion became a matter between you and God, then ministers, the Church and even the state itself became much diminished at best, and at worst irrelevant in the eyes of her critics.

She was brought to civil trial before the General Court in November 1637 accused of sedition. For two days she stood before the seated Winthrop and dozens of men who were for the most part both her judges and her accusers. Rhetorically she could not be bettered. She found biblical quotations for all her positions as the Court struggled to prove any case against her.

Anne and the Governor clashed swords time and again. He tried to prove that by hosting meetings for women she was causing them to neglect their families by taking them away from the domestic sphere.

"There is a clear rule in Titus, that the older women should instruct the younger and then I must have a time wherein I must do it," Anne argued, invoking Paul's letter to the early Christian leader Titus in the New Testament.

Winthrop rebutted her quotation with an admonishment from Corinthians: "Let your women keep silence in the churches; for it is not permitted unto them to speak."

Quick as a flash, Anne parried: "Yes, but that is inside."

She also pointed out that as her female pupils sat and listened, their hands were busy knitting or sewing or crocheting.

After two long days it became clear to Anne that the outcome was predetermined. At this point she spoke her mind without fear or flinching, telling her accusers that they had no power over her and could do nothing to harm her. Only God had that power. Then she issued a dire warning: they should consider carefully what they might do to her, for "if you go on in this course you begin, you will bring a curse upon you and your posterity, and the mouth of the Lord has spoken it."

A shocked silence turned to jeers from the bench and her detractors in the public gallery — how dare a woman lecture them in public, and in such terms? Anne Hutchinson was put under house arrest at the home of Joseph Weld, brother of the prominent Puritan minister the Rev. Thomas Weld, while awaiting a church trial the following March. "Prisoner" Hutchinson was allowed few visitors of her own choosing. Instead, access was granted to local non-Hutchinsonian ministers who either wanted to convert her to their way of thinking or to trap her into some blasphemy that could be used against her.

Her two-day church trial began on March 15, 1638. Anne Hutchinson and all her leading supporters were excommunicated, disenfranchised and banished. They were given three months to leave town. Some 75 others were ordered to be humiliatingly "disarmed" of their muskets unless they openly repudiated her views.

More than a score of her supporters, including her husband William, had signed the Portsmouth Compact under which they formed a political body focused on moving to settle in the Providence Plantation Colony founded in 1636 by Roger Williams, an English theologian who strongly favored religious freedom, separation of church and state, fair dealing with Native Americans, and abolition. They were deeply troubled by Governor Winthrop's alien exclusion law, which was his attempt to block further waves of migrants who might well be Hutchinsonians, and they despised his newly imposed price and wage controls and his banishment of the Rev. John Wheelwright.

In anticipation of the verdict of the church court, most of them had already headed south to what would become Rhode Island. Anne walked in snow for six days to join them. With her input — her husband had become the second Governor of this fledgling state — trial by jury and the separation of Church and state were quickly established.

However, following her husband William's death, aged 55 in 1642, the new Governor began talks with Massachusetts about uniting the English colonies.

Anxious, Anne quickly decided to move her entire household of 16 children, servants and in-laws into Dutch territory. They went to Split Rock in New Netherland, which today is in the northern Bronx, New York City. From the start, there were clear signs that the local Siwanoy people were unhappy about their presence but she had opposed the Pequot War in Massachusetts and enjoyed good relations with the Narragansett in Rhode Island, so was confident about developing local friendships. But the Dutch Governor Willem Kieft effectively declared war on the Siwanoy, a move that was to have tragic consequences. Chief Wampage warned Anne's settlement of his imminent attack and said that they should leave, but, unarmed and unprepared, they did not heed his words. The warriors expected to find an empty house but all its occupants were present except Anne's daughter, who was out picking berries. All inside were butchered and burnt, including Anne, while Susanna, aged seven, was kidnapped because — it is said — of her red hair. The Siwanoy held her for some six years and then ransomed her back to some older siblings in Boston who had not relocated with Anne.

Anne had stepped firmly outside the domestic sphere; she was an outspoken preacher who easily attracted followers. Male ministers felt deeply threatened by her personality and her ideas which challenged all authority except that of God.

She was a strong individualist, grounded in her belief in liberty and the role of the individual under God.

Chapter 2. Mercy Otis Warren

"The most remarkable woman who lived in the days of the American Revolution." — 19th-century historian Elizabeth Ellet

Writer and Revolutionary
September 14, 1728–October 19, 1814

PLYMOUTH, MASSACHUSETTS

Throughout the 1760s, revolutionary feelings were running high in the Thirteen Colonies; many Americans wanted independence from the British. The busiest port in the thirteen colonies was Boston, and it was very badly affected by taxes imposed by the British government. The resulting mood there was particularly febrile. Lawyer James "Jemmy" Otis, whose five-hour speech in court in 1761 was said by future second President John Adams to have sparked the American Revolution, led his intensely political family in openly agitating for independence and against the British. Tories, sympathetic to England, hated him and would confront him on the streets. One day in early September 1769, Jemmy entered a British coffee shop on State Street, knowing it was frequented by his enemies, and was instantly attacked by customs officer John Robinson — whom Jemmy had criticized in a newspaper article. A brawl ensued and Jemmy was badly beaten, incurring severe blows to his head. He was never the same man again, suffering lapses in lucidity, and would be declared legally incompetent in 1771.

Jemmy's sister, MERCY OTIS WARREN, now picked up the revolutionary baton. She had had five sons, but she was done with birthing. Many of the key men in the revolutionary movement, who included not only Jemmy but also her own husband the revolutionary politician James Warren, often met at the Warrens' house in Plymouth, Massachusetts. Mercy knew the movers and shakers, and the issues, and she was passionate about liberty.

She began by moving the brain-damaged Jemmy into her home and took over his substantial correspondence. Mercy had other plans, too. In a letter to her friend Abigail Adams, who would become the second First Lady of the United States (Chapter 4), she wrote that she believed that exposing the British through ridicule in the style of the French satirist Molière would be more effective than any number of ponderous sermons. She was keen to engage in a fight for the hearts and minds of the colonists. Her first satirical play, *The Adulateur*, appeared anonymously in 1772. This and future poems and plays angered the British while hugely entertaining and energizing those who sought independence.

Mercy Otis Warren was to become the single most important woman of the Revolutionary era. Not only did she stir patriotic fervor with her writings, she also counseled prominent leaders from John and Samuel Adams to Thomas Jefferson and George Washington, influenced the Bill of Rights and, with her *History of the Rise, Progress, and Termination of the American Revolution*, became the first woman to write a history of the United States.

From an early age, Mercy was used to being a woman in a man's world. She was the third of thirteen children and the only girl born to Colonel James Otis and Mary Alleyne Otis in the Plymouth Colony of Barnstable, near Cape Cod. Colonel Otis was a prosperous trader, military officer, farmer, politician, lawyer, and judge. His wife was descended from Mayflower passenger Edward Dotey. The children grew up hearing their father's many complaints about ongoing interference by the British; and intellectual conversation, revolutionary ideals and serious books filled the Otis household.

Colonel Otis hired (for payment in farm produce) his brother-in-law, the Yale graduate Reverend Jonathan Russell, vicar of West Barnstable, to prepare the two elder children, Jemmy and Joseph, for college. Mercy sat in and listened, having access to all the same college preparatory classes as her brothers except for formal Latin and Greek. This came on top of all the other skills expected of her, such as needlework and cooking.

Jemmy and Mercy were inseparable, sharing a love of learning as well as liberty. Even when Jemmy went off to college, his sister wanted to continue studying.

When Jemmy was later apprenticed to a Boston lawyer and their father entered the Massachusetts House of Representatives, Mercy corresponded with both regularly, thus beginning a lifetime of letter writing.

Through Jemmy, Mercy met her future husband. James Warren's family owned a large farm and his grandfather Richard had also sailed to America on the Mayflower. It would have been hard to find a stronger grouping of Lockean Whigs than the Warren and Otis families. They were followers of John Locke, whose writings inspired the most famous phrase of the Declaration of Independence, "Life, Liberty and the Pursuit of Happiness." Locke taught that revolution was a right, even an obligation. The Whigs (as opposed to pro-British Tories) identified with the political opposition to King George III and his Prime Minister Lord North in Great Britain.

Mercy and James became engaged in 1748; they married six years later in 1754, when she was 26 and had a dowry of substance; he was 28. They had five boys James (1757–1821), Winslow (1759–1791), Charles (1762–1784), Henry (1764–1828) and George (1766–1800).

The people who frequented Mercy's fairly affluent circles were talking more and more about independence, in particular the young John Adams, who would become the second president of the United States, and her brother Jemmy. Local politics became tense as Whigs such as Colonel Otis found themselves marginalized, while Tories such as Thomas Hutchinson won preferment from the British. The British now abandoned salutary neglect and started to enforce the 100-year-old Navigation Act of 1651, demanding that all American imports and exports flow through London regardless of origin or final destination.

From 1757 onward, Mercy's home in Plymouth became a regular meeting place for patriots disturbed by this development. They became even more upset by the passage of the Writs of Assistance in 1760, which allowed British customs officials to enter any property, including private homes, unannounced and confiscate any goods they suspected of being smuggled. On February 24, 1761, came a turning point in the struggle for independence. Supported by Mercy, Jemmy, acting on behalf of colonial merchants, brought a complaint before Chief Justice Thomas Hutchinson, sitting with four colleagues, against the Writs of Assistance. Jemmy's passionate oration against this invasion of freedom gave us the immortal phrase "Taxation without representation is tyranny." John Adams, who was present, wrote "American independence was then and there born." Although he lost his case, Jemmy gained stature and the popular nickname of "The Patriot."

Matters escalated. In 1764 came the Sugar Act and new controls on the lumber trade (many revolutionary flags featured pine trees), new taxes on coffee and sugar, and better enforcement of old taxes on molasses. Then 1765 saw the dawn of the Stamp Act, which taxed every piece of paper from a will to a playing card. The Warren caucus — all men except for Mercy — was outraged and quickly called representatives from throughout the Colonies to New York City to protest this Act in a petition to King George III. The petition was a success — the Stamp Act went in 1766 — but many, including Mercy, were fearful of what might replace it. Their suspicions were well founded. The next year, 1767, saw the Townshend Act which built on the Sugar Act and imposed taxes on a range of everyday items, including lead, paint, glass, lace and silk.

Jemmy and Samuel Adams, cousin to John and another of the Founding Fathers, hatched the idea of sending a circular letter to leaders throughout the Colonies urging a boycott of imported goods from England. They would substitute home-grown and manufactured items such as Liberty Tea, made from American herbs, instead of tea imported from India via London. Tension rose as the boycott took hold — those who bought English products risked having their names published in local newspapers.

The boycotts led to unemployment, business gridlock and eventually the Boston Massacre of 1770 in which British troops, known as the Redcoats or "lobsterbacks," shot dead five patriots. Boston was split between Tories and Whigs. The Governor was recalled to London and the much-hated Thomas Hutchinson took over.

Mercy's play *The Adulateur* seized on the mood of the times. Would-be revolutionaries clearly recognized Rapatio as Hutchinson, Brutus as Jemmy, and Upper Servia as Boston. Whigs were depicted as noble freedom lovers and Tories as greedy rapacious, self-centered nepotists. Brutus foretells the sticky end awaiting the mad, bullying Rapatio. The satire captured the public and political imagination. From then on Hutchinson became known to all patriots as Rapatio. Mercy was hitting above her weight.

Her next play, *The Defeat* (1773), was in part inspired by letters that Founding Father Benjamin Franklin found in London from Hutchinson and a colleague urging the British government to impose harsh measures on the Massachusetts colony. Franklin sent the letters to the Speaker of the Massachusetts House, Thomas Cushing, hoping this would show that Hutchinson, not the British, was the real culprit. Cushing showed the letters to several people, including James Warren, and Mercy's pen was soon at work excoriating Hutchinson in the guise of Rapatio and quickly sending her villain to meet his maker.

Writing allowed Mercy an outlet for her political sentiments at a time when women played no overt part in political life. Both of the plays were highly popular and tipped many people toward the patriots' view.

She had a part in revolutionary decision-making, too, hosting meetings of a mini caucus. One evening after dark in October 1772 she, her husband James

Warren and John and Samuel Adams met to discuss coordination and communication between the Thirteen Colonies. She and her husband recalled the success of the boycott circular sent out by Jemmy and Samuel in 1768 and argued that formally constituted Committees of Correspondence be established throughout the Colonies to spread information, coordinate action, and keep revolutionary fervor alive. John and Samuel Adams added further detailed insights and within 18 months over 300 such committees existed throughout every colony.

May 1773 also saw the passage of the Tea Act which gave the British-owned East India Company a monopoly. Patriots began holding "tea parties" at which chests of tea would be destroyed. The most famous of them all was the Boston Tea Party, when on December 6 a group of revolutionaries camouflaged as Mohawk Native Americans dumped 90,000 pounds of tea into Boston's harbor.

John Adams wrote to his friend James Warren, saying he wished somebody had the talent to popularize this event in a poem. Mercy took this rather obvious hint and penned *The Squabble of the Sea Nymphs*.

On top of her poems, plays, and revolutionary activities, Mercy engaged in a vast body of correspondence with leading patriots such as John and Abigail Adams. They discussed the boycott of British goods and whether or not war was necessary; all wanted an independent America where women had more rights. It particularly rankled with Mercy that the British would not allow women to be involved in politics.

But worse was to come from the British in the form of the Coercive Acts of 1774, which the patriots immediately branded the Intolerable Acts. These Acts of the British Parliament, led by Lord North, forced the colonists to feed and house British troops and gave control of Boston harbor to the British Royal Navy to ensure all trade was kept in British hands. Any British official accused of a misdeed would receive his hearing not in America but back in Britain. This was hardly likely to placate the colonists.

The result was the first Continental Congress of September 1774 in Philadelphia, where 56 men from 12 of the Thirteen Colonies (nearly all of them members of Mercy's Committees of Correspondence) gathered to vote for another boycott of British products. But this time they went further: they opted to train soldiers for a militia.

Mercy's personal response came in the form of a new poem, *"To the Hon J Winthrop Esq.,"* in which Clarissa and Prudentia buy British goods but true patriots do without (or make their own). This was followed in 1775 by *The Group*, a play which pits the weak, corrupt British against the strong, principled patriots. Once again it found great favor with the public.

War had become inevitable. The new British Governor of Massachusetts, General Thomas Gage, set out to seize munitions and arrest the prominent patriots Samuel Adams and John Hancock. Revolutionary messenger Paul Revere alerted the colonists and, with skirmishes at Lexington and Concord April 19, 1775, saw the start of the War of Revolution with the Declaration of Independence being signed July 4, 1776, by 56 men from all thirteen colonies.

Throughout the war Mercy Otis Warren continued to write poems, plays and pamphlets as well as keeping notes for what became her history, her magnum opus. She also for a spell of time acted as her husband's secretary as he took on more responsibilities, which included recruiting, arming and paying patriot soldiers. The Battle of Saratoga had been a heavy defeat for the British, led by General Burgoyne, who surrendered in October 1777. But Burgoyne, fancying his talents as a playwright, penned *The Blockade of Boston*, which ridiculed the colonists and praised the Redcoats. Mercy responded anonymously with her play *The Blockheads*, a savage, earthy and biting satire. It was quickly printed and passed hand to hand, tent to tent, boosting patriot morale enormously. Her plays were read rather than performed.

As the Revolutionary War ended in victory for the patriots, Mercy became bitter about the lack of preferment for her husband. She saw younger men winning promotion and taking power, and she detested the farmers and merchants who had profited greatly from events and now gave themselves all manner of airs and graces. "The progress of the American Revolution has been so rapid and such the alteration of manners, the blending of characters, and the new train of ideas that almost universally prevail, that the principles which animated to the noblest exertions have been nearly annihilated," she observed in her history. Out of this concern came yet more plays: *The Sack of Rome* and *The Ladies of Castile*, which address the problem of liberty and the need to safeguard moral and social values in this changing society.

Of her five sons, three predeceased her and another, John, was invalided home from the Navy, having lost a leg in action. He became his mother's secretary and her eyes, as her own sight deteriorated.

In 1781, Mercy and James gained somewhat vicarious pleasure from the purchase of Milton Hill, the recently deceased Hutchinson's former home 14 miles outside Boston. In the same year the Peace Treaty was signed, and Mercy began her history project, much encouraged by John Adams. It would take her a quarter of a century to complete. She was greatly inspired by the English Whig historian Catherine Macaulay, who had published a multi-volume history of England. The author had sent a copy of the first volume to Jemmy with an admiring inscription and this led Mercy into a correspondence. Catherine Macaulay later visited while Mercy was at work on her American history. But by 1790, she was back in Plymouth, putting aside her history for ten years as she grieved over the deaths of her sons, in particular Winslow.

The Articles of Confederation had been signed in 1781, but in some eyes this early constitution was turning out to be inadequate. After the Revolution many farmers had returned home from the army penniless, with lives and businesses to rebuild. But the new state governments were soon imposing high taxes — some thought to fund the war — and the courts and debtors' prisons filled up with those who could not afford to pay. Revolution veteran and former farmhand Daniel Shays started a rebellion for lower taxes and a moratorium on debt collection until people could become re-established. Shays' armed uprising did not last long, but Mercy and her husband let their sympathies with his case be widely known. Both wrote under pseudonyms, she pamphlets, he newspaper articles.

John Adams was scandalized, outraged by any questioning of the sanctity of the courts, while Thomas Jefferson, at that point minister (ambassador) to France, wrote that "a little bit of rebellion now and again is a good thing." As a result, Mercy was delighted when the Republican Jefferson stopped the Federalist Adams from winning a second presidential term in 1800. She was even more pleased when Jefferson rescinded the Alien and Sedition Acts signed by John Adams in 1798 which, as well as dealing with citizenship, deportation and imprisonment of foreigners, had criminalized the writing of articles critical of the government. Twenty-five anti-federalist papers had closed when their publishers were arrested.

In 1787, the Constitutional Convention met in Philadelphia under the chairmanship of George Washington. Later two camps were to emerge, the Federalists, such as John Adams, who were in favor of the new constitution, and Anti-Federalists such as Samuel Adams and Thomas Jefferson. The Anti-Federalists were concerned about two things. First, they feared that too much power was being given to too few people and second that there was nothing to guarantee rights. Mercy's pamphlet *Observations on the New Constitution* aired her concerns about these dangerous encroachments of powers. Only the creation of the Bill of Rights in 1791 calmed their fears.

With matters settled and the British gone, Mercy began to publish openly and in 1790 a collection of her writing came out as *Poems, Dramatic and Miscellaneous*. It was dedicated to George Washington.

When her three-volume *History of the Rise, Progress and Termination of the American Revolution* (today published in two volumes by Liberty Press of Indianapolis, Indiana) was finally completed in 1805, a subscription list was raised. Thomas Jefferson, then President, ordered copies for his entire Cabinet, but John Adams hated it. After a bitter exchange of letters with Mercy Warren concerning his competence and her suspicions that he was not a true Republican at heart but pro-monarchy, the old allies did not correspond again until the fall of 1813, not even on the death of James Warren in 1808. As a memorial to her late husband, Mercy wrote an eleven-line acrostic poem in which the first letter of each line spelt out his name when read downwards: JAMESWARREN.

A longstanding mutual friend of the Adams and the Warren families was Governor Elbridge Gerry (famous for constructing a district for his party in the shape of a salamander, hence the term "gerrymander," which today means altering electoral boundaries to engineer a desired result). He managed to reconcile John Adams' wife Abigail with Mercy in 1812. Later that year, through her son, Mercy kept up extensive correspondence including letters to Abigail's son, John Quincy Adams, who would become the sixth President in 1825. Suddenly, in October 1814, she fell ill and after a four-day illness passed away on October 19, 1814, aged 86 years.

Mercy Otis Warren's achievements were impressive, especially at a time when women were excluded from politics. She helped to awaken and sustain revolutionary ardor across Massachusetts and far beyond with her poems and plays mocking the British. They offered not only important political comment but also a psychological boost in difficult times. As a leading member of the Warren caucus she was a prominent strategist and activist. She influenced the Constitutional Convention through her pamphlets and her correspondence influenced at least four of the first six presidents. Her strongly voiced opinions in the two decades after the conclusion of the Revolutionary War and her history rightly earned her the sobriquet "Conscience of the American Revolution."

Chapter 3. Martha Washington

"Keep all your matters in order yourself without depending on others as that is the only way to be happy." — Martha Washington

Revolutionary
June 2, 1731 — May 22, 1802

MOUNT VERNON, VIRGINIA

MARTHA WASHINGTON was a woman of routine: every late fall between 1775 and 1781 when by mutual agreement the fighting with the British ended for the winter, she traveled to join her husband General George Washington for a few months. Then, every spring, as the fighting resumed in earnest, she traveled back to their Mount Vernon home. Throughout those winter months every year she was tireless in her efforts to encourage, succor and provide for all around her while setting a sterling example of steadfastness. This was a revolution and she was there right in the thick of things.

She was brought up as Martha Dandridge on a tobacco plantation of several hundred acres 25 miles from the then Virginia colonial capital of Williamsburg. The eldest of eight to survive infancy, she was taught reading, writing and math, probably by her mother Frances. The bulk of her education was more practical in nature, following the norm among girls of her class in the eighteenth century. Needlework, music and how to manage a household would surely have featured on her home-schooled curriculum, but it is likely she also mastered a range of skills that would astonish us today, including plantation management and animal husbandry.

The family, in common with most, was self-reliant. There were no stores; people either grew or made what they needed or they went without. Once a year the British ships would arrive to pick up the tobacco harvest and Martha's father John would have pre-ordered just a few imported items. These might include luxury goods such as satin, china and nutmeg, and farm implements such as scythes and axes.

Aged 17, Martha began to see more and more of a bachelor neighbor, Daniel Parke Custis, who was twenty years her senior and manager of one of his family's many plantations just four miles away. But when they decided to marry, there was an obstacle in the shape of Daniel's father, John Custis IV. He wanted Daniel to marry a cousin, but neither party was in favor. John Custis IV threatened to disinherit Daniel, even going so far as to give away family silver rather than countenance the thought of it falling into Martha's hands. And he let the whole world know what he was doing and why.

During 1749, the 18-year-old Martha contrived to meet John to persuade him to change his mind. The evidence for this is a letter to Daniel from his friend James Power, who also lived in Williamsburg. Power states that John Custis has asked him "to let you know that he heartily and willingly consents to your marriage with Miss Dandridge." Daniel's friend reports that this dramatic change of heart is apparently all down "to a prudent speech of her own," but he ends by advising them to "hurry down immediately" in case Daniel's father should reconsider. However, John Custis IV was soon to pass away, in November 1749. Out of respect, the marriage was postponed to May 15, 1750. When they wed, Martha, at the age of 19, became mistress of several homes, 300 slaves and some 18,000 acres of farmland, along with a healthy bank balance.

Martha immediately began to produce the sons and daughters expected of her; the first two, David and Frances, died in childhood. John, known as Jacky, was to die in his twenties and Martha, nicknamed Patsy, died in her teens. Their father, Daniel Custis, died intestate in July 1757, leaving his 26-year-old widow with two children and a large fortune. The lack of a will meant that common law now dictated that she inherit one third of the estate with Jacky and Patsy enjoying the remainder under her trusteeship. There is evidence that Martha was an accomplished businesswoman, dealing with tobacco exports.

Accounts vary as to how widow Martha Custis met bachelor Colonel George Washington. But they would surely have known of each other. They were of a similar age, Washington being a little under a year younger, and both well-known Virginians: he for his military prowess in the French and Indian War, securing the borders of the colonies over the mountains to the west in the Ohio

Valley, and she for her wealth, manners, and positive outlook. As she said of herself: "I am determined to be cheerful and happy in whatever situation I may find myself. For I have learned that the greater part of our misery or unhappiness is determined not by our circumstance but by our disposition."

Washington was a surveyor as well as a military man and he also leased 2,200 acres at Mount Vernon. This was four times the size of Martha's original family plantation and he would eventually inherit it from his elder brother's widow. The couple became engaged in the summer of 1758, and before they were married in January 1759, Washington had fought the French again and then resigned his commission when he was elected a Burgess from Frederick County in the House of Burgesses (the legislative body that was a precursor to today's Virginia House of Delegates). Consequently, he married Martha in a suit rather than a uniform, at her plantation home of White House.

Martha's next 15 years have been described as idyllic. At the same time relations with the government in London deteriorated, something that had a strong bearing on her later life.

George Washington's personal highs included his harmonious relationship with his wife's children, friendships with the intellectual elite of Northern Virginia including their close neighbor the statesman and Founding Father George Mason, his ongoing experiments in agricultural techniques and his election to represent Fairfax County in the House of Burgesses. For Martha fulfillment came in the shape of the engagement of her son Jacky.

The couple worked well as a team. While George Washington was responsible for the financial aspects of Mount Vernon and the Custis estate, Martha took charge of the harvest, including the preparation and preserving of the herbs, vegetables, fruit, dairy produce and meat produced there. As well as food, the estate produced medicines and household products. She also oversaw a large staff of servants and slaves.

The lows included the lack of any children of their own and the death of Patsy.

The deterioration of relations with London was fast, furious and mostly unexpected. In just a few years a tsunami of regulations and taxes reached the Eastern seaboard from Britain. Martha and George went from being loyal subjects of the king to reluctant rebels to leading the Revolution. Mount Vernon and its grounds and outbuildings became a hive of small businesses, the result of George and Martha Washington's involvement in a group committed to avoiding importation or consumption of British products. Substitution was their mantra as they trawled lists of goods regularly imported for items they could manufacture. This was their way of hitting back at and hurting the British.

George Washington traveled to Philadelphia for the Continental Congress of 1774 that saw the boycott of British goods enacted. He went with George Mason's advice in his ears and Patrick Henry and Edmund Pendleton for company. He also took with him Martha's counsel and encouragement, as theirs was a household in which the women's voices were clearly heard. "I hope you will all stand firm," she told the other two delegates. "I know George will."

Royal Governor Lord Dunmore dissolved the House of Burgesses in the face of its perceived disloyalty, and the Virginia Conventions then served as a temporary government. George Washington attended the first Convention that year and the second in March 1775. He was again selected to attend the forthcoming second Continental Congress to be held once more in Philadelphia. But before he could travel there in May events began to overtake political discussion with the confrontation of April 19 between American patriots and British Redcoats at Lexington and Concord, which reverberated around the world.

The Congress acted quickly as Massachusetts delegate John Adams proposed that George Washington be promoted to General and made Commander-in-Chief of the many poorly organized militia units with the object of forming a Continental Army. It was a practical appointment as Washington had fought before; it was also highly political, with a delegate from the Northeast proposing a Southerner. The rebels in Massachusetts knew they needed the South. Virginia was its biggest and richest state and George Washington was its natural leader. He accepted on the condition that he was paid only expenses and not one cent in salary.

After writing scores of letters to Martha and his managers, neighbors and friends, General Washington rode to Cambridge, Massachusetts and quickly realized he would not be seeing Mount Vernon for a long while. His earlier prediction that he would be able to take the winter off and return home was a false hope. Even though the war stopped for the winter, he feared that without the Commander-in-Chief present the whole army would simply disintegrate. Consequently he invited Martha to join him and she made the difficult journey by road to be with her husband. It was almost a triumphal procession. George Washington had become a national icon and here was "Lady Washington" traveling to join him. As her party neared each town on its route, so local honor guards would form and escort it safely on its way. She commented to a friend that in Philadelphia she had been celebrated "in as great pomp as if I had been a very great somebody."

That first winter in Cambridge was not disagreeable. There was no fighting; they were accommodated in some style in Craigie House and reasonably well provisioned by James Warren (Chapter 2), while the British were holed up in Boston. Martha took over large aspects of her husband's operations, in particular shielding him from the distraction of a daily line of visitors who met her instead so that he could focus on the Revolutionary War. She also acted as a mother figure to young officers.

One of Washington's key officers, Henry Knox, hauled 50 cannons 300 miles using 160 oxen from Fort Ticonderoga to the heights overlooking Boston. On March 5, the British woke up to find themselves staring into the mouths of this artillery. They packed up and left; the siege of Boston was over.

But it was a roller coaster year. Boston, the Declaration of Independence in July, their first grandchild, and Martha's successful inoculation against smallpox (a hazardous three-week process) were major personal triumphs. But there were bad times too, including the many defeats Washington suffered as he was driven back from New York into Pennsylvania.

We have to remember that this was a matter of life and death. Were the revolutionaries to lose, then Washington would certainly be executed. And neither could Martha have assumed that the British would be lenient with her.

As 1775 ended, military matters turned in favor of the patriots as Washington crossed the Delaware River into New Jersey and took Trenton and Princeton, forcing the British back into New York City. Martha made her way to Morristown, New Jersey, for her second wartime winter camp.

The next four winters continued in the same way, seeing her invited to Valley Forge, Pennsylvania, then Middlebrook, New Jersey, and back to Morristown, New Jersey, and on to New Windsor, New York respectively. At all of them she inspired confidence, built hope and strengthened resolve. There are letters from women who, when going to meet Martha, expressed surprise at how simply she dressed and lived. She threw her weight behind an initiative to persuade women to help fundraise to support the soldiers of the Continental Army, becoming like her husband a symbol of the Revolution. She even donated a substantial sum from her own income.

Finally, Washington visited Congress, assembled in Annapolis, on December 23, 1784, resigned his commission, and was home late on Christmas Eve.

For two and a half years he and Martha enjoyed rebuilding their plantations at Mount Vernon. She "adopted" two of her late son Jacky's four children, a boy, George Washington Parke Custis, known as "Wash" or "Tub," and a girl, Eleanor "Nelly" Parke Custis. Their door was always open and among many visitors was the great British historian, Catherine Macaulay, introduced by a letter from their mutual friend Mercy Otis Warren (Chapter 2).

In the spring of 1787, George Washington agreed to lead the Virginia delegation to another Philadelphia convention. Once all had assembled, the Articles of Confederation were torn up and with Washington in the chair they began to write the Constitution. It was adopted on September 17, 1787. However, it still needed ratifying and a big debate ensued. On the one hand were the Federalists who favored a strong central executive, while on the other were the Anti-Federalists who feared such a model and in particular the power it gave to one man, the President.

It was almost inevitable that Washington would emerge as the leading candidate for the post. It was felt that a man who had voluntarily resigned as Commander-in-Chief three years earlier could be trusted.

There was no campaigning or "running" for the presidency. Friends put forward the name of their favored candidate, who stayed at home while his supporters campaigned on his behalf. And there was no running mate, either. Whoever came second became Vice President. In the first ballot George Washington secured 69 votes from the Electoral College, composed of representatives from every state, while John Adams garnered 34.

On April 6, 1789, Washington, who never sought the office, became President with John Adams as Vice President.

Martha was far from pleased. All she wanted was "solitude and tranquility" after the war and to remain surrounded by friends and family at Mount Vernon. George Washington left for the capital, New York City, on April 16 and was sworn in without his wife present on April 30. But for all her protestations, it is interesting to note that in March the couple had sent their agent to New York to arrange accommodations, armed with lists prepared by Martha.

She followed, arriving in late May, and like her husband she had to create her job. He was the first president of a newly independent nation; she was a revolutionary who had become the first First Lady. There were no precedents. However, both seemed aware from the outset of vested interests and favoritism. It was widely reported in the press that neither would attend private meetings, though Washington later relented so that his wife could see friends.

Martha and George Washington were in their fifties — considered old in the late eighteenth century — and George Washington certainly had pneumonia early in his presidency. He developed a good and improving relationship with Vice President John Adams and Martha with Adams' wife Abigail (Chapter 4). Abigail Adams, in a letter to her sister, described Martha as "modest and unassuming, dignified and feminine." However, other politicians, including Representative Madison, Treasury Secretary Hamilton and Secretary of State Jefferson, were busy doing backroom deals on issues from central banking to where to site the nation's capital: New York, Philadelphia or a new city on the banks of the Potomac. To Martha's dismay — she feared her husband's health would not stand the strain — George Washington allowed his name to go forward for a second term and they were signed up for four more years, this time in Philadelphia, the new capital. They did not return to Mount Vernon until March 1797, which without their constant presence and management had become somewhat dilapidated.

George Washington passed on in 1799 and she in 1802, having destroyed nearly all her letters to her husband shortly before her death. His will allowed for his slaves to be freed but it was a very complicated matter as to which were his and which belonged to the broader Custis estate, which Martha still managed. He stipulated that they should be freed on his wife's death, but the disadvantage of this was that 123 slaves were eager for her to die as soon as possible. Martha herself freed them.

Martha was by no means scholarly, but she was focused, determined and sensible. Some women demanded their men come home during the winter truces of the Revolutionary War, while still other wives stayed home while their men folk were away. Martha did neither: when the war for liberty was being waged, she was there supporting and advising her husband.

In 1901, Martha Washington became the first woman to be depicted on a US postage stamp.

Chapter 4. Abigail Adams

"I wish most sincerely there was not a slave in the province; it always appeared a most iniquitous scheme to me to fight ourselves for what we are daily robbing and plundering from those who have as good a right to freedom as we have." — Letter to John Adams, September 1774

Revolutionary, Abolitionist, Women's Rights Campaigner and Entrepreneur
November 11, 1744–October 28, 1818

BRAINTREE, MASSACHUSETTS

Until Barbara Bush, ABIGAIL ADAMS was the only woman to be a wife and a mother to a President of the United States. She was the wife of the second president, John Adams (1797–1801) and the mother of the sixth, John Quincy Adams (1825–1829). She did not live long enough to see her son inaugurated but she did stand with him, aged not quite eight years old, on a hilltop near their home on June 17, 1775, watching the British lose a thousand men as they won a Pyrrhic victory at the Battle of Bunker Hill. For every eight or more dead Redcoats there was only one dead patriot. The experience was a valuable lesson for the young John Quincy Adams, who would grow up like his father to defend the laws and liberties of his country.

While never formally educated, Abigail Adams, born Abigail Smith, was exceptionally well read, having access in her youth to three private libraries — her father's, uncle's and grandfather's. She devoured everything in them. As a young woman she had already developed clear views on the iniquity of slavery (she never owned one) and the parallels between the plight of slaves and the status of women, particularly married women.

Critics argue that Abigail Adams was simply the great woman behind a great man or that, together with Mercy Otis Warren (Chapter 2) and Martha Washington (Chapter 3), her achievements were the result of an accident of birth and/or marriage and therefore she does not deserve a place in the same pantheon as those women who fought alone for liberty.

However, all three women showed a core commitment to values and principles. They did far more than support their husbands. They acted in ways that put their lives in jeopardy. As a patriot during the Revolution, a woman as well as a man stood a strong chance of being executed. Abigail wrote letters to her husband containing valuable information about British troop movements; she housed people fleeing the British occupation of Boston; she melted her pewter pots, pans and plates and turned them into musket balls for the militia; and she allowed that same militia to train on her land. She brewed "Liberty Tea" from plants in her garden in order to avoid buying British imports. All these activities put her at risk.

But it is principally in her letters to her husband, full as they were of dangerous ideological discussion on politics and government, that her main contribution to the ideas of the day can be seen. John Adams turned to his wife for advice and, as a result, her own views were to underpin the newly founded United States of America.

So where did Abigail Adams spring from? What did she do to join our list of women who have played such a defining and crucial role in the struggle for liberty?

She was born in Massachusetts of pioneer stock. Her father, William Smith, was a parson, while her mother Elizabeth Quincy came from a prominent political family. Abigail was a sickly child, which afforded her time to read.

Abigail Smith and John Adams were third cousins; in other words they shared the same great, great grandparents. They had known each other all their lives but Adams became impressed at the erudition she showed as a 17-year-old. Relations between America and the homeland were beginning to plummet and their courtship from summer 1759 to marriage in fall of 1764 was dominated by political talk of a pro-liberty nature. More than a thousand letters between them survive. In one John Adams asserts that he gains more from just one of her letters than from a pile of newspapers. Their mutual interest in politics laid the ground for their long union. Abigail was well bred and well off; she was smart, sensible, widely read and in tune with the times. Adams was the middle-class son of a small farmer and had become a Harvard-educated lawyer.

The marriage produced six children in quick succession between 1765 and 1772: Abigail (always known as Nabby), John Quincy, the future President, Susanna who died in infancy, Charles, Thomas Boylston and Elizabeth, who was stillborn. They set up home in Braintree, Massachusetts, later renamed Quincy in honor of Abigail's grandfather, the politician Colonel John Quincy. John Adams himself went into politics, soon becoming a local councilman. His legal business took him away for days, sometimes weeks at a time. At one point the young family tried living in Boston, but found it a noisy, very smelly city.

In 1770 John firmly threw the family into the British spotlight. He was elected to the statewide legislature; then, following the Boston Massacre in which five patriots were gunned down, he agreed to represent the British soldiers involved. Adams was motivated by two things: first he wanted to show the British that America had a mature, fair legal system; he also wanted to dispel any idea that the cause of liberty could be advanced by mob violence. An important pillar of the case was that it was unclear who had cried "fire"; it might well have even been a member of the mob. Nobody was found guilty of murder.

He was on his way to great and lasting fame but he had no illusions about the risks. He told his wife that pro-British sentiment ran high once you moved away from the greater Boston area and he feared their cause would be totally crushed. There was a high chance that they would fail and could be put to death but he asked her to stand with him. Abigail readily agreed.

British Prime Minister Lord North's reaction to the Boston Tea Party was to introduce the "Intolerable Acts," which included an order for the closure of the port of Boston. A coordinated response from all the Thirteen Colonies was called for and John Adams was again to leave Abigail behind in Braintree when he became one of five delegates from Massachusetts to attend the fall 1774 Continental Congress in Philadelphia. By the time he returned to that city for the second Congress in the spring of 1775 he was leaving his wife and four children behind enemy lines. And the very day she stood with their eldest son John Quincy watching the Battle of Bunker Hill, her husband was on his feet nominating George Washington to be Commander-in-Chief of the Continental Army.

In his absence Adams' law firm, the children's education and the farm and household were now her domain. She managed it all very successfully, taking a role in overall management that was unusually wide-ranging for women of the time. As the price of pins, in increasingly short supply, went through the roof, Abigail hit on a small business idea. She persuaded her husband to ship pins to her which she then sold. She wrote lengthy letters to him not only on liberty and their shared principles and ideas but also on troop movements and military action in the neighborhood. "You can hardly imagine how we live," she wrote of life under the British in Massachusetts. He shared the information she gave him with fellow delegates at the Continental Congress. Together with General George Washington, she visited the wife of John Adams' second cousin, the politician Samuel Adams (also in Philadelphia), and she corresponded with Mercy Otis Warren (Chapter 2) about the unequal treatment of women in American society. At the same time she steered her extended family through an outbreak of dysentery that took many lives, including her mother's.

As Washington's artillery movement (Chapter 3) led to the liberation of Boston and the removal of immediate threat, Abigail was encouraging her husband to press for independence. That in turn would mean, she wrote, that he and his fellow Congressmen would have to write a new set of laws for the new country. She believed passionately in property rights and education for women — regretting her own lack of formal education — and she hoped that her husband and his colleagues in drafting these laws would "...remember the ladies, and be more generous and favorable to them than your ancestors. Do not put such unlimited power into the hands of the husbands. Remember all men would be tyrants if they could. If particular love and attention is not paid to the ladies we are determined to foment a rebellion and will not hold ourselves bound by any laws in which we have no voice or representation." Those three words "... remember the ladies" would resonate down the centuries.

In the same March 1776 letter, she observed that Southern slave owners could hardly be as passionate about liberty as she and others like her because they were used to "depriving their fellow creatures" of freedom. In just one missive, John Adams was being urged to free the women and free the slaves.

While some in their circles talked of sharing power with the British, to Abigail and John Adams sovereignty could never be split. Either you are sovereign or you are not. Adams and Pennsylvania delegate to the second Continental Congress Benjamin Franklin helped Thomas Jefferson, the main draftsman of the Declaration of Independence. It was voted through on July 2, 1776 and formally approved on July 4. Abigail heard it read aloud from the balcony of the statehouse in Boston on July 18 and she wrote to her husband that she was sorry that he had taken out the words she had suggested on a draft copy. She was clearly disappointed that the robust document she had wanted with its criticism of the slave trade had not materialized.

For most of 1776 and 1777 John Adams attended Congress, and in February 1778 he traveled across the Atlantic to Paris, France taking ten-year-old John Quincy with him. His mission was to join Benjamin Franklin in persuading France to enter into an alliance against the British. That accomplished, Franklin was made the permanent representative. No sooner had John Adams returned in

1779 than he was sent by Congress back to Europe to be in place when the time came to negotiate a peace treaty with the British.

This time accompanied both by John Quincy, his nine-year-old brother Charles, a Mr. Thaxter to act as their tutor, and John Adams's secretary, he set sail in November 1779. Spring 1780 saw them first in Paris and then in Amsterdam, where Adams negotiated a significant loan for the Americans from the Dutch. He also shipped goods such as calico dresses, ribbons, handkerchiefs and spices back to Abigail, who sold them at a profit, enabling her to buy land to expand the farm. Abigail relished her role as a businesswoman. A year later the new American Minister to the Court of Russia asked 14-year-old John Quincy to become his translator — the Minister spoke no French and it was the language of the Court. John Quincy's French was excellent, and he agreed.

The British surrender at Yorktown on October 19, 1781, involved John Adams in extensive negotiation of treaties and loans. On September 3, 1783, he joined Franklin and fellow Founding Father John Jay in signing the Treaty of Paris which recognized the Thirteen Colonies as free, sovereign and independent states. This was followed by negotiations for a commerce treaty with the British. Franklin was the only man to sign all four major documents of the founding era namely these two treaties and the Declaration and the Constitution.

In the summer of 1784, Abigail left Charles and Thomas with her sister Elizabeth and took daughter Nabby, who was approaching her twentieth birthday, with her to Europe. The 30-day crossing was vile in all regards. A letter she wrote on board stated "that no being in nature was so disagreeable as a lady at sea." She was terribly seasick and hated the cold. Abigail checked into a hotel in Covent Garden in the center of London but her husband was engaged in treaty discussions on the Continent. The women were greeted by John Quincy, who had left home a 12-year-old boy and was now a 17-year-old man.

Husband and wife and the two children moved to his official residence in Paris for a year, spending a great deal of time with Thomas Jefferson, a recent widower, who was now Minister (ambassador) to France. In 1785, John Adams was himself made Minister to the Court of St James's in England.

Abigail and John Adams reached London in May 1785, less than two years since the signing of the peace treaty, and soon rented a spacious house in Grosvenor Square, starting a diplomatic tradition that continues today but will soon end with the construction of a new, more secure building on the other side of the River Thames.

His first job was to present his credentials to King George III, then to build trade and commercial links. There is some possible irony in a former traitor becoming ambassador to his former enemy and would-be executioner. The couple occupied themselves reading and signing treaties for the next three years. They returned home to Boston in June 1788 and thousands turned out to welcome them back, including sons Thomas and Charles. John Quincy was soon to arrive from Newburyport, Massachusetts where he had been practicing law after graduating from Harvard. Jefferson stayed in Europe a further year, which put him out of the picture for the upcoming election of the first President of the United States of America.

When John Adams was named as the first vice president, after coming second to George Washington, he moved to the then capital New York. He and Abigail had moved to a new home they had purchased in Quincy while they were still in Europe. It was called Peacefield, to reflect John Adams' role in the 1783 peace treaty. But soon Abigail was to join her husband in New York.

Martha Washington and Abigail Adams had to invent their respective roles in society and became friendly with each other.

The capital moved to Philadelphia in 1790 but on the re-election of George Washington and John Adams in 1792, Abigail decided to stay at Peacefield. It saved money and it was much healthier, she felt. While the Vice President was away, she resumed her correspondence with him. She always found it easier to give her husband frank advice in letters rather than to his face. "My pen is always freer than my tongue," she wrote. "I have written many things to you that I suppose I never could have talked."

Ideologically, Adams and his friend Thomas Jefferson had drifted apart. Adams was increasingly a Federalist, supporting a strong central government and a national bank. Jefferson leant more toward the Democratic–Republicans and their emphasis on states' rights. Abigail was increasingly uncomfortable about his views, questioning his support for the bloody French Revolution. In the presidential election in 1796, Adams squeaked home 71 to Jefferson's 68, and Abigail became the second First Lady, with Jefferson as Vice President.

As this unfolded, Abigail famously defended a young black stablehand called James whom she had enrolled at a local evening school in Quincy to improve his writing skills. She was approached by the white father of two other boys in the class and was told that James's presence would lead to the break-up of the school. Was he misbehaving, she asked? No! Did they mind seeing him in church? No! Did they mind him providing music at local dances? No! Very rapidly the man started claiming that neither he nor his boys were the ones complaining. She demanded that the real protestors be sent to her so that she could convince them they were wrong. She pointed out that James was "a Freeman as much as any of the young Men and merely because his Face is Black, is he to be denied instruction? How is he to be qualified to procure a livelihood?... I have not thought it any disgrace to my self to take him into my parlor and teach him both to read and write." The education of James continued.

On Saturday March 4, 1797, John Adams was sworn in as America's second resident. It was quite possibly the last time Washington, Adams and Jefferson appeared in public together. Commenting on his eight years as vice president, John Adams wrote to Abigail, "My country has in its wisdom contrived for me the most insignificant office that ever the invention of man contrived or his imagination conceived."

But now that he was president, he told Abigail, "I never wanted your advice and assistance more in my life." His presidency was not a happy four years. Abigail much preferred Quincy to either Philadelphia or the government's new home in the District of Columbia. She was appalled at the state of the White House when the Adams family became its first occupants in May 1800. All thirteen fireplaces had to be kept going full blast to ward off the pervasive damp and Abigail famously hung the linen out to dry in the East Room. The President's new official residence was a building site in the middle of a swamp adjoining a village. It was surrounded by wilderness and next to a dirty hole called Georgetown.

John Adams' main achievement was avoiding an outright war with France. Abigail meanwhile managed the farm and household, and quietly made respectable profits on her own investments in state-backed securities. She continued to write to large numbers of people, and she involved herself to such an extent in policy matters that she became known as "Mrs. President."

In the end, peace with France and his wife's active involvement were not enough to save Adams, who in 1800 was defeated by Vice President Thomas Jefferson.

The Adams family retired to Peacefield to farm. Abigail continued to write letters. She even sent letters to the new president, disapproving of some of his actions. Abigail Adams died in 1818, aged 73, and John Adams in 1826, aged 90. Both received funerals that reflected their contribution to early American democracy, with distinguished pallbearers, thousands of mourners and effusive eulogies. Abigail's eulogy was given by John T. Kirkland, the president of Harvard. John Adams lived long enough to see John Quincy installed as the sixth president and only regretted that his wife had not. Both had rekindled their earlier close friendship with Thomas Jefferson before their deaths.

Abigail Adams' revolutionary zeal and personal example gave courage to many. In her opposition to slavery, she was a very early abolitionist; she was also a successful entrepreneur and farm manager at a time when men more usually occupied such positions; as a politician's wife she played an active role in shaping policy that went far beyond the supporting role of a First Lady. As an outspoken advocate of equality for women, she can be considered the founder of the real US women's rights movement.

Chapter 5. The Grimké Sisters

"So precious a talent as intellect never was given to be wrapt in a napkin and buried in the earth." — Angelina Grimké, *Appeal to the Christian Women of the Southern States*

Anti-slavery and Women's Rights Campaigners
Sarah Grimké,
November 26, 1792–December 23, 1873
Angelina Grimké,
February 20, 1805–October 26, 1879

CHARLESTON, SOUTH CAROLINA

SARAH and ANGELINA GRIMKÉ were born into good fortune. Their father, John Grimké, previously a lieutenant colonel in the Revolutionary War and speaker in the South Carolina House of Representatives, was now a plantation owner and judge in the state's Supreme Court. The girls could look forward to a life of ease. In front of them lay a future of balls, concerts, picnics, rides, dinners, parties, and entertainments. They would spend their days in spacious rooms with high ceilings in beautifully decorated homes and stroll in well-manicured gardens. Their wardrobes would be of the finest kind, full of the latest fashions, and their tables would be laden with both local and imported food and wine. What's more, they'd hardly need to lift a finger, thanks to the house slaves on hand 24 hours a day, seven days a week to attend to their every whim. Outside, field slaves would work just as hard if not harder on the plantations that made all this possible.

Mary Grimké (née Smith), their mother, also came from the highest echelons of Southern society. On the branches of her family tree sat colonial governors and military heroes; her father was a banker and one of the state's richest men, while her brother had served on George Washington's staff before becoming Governor of North Carolina. In the new Republic, this was as close to being "royalty" as anyone could imagine.

But Sarah and Angelina were to reject the highly privileged existence spread out before them by the simple accidents of their births. Instead they both moved north, embraced principle, and devoted their lives to campaigning for the abolition of slavery and for women's rights.

They rejected the thinking of the day that blacks were inferior to whites; they rejected the idea that it was proper for one individual to own another; they dismissed the notion that it was acceptable as long as you treated your slaves well and did not beat or torture them; and they had no time for the belief that the solution was to send freed slaves back to colonize African states such as Liberia, whether it was their country of origin or not. The sisters took an extremely principled position, becoming outright abolitionists.

Sarah Moore Grimké was born in 1792 and grew up in a magnificent house in the center of Charleston and on the family plantation inland at Beaufort. She had three elder brothers and one elder sister, and three younger brothers and two younger sisters. Her education was to consist of reading, writing and enough mathematics to run a household. Needlework, art, music and a little French featured on the curriculum, but the most important subject was the learning of manners. However, she craved more from her education and started to learn secretly from her brother Thomas, six years her senior, studying his books at night. This way she was able to delve into history, geography, science, Greek, and advanced mathematics. She was allowed to participate in the semi-formal debates her father arranged for his sons as law school preparation. Judge Grimké reportedly commented that if Sarah had been a boy she would have been America's greatest jurist. And so in 1804 Thomas went to Yale, while Sarah stayed at home.

From an early age Sarah became aware of the unjust treatment meted out to slaves. When at the age of five she saw a slave being beaten, she tried to run away from home to a place where there was no slavery. Later, in her speeches, she recalled the many harrowing experiences of slavery she had witnessed, ranging from whippings to torture at the local workhouse where slaves were sent to be disciplined. She even witnessed the gruesome spectacle of the severed head of an escaped slave on a pole by a country roadside, placed there as a warning to other would-be runaways. What she saw was to turn her into a rebel.

Sarah's family was devout Episcopalian and she taught Sunday School to younger slave children. But she asked why she couldn't teach them to read so they could discover the Bible for themselves. She was told by her father that the 1740 Better Ordering and Governing of Negroes and Slaves Act levied a fine of £100 (in the region of $10,000 today) for educating such people or employing slaves with these skills. Sarah's reaction was to teach her young black maid, Hetty, to read, secretly, until her mother discovered them; Sarah was severely admonished by her father and Hetty was very lucky to escape a severe whipping. Sarah later wrote: "I took an almost malicious satisfaction in teaching my little waiting-maid at night, when she was supposed to be occupied in combing and brushing my locks. The light was put out, the key hole screened, and flat on our stomachs before the fire, with the spelling-book under our eyes, we defied the law of South Carolina."

In February 1805, Mary produced her fourteenth and last child, Angelina Emily. Sarah begged her parents to make her the new child's godmother and to give her a major central role in raising the girl; they assented, in part to relieve Mary of some of the child-rearing burden and in part to cheer up the morose Sarah.

Angelina became the focus of Sarah's existence and by the time the former started to talk, she addressed her elder sister as "mother." Thomas returned from Yale, determined to enter the ministry and full of revolutionary ideas that he shared with Sarah. His beliefs were radical, and they included education for women. Sarah had secretly been reading many of her father's law books and wanted to read for the bar. But Judge Grimké would have none of it and that feat was not achieved by a woman until two generations later, when Arabella Mansfield became an attorney in Iowa in 1869. At his father's insistence, Thomas would read for the bar and Sarah would at age 16 soon be launched into society.

While Thomas was a great success in his chosen career, Sarah floundered socially and spiritually. Her looks (she was widely considered to be "plain"), eccentric views, and general intellectual restlessness left her unattached. Good works were not for her either: she did not want to visit poorhouses; she wanted to cure poverty! She was a real doer, a would-be activist. Angelina too was growing up disturbed by the sights and sounds of slavery. It is said she would at night slip into the slave quarters to tend anyone who had recently been beaten.

In 1818, Judge Grimké fell seriously ill and in the spring of 1819 his Charleston doctor referred him to a Philadelphia specialist. Sarah accompanied her father on the sea journey. After two months the doctor could do no more than recommend the sea air and the bathing at Long Branch, New Jersey. Father and daughter traveled there, but to no avail. Judge Grimké died and Sarah was his sole mourner.

Looking after her dying father all alone, and staying with Quakers in Philadelphia for months either side of his death, seem to have hardened and focused her, resolving many issues. On the ship back to Charleston she was befriended by a prosperous Quaker family named Morris, who gave her books and tracts. She started a correspondence with Israel Morris, the head of the family.

Back home, she threw herself into discovering all she could about the Quaker movement, also known as the Religious Society of Friends, and its outright opposition to slavery. She also took to wearing the plain habit of Quaker women and in 1821 she relocated to Philadelphia to live alternately with Israel's family in the country and his sister Catherine Morris in the city, supported by the interest on her inheritance. In May 1823, Sarah Grimké became a full member of the Friends.

Angelina meanwhile was on her own spiritual and intellectual journey from the Episcopal Church, with its emphasis on the rule of the clergy, to the more democratic Presbyterian Church, and from being a merely argumentative to a highly opinionated anti-slavery activist. She built a huge Sunday School following at her new church, as well as holding daily prayer meetings for her slaves and those of other masters. But she could not abide the idea of Christians owning other Christians and she too became attracted to the Quaker religion and its dedication to peace and equality.

It was not only the impact of slavery on the slaves that troubled Angelina Grimké but also its effect on their owners. Having everything done for you by house slaves and living off the work of field slaves was, she observed, deeply amoral and undermined families. If you could not even move a chair for your mother or open a window so that she might enjoy the air, then what hope was there for affection to arise from familial duty, she wondered. Her mother disagreed strongly, arguing that it was a slave's duty. But Angelina was disturbed by the immorality that owning slaves fostered too — nearly every family had mulatto children born to slave women.

In November 1829, Angelina stopped her one-woman crusade in Charleston and headed north to be with Sarah in Philadelphia. Soon she too had joined the Quakers.

Both sisters still struggled to find their niche, and initially their mission to abolish slavery had little real direction, partly because the Quakers considered their views to be too radical. While Quakers might be against slavery, their social activism was unlikely to extend beyond praying for a solution.

There were at that time four major positions on the abolition of slavery:

- Colonization advocates, people like their brother Thomas Grimké, who felt the solution was to assist all black people, including free persons of color, to relocate to Africa;

- Gradualists, who conceived of change over time; under their proposal all current slaves would die slaves but all children born after a given date (several years in the future) would become free on turning 25;

- Conservative immediatists, for whom abolition did not mean that slaves would "be free from the benevolent restraints of guardianship" — they would be able to earn wages but not to vote or to hold public office; and

- Radical immediatists who abhorred colonization and wanted much quicker change.

The Grimké Sisters were very much in that last camp, though the younger Angelina yearned for an activist role while her elder sister was more cautious.

In the mid 1830s, there was an explosion of anti-slavery societies in the North, including female versions of such groups in which women were able to play a leadership role previously denied them. Both sisters began to engage more and more in the anti-slavery movement, Sarah through reading and study and Angelina by attendance at meetings of the Philadelphia Female Anti-Slavery Society.

The era also saw a great deal of violence directed at such activities, even in the North where slavery for many people was little more than an abstract idea. It is certain that most had never witnessed it personally.

Against this background Angelina wrote a personal letter to William Lloyd Garrison, editor of *The Liberator*, the leading anti-slavery periodical. Garrison had been editorializing strongly against mob violence and demanding that British reformer George Thompson be given a peaceful platform.

"The ground upon which you stand is holy ground; never — never surrender it," she urged him in her letter. "If you surrender it the hope of the slave is extinguished." She concluded: "This is a cause worth dying for."

Without consulting her at all Garrison published the letter in full and identified its author clearly as being from the prominent Grimké family of Charleston. It was widely read, reprinted and admired, suddenly giving Angelina a public profile and deeply impressing the leading reform spokesman Theodore Weld. Her future as a radical abolitionist was assured. At the same time, the letter was intensely embarrassing to Angelina. It outraged the Philadelphia Quakers, whose way of life Sarah and Angelina were finding more and more stultifying and at odds with their reforming zeal.

Angelina became deeply involved in the Philadelphia Female Anti-Slavery Society and through its meetings kept track of activists such as Theodore Weld and the violence he and others often faced. Angelina also tried to purchase her former maid, Hetty, who now had children, in order to free her and her family but to no avail — the requests were ignored. Angelina later rejected this purchase-to-free strategy as being insufficiently pure since it implied acceptance of the system.

The more contemplative Sarah had become attracted to the Free Produce Movement which advocated that consumers weaken the economy of the South by buying food products made only by free men, in other words a boycott of anything slave-produced.

In February 1836 both sisters attended the Quaker Convention in Providence, Rhode Island where they met abolitionists from all over the Northeast, with whom they felt much more comfortable than their Philadelphia group. This resulted in an invitation to Angelina, a talented and passionate public speaker, to become a speaker for the New York City-based American Anti-Slavery Society. While she considered this offer she penned a highly influential monograph, *Appeal to the Christian Women of the Southern States.*

In this publication she wrote as a Southern lady, addressing her friends and their friends in their language. She took on every argument advanced in favor of slavery and refuted them all. Set your slaves free, she urged her fellow Southern women. "If they wish to remain with you, pay them wages," she continued. "If not, let them leave you. Should they remain teach them."

Sales of Angelina's monograph took off. This led to acclaim but also to trouble. Police in Charleston paid a visit to the Grimké sisters' mother. The Postmaster had burned copies of *Appeal* in public and the police warned that Angelina was not to visit; if she did she would be arrested, imprisoned and deported on the first available boat back north.

The Quakers of Philadelphia disapproved too and insisted the sisters could not leave the city without their permission. Angelina resolved to move to New York City and, as Sarah wondered what to do she received a letter from their mother begging her to accompany her sister so as to look after her. Sarah and Angelina Grimké were on their way to becoming America's first female agents for abolition.

Arriving in New York City in October 1836, the sisters were immediately thrown into an intense three-week-long training course for new agents run by the American Anti-Slavery Society and led by Theodore Weld. Sarah and Angelina were the only two women out of forty. Here the local Quakers were supportive and, for the first time, they both felt part of a harmonious team in which everybody was pulling in the same direction.

The plan for the Grimké Sisters was for them to address fellow women in parlors at the homes of members of the Female Anti-Slavery Society. However the response to their lectures was so huge that no parlor was big enough to hold all those who wanted to attend. A room at a local church that could sit 300 was found instead, but that too proved inadequate and the lectures were moved into the main body of the church itself.

Theirs was an impressive double act. Sarah dealt with the religious aspects of their case and Angelina the political. While Angelina's monograph had been aimed at the women of the South, Sarah now wrote and published *An Epistle to the Clergy of the Southern States*, urging Southern religious leaders to take a stance. And while Angelina penned her *Appeal to the Women of the Nominally Free States*, Sarah wrote *An Address to Free Colored Americans*. Invitations to speak flowed in and they decided to target New England from a base in Boston. They were an instant hit: between June 7 and June 23, 1837, they addressed 11 meetings of 3,500 people in total, including many men. But this appeal to men and the fact that they were speaking before a "promiscuous" — mixed-gender — group caused controversy. It was one thing for women to talk with other women in small groups in private homes but quite another for them to address large groups in public with men in attendance.

First the Quakers and then other Christian denominations such as the Congregationalists closed their premises to abolitionists and women speakers; it was quite clear who they were trying to gag. Sarah, unhappy that women could be denied a public platform, began to move beyond abolitionism and into the area of women's rights. Theodore Weld, however, advised them to stick to the issue of slavery. As the fall of 1837 came, both sisters fell ill from fatigue but by then they had already spoken to 40,000 men and women at 80 meetings in 67 New England towns.

In 1838, Theodore Weld proposed marriage to Angelina. She was also invited to address the Massachusetts State Legislature in Boston's State House. She accepted both and on February 21 and again on February 23 she became the first woman in US history to address such a legislative committee.

She started her speech: "I stand before you as a Southerner exiled from the land of my birth by the sound of the lash, and the piteous cry of the slave. I stand before you as a repentant slaveholder. I stand before you as a moral being."

One thousand people attended on both days and such was the reception given to her speeches that Angelina wrote to her friend, the African-American abolitionist Sarah Douglass: "We Abolition Women are turning the world upside down." Next, a series of six formal lectures was booked at Boston's huge Odeon theatre — Sarah gave the first and Angelina, who was more of a natural orator than her elder sister, delivered the remaining five. Every square inch of space was packed out by an audience of up to 3,000 people.

The Female Anti-Slavery Society's annual convention was scheduled for mid-May in Philadelphia. Angelina Grimké and Theodore Weld decided to marry just before it so that their activist friends would not need to make a special journey. Weld viewed the law that made all the property of a wife over to her husband as pure vandalism and looked forward to a ceremony in which he would make himself the exception. They had decided to live in Fort Lee, New Jersey and invited Sarah to join them. Weld would commute by steamer to New York City and the sisters would continue to work for abolition.

So on May 14 the "most mobbed man" in the US, according to the Grimké sisters' 1967 biographer Gerda Lerner, married its "most notorious woman." They invited scandal by having the ceremony performed before a mixed race group which included Grimké family slaves who had been freed and were now living locally. A black baker made the cake, using slave-free sugar.

On the very same day in the same city of Philadelphia, Pennsylvania Hall opened. It had been funded by 2,000 abolitionists — many of them women — who had each sent $20 (the equivalent of about $250 today) to purchase a share. The aim was to build a large hall which would enable abolitionist lectures to take place without fear of offending the sensibilities or policies of the owners of halls and churches.

Two nights later 3,000 abolitionists — mostly women — braved a braying mob to enter the hall. Inside blacks and whites mingled and *The Liberator*'s William Lloyd Garrison gave the first lecture. Angelina then spoke for an hour during which time the mob outside hurled stones through newly broken windows. The Mayor of Boston, perhaps not wanting to buck majority opinion, refused to intervene and the convention had to resume the next afternoon. But the mob grew and became even more vicious and intemperate. In response the Mayor ordered the evening session to be cancelled. Fearing in particular for the safety of the black women, Angelina asked the white women to link arms with their black sisters and the mob reluctantly backed off as a line of reformers, alternately black and white, left the building. The Mayor urged the mob to disperse — it had already succeeded in stopping the convention — and then he departed. However, the mob soon looted the hall before burning it to the ground. This was an astonishing act of vandalism and an equally astonishing abrogation of duty by the Mayor. But in polite circles and newspaper editorials, the consensus was that the mob had been provoked by troublemakers who did not know their place in society.

Installed in New Jersey, the sisters learned to cook and keep house aged 45 and 33. Theodore Weld began a new book of first-person statements by people who had witnessed slavery. The book was designed to educate the many Northerners who had little, even no, experience of it. In the course of his research, he discovered a library in New York City which subscribed to many Southern newspapers. It periodically cleared out old papers, selling them as waste paper. Weld bought three years' worth, well over 20,000 copies, and Angelina and Sarah spent six months reading them for first-hand accounts of slavery expressed in the words of their fellow Southerners.

The result was *American Slavery as It Is: Testimony of a Thousand Witnesses*, arguably the most revealing anti-slavery volume ever compiled. It was published anonymously, Weld eschewing the pride that came with associating his name with this work, and the profits went to his employer, the American Anti-Slavery Society. It sold 100,000 copies in its first year alone and is said to have inspired Harriet Beecher Stowe's bestseller *Uncle Tom's Cabin* (Chapter 7). She is reported to have slept with a copy of Theodore Weld's book under her pillow.

By 1839 Angelina's health had become a major concern and was to remain so the rest of her life. But she had three children, Charles Stuart Faucherauld Weld, born in 1839, Thomas Grimké Weld in 1841 and Sarah Grimké Weld in 1844.

The financial panic of 1837 had seriously depleted both the sisters' financial reserves and Theodore Weld's salary as an employee of the American Anti-Slavery Society, an organization reliant on donations. They moved to a 62-acre Belleville, New Jersey farm where they hoped to become mostly self sufficient. However, Theodore Weld's farming career was cut short when former President John Quincy Adams, now a congressman from Massachusetts, invited him to come to Washington, DC to be the researcher for a small group of abolitionists in the House of Representatives.

Angelina was severely depressed with her husband away so much, her finances destroyed and the burden of a farm and three young children. Sarah, however, was there to help her raise the children just as she had done with Angelina herself. On his return from Washington, DC, Weld began to educate his three children. The farmhouse was big enough for other children to board and they were soon lodging and teaching twenty youngsters, including the children of fellow abolitionists. This led to Theodore Weld being offered the headship of a new school, Eagleswood in New Jersey, where Angelina taught and Sarah did the accounts. It also allowed the Welds to sell the farm and use part of the proceeds to repay Sarah, who had been helping to support them.

By the time the Civil War broke out in 1861, the Welds had come to the conclusion that conflict was inevitable. "War is better than slavery," Angelina wrote.

The war energized the couple and brought them back into the public eye. Theodore Weld began speaking throughout New England in support of the North. Meanwhile many of Angelina's old friends and admirers formed the Woman's National Loyal League to support the government's "war for freedom." On the twenty-fifth anniversary of her wedding and only two days shy of the twenty-fifth anniversary of her last speech in public at the ill-fated Pennsylvania Hall, Angelina addressed the League's National Convention in New York City. As a South Carolinian she urged the North to press forward with the war.

However, the fighting disrupted enrollment at their school, which closed in 1863, and the trio moved to live out their lives in Massachusetts. They lived in

Hyde Park, Boston on weekends and spent their weekdays teaching in a Lexington, Massachusetts boarding school. While abolitionists streamed south, they collected clothes and money for their newly freed brothers and sisters.

It was in 1868 that Angelina came across a newspaper reference to a brilliant student called Archibald Grimkie at the black Lincoln College in Pennsylvania. Struck by the similarity to her unusual family name, she wrote to the student concerned, care of the college, and received a quick reply. Archibald was the son of her younger brother Henry (1801–1852) and a slave whom Henry freed before moving away with her. He had two brothers, Frank and John. Angelina, Theodore and Sarah immediately took their three nephews under their wing. Archibald went on to Harvard Law School, one of the first black people to do so, and later helped found the National Association for the Advancement of Colored People (NAACP). His daughter Angelina Weld Grimké became a famous poet in the Harlem Renaissance of the 1920s. Frank attended Princeton Theological Seminary and served the Presbyterian Church on 15th Street in Washington DC as its leader for all but half a century.

The Grimké Sisters were to hit the headlines one last time when, in March 1870, aged 77 and 65, they led a group of women in voting in a Lexington town election. They marched through the snow from a local hotel, each carrying a bouquet of flowers, and placed ballots into a box undeterred by the noisy barracking of male citizens. Of course the ballots would not be counted, but they claimed to be the first women to vote; and they were almost exactly 50 years ahead of the February 1920 passage of the Nineteenth Amendment which gave women the right to vote.

Sarah died in 1873, aged 81; Angelina followed her in 1879, aged 74. Theodore Weld died in 1895, aged 92.

The Grimké Sisters were principled and steadfast and made huge personal sacrifices. They were courageous, generous and caring. They were also gifted writers and public speakers, and clever strategists. But above all they were driven by an abhorrence of the idea that one individual could own another. To that end, they were pivotal in the effort to see that notion pass from an unassailable part of American culture into the dustbin of history.

CHAPTER 6. SOJOURNER TRUTH

"Proclaim liberty throughout all the land unto all the inhabitants thereof" —
Sojourner Truth's banner

Slave, Abolitionist and Women's Rights Activist
Circa 1797–November 26, 1883

NEW YORK; MASSACHUSETTS; MICHIGAN

SOJOURNER TRUTH was born a Northern slave. She was illiterate but had a powerful memory. With her strong speaking and singing voice, she was a tenacious advocate for the abolition of slavery and for the rights of both black people and women. She was able to pack halls from Massachusetts to Michigan and braved mobs, stones, even death threats. Her height — she was six feet tall — her deep ebony skin and her equally deep voice gave her an imposing presence. Many of her opponents claimed she was really a man in disguise. At one meeting a persistent heckler, a medical doctor, suggested she prove him wrong by baring her breast in privacy to some of the white women present. Her response was to bare her breast to the whole congregation.

So who was Sojourner Truth?

She was born Isabella (or Isabelle) Baumfree (or Bomefree) into slavery circa 1797 (the exact year is not recorded) in Ulster County, about 100 miles north of New York City. Baumfree was the low Dutch nickname, meaning "tree," of her very tall father. Isabella, who was also known by her parents' Dutch master's surname, Ardinburgh, grew up speaking only the language of her owner, who farmed a large estate and owned as many as 15 slaves. Isabella's mother had 12 or 13 children but, by the time Isabella, known as Belle, was old enough to remember, all but her brother Peter had either died or been sold.

Soon after she was born, the state of New York began the long and very complex process of abolishing slavery which lasted nearly 30 years, culminating on Freedom Day, July 4, 1827. New York and New Jersey were the only states north of Delaware and Maryland to have retained such a system of ownership. However, slavery still dominated the South, and the Civil War was a generation away.

Her first master died when she was a baby and the whole family now became the property of his son Charles, who in turn died in 1806 when Belle was about nine years old. A week later she was auctioned off with a flock of sheep for $100 (worth about $1,500 today) to John Neely. He owned a trading post and thought Belle could help his wife. Unfortunately, they spoke not a word of Dutch and she not a word of English, which led to much ill treatment. Neely is once reported to have whipped her until she bled with a bundle of rods heated in embers.

Belle's father, freed because at his age he was deemed worthless on the auction block, heard of her predicament and prevailed upon a local farmer and innkeeper named Martinus Schryner to offer Neely $105 for her. The offer was accepted and in 1808 she walked to her new lodgings. She seems to have been very happy there; she grew to her full adult height by the time she was 13. In 1810, she caught the eye of another local landowner John Dumont, who purchased her for $300. She worked so hard for him that his other slaves advised her to slow down for their sakes. When she refused, they called her "white man's pet" and she became very unpopular.

In her late teens, Belle met and fell in love with a slave named Robert who came from a nearby farm. A property rights issue arose — who would own and thus profit from their children? The liaison was unacceptable to both owners and Robert was savagely beaten and told to "marry" another slave owned by his master. Belle was presented with an older Dumont slave named Tom, whose first two wives had already been sold. She rapidly produced five children: Diana, Elizabeth, Hannah, Peter and Sophia.

With the pre-set date for Freedom Day only two years off, Dumont did two things that would have far-reaching consequences. First, he promised Belle that, as she had been the best worker he had ever had, she would be freed a year early. Second, he sold her four-year-old son Peter to his neighbor Solomon Gedney. The legislation designed to ease the transition to freedom dictated that he could not sell Peter as a slave, but because he owned Belle he could sell Peter's labor up to the age of 28.

After a year went by, Dumont failed to honor his promise, arguing that a hand injury that Belle had sustained had made her less productive. She worked hard throughout the summer and fall, until she felt she had fulfilled her obligation to her master. Then she picked up her youngest, Sophia, who was still a baby, and escaped early one morning. She was forced to leave Diana, Elizabeth, Hannah, and Peter behind with Dumont who, while lacking in integrity, was a better master than most. She said later: "I did not run off, for I thought that wicked, but I walked off, believing that to be all right."

She headed for a local Quaker neighborhood and found refuge with Isaac and Martha Van Wagenen. Within hours Dumont had tracked her down and demanded she return immediately. Isaac intervened and, while refusing to buy her as a slave, which was against his principles, he offered $20 for Belle's services for the six or so months before Freedom Day. Dumont accepted and Belle remained with the Van Wagenens, a short distance from the children she had left behind.

On July 4, 1827, Belle became free along with all other slaves aged over 28 in the Empire State, and Isaac and Maria started to pay her a small weekly salary. She began to inquire after her son Peter and finally discovered he had been taken south to Alabama, in clear breach of the new laws which prohibited taking slaves out of state.

She found the county court in Kingston and swore a complaint before the grand jury, who believed her story. A constable was sent to serve a writ on Peter's owner, Solomon Gedney. But the constable served the writ on Gedney's brother, who promptly alerted Solomon. Solomon fled in the fall of 1827, sailing all the way around the southern tip of Florida to Mobile, Alabama, and back with Peter to avoid a large fine and up to 14 years in jail for shipping a slave out of state. But on getting back to upstate New York, Solomon Gedney forcefully kept Belle from seeing her son. Again she went to court, and Peter was returned to her.

While with the Van Wegenens, she had felt "overwhelmed with the greatness of the divine presence" and began to formalize her religious beliefs through a newly opened Methodist church in the area. Through the Church she received an offer of work in New York City, which included education for Peter. She jumped at the chance and through the 1830s she worked as a housekeeper. Peter, however, joined a gang and was frequently arrested before finally signing up for a whaling ship called the *Zone of Nantucket* in 1839. When it returned to port he was not aboard, and Belle never heard from him again.

On June 1, 1843, Belle, now 46, set off from New York City on foot, unsure of what she ought to do but feeling a call to action. She started by preaching at the religious summer camps that were popular then, recounting her life story and using it to decry slavery. Vast numbers of people would congregate in a large field in huts, tents and wagons and be entertained by a series of speakers for three or four days. Belle could electrify an audience with her story, her powerful voice and her songs. Looking for her own identity in a new role after decades of being named for her masters, she restyled herself Sojourner Truth. What was her rationale? She would be moving from place to place, so she selected Sojourner as her first name, and when she called on God for a second name she heard the answer "truth." And while she travelled she kept in touch with her daughters, using amanuenses — every town had someone to whom the illiterate could dictate a letter for a small fee.

Her reputation was considerably enhanced when she quelled a riotous group of young white men armed with rocks and wooden bats who had broken up one of these religious camps in Connecticut. At first she sang to attract their attention, before engaging them with her stories and ideas. Winter saw her in Northampton, Massachusetts, which was to become her base for the next 14 years. There she joined for a short time the utopian community, the Northampton Association of Education and Industry, which believed in equal rights for all races and women. She met William Lloyd Garrison, the famous abolitionist and editor of *The Liberator*, and Frederick Douglass, who escaped slavery to become a leading abolitionist. Both encouraged her to develop her oratory, as did abolitionist attorney Wendell Phillips, himself a gifted speaker, and Parker Pillsbury, a minister and close associate of Elizabeth Cady Stanton (Chapter 8).

Another friend, Olive Gilbert, came up with an inspired idea: if Sojourner would dictate her life story, she would write it down. William Lloyd Garrison was keen to help and wrote the introduction to the book, entitled *Narrative of Sojourner Truth — A Northern Slave*. He also established a line of credit for her with his printer so she could pay for the books after they were sold and promised that if she came to his meetings and set up a bookstall, he would praise her and the books would sell in huge numbers.

The book came out in 1850, just as the debate on slavery reached new heights with the passage of the Fugitive Slave Act which decreed that all runaway slaves caught in the North had to be returned to their owners in the South. It was called "the Bloodhound Law" after the dogs used by the bounty hunters. Sojourner Truth became a regular speaker at abolitionist meetings around Boston. That same year she purchased her first home in Northampton for $300. Profits from the book went to pay off the mortgage.

She was a Massachusetts delegate to the first National Women's Rights Convention in 1850 held in Worcester, Massachusetts, and the only black woman present. Garrison invited her to join him and abolitionist and staunch advocate of free trade George Thompson, who was a British Member of Parliament, on a speaking tour in early 1851. However Garrison fell ill, leaving Thompson and Truth to travel together. They toured from Massachusetts through upstate

New York, often facing mobs of hecklers. In May she headed for Akron, Ohio, for the Ohio Women's Rights Convention, where once again she was the only black woman to attend. Her presence was a problem: many women's rights advocates thought it would be a strategic mistake to embrace abolitionism. It was hard enough to achieve divorce reform, let alone free the slaves. This set the scene for her famous *Ain't I a Woman?* speech in which she cleverly used her own experience as a slave — possibly melding it with that of her mother — to link the two causes: "I think that 'twixt the negroes of the South and the women at the North, all talking about rights, the white men will be in a fix pretty soon. But what's all this here talking about?"

She continued:

> That man over there says that women need to be helped into carriages, and lifted over ditches, and to have the best place everywhere. Nobody ever helps me into carriages, or over mud-puddles, or gives me any best place! And ain't I a woman? Look at me! Look at my arm! I have ploughed and planted, and gathered into barns, and no man could head me! And ain't I a woman? I could work as much and eat as much as a man — when I could get it — and bear the lash as well! And ain't I a woman? I have borne thirteen children, and seen most all sold off to slavery, and when I cried out with my mother's grief, none but Jesus heard me! And ain't I a woman?

The leading reformer Frances Gage, who later wrote an account of the speech, described Sojourner's "deep, wonderful tones, as she stood there with outstretched arms and eyes of fire." She moved her audience to tears and ended to "roars of applause."

For two years Sojourner Truth targeted Ohio. It was a key state; to its south lay the slave state of Kentucky and to its north Lake Erie and Canada. If slaves could cross this one state, they found freedom. Technically Ohio had been free since 1802, but black people were often unwelcome. Indeed, the state passed many impediments of its own to black settlement and advancement. Sojourner felt that the more people she could win round in Ohio, the better. To that end she borrowed a horse and cart, shipped in supplies of her books, photos and song sheets to sell and took to the road, speaking in literally hundreds of places and working closely with Marius Robinson, editor of the Ohio-based *Anti-Slavery Bugle*. Sometimes she would just stop at a crossroads and belt out a few of her songs. Traffic would stop, people from nearby fields and homes would wander over and she would have an instant audience.

Sojourner Truth had become a seasoned performer and was in demand to address big meetings. She visited her by now grown daughters and their families, extolling the virtues of the Midwest. In 1857 she sold the house in Massachusetts and moved to Harmonia, Michigan, just west of Battle Creek, a city that had impressed her on one of her speaking tours. There were jobs, the schools admitted black children, and people were so pro-abolition that the Underground Railroad that secretly conducted escaped slaves to freedom ran over ground. Sojourner remarked that the runaway slaves could be accompanied down Main Street in the middle of the day with a marching band and no one would bat an eyelid. She began to regroup her family there.

On a final visit to Northampton, she stopped in Andover where Harriet Beecher Stowe (Chapter 7), the writer of a new book entitled *Uncle Tom's Cabin*, lived. A friend had read it aloud to Sojourner and she had a bone to pick with the author: why were the light-skinned negroes in the book portrayed as intelligent and the dark-skinned ones seemingly less so? Stowe welcomed her — indeed Sojourner stayed several days, talking day and night, giving her host all the material she needed for a profile which Stowe published in *The Atlantic Monthly*.

Sojourner was also convinced that the abolitionist cause must now be centered in the Midwest and not the East. The Compromise of 1850, which included the draconian Fugitive Slave Act, had been succeeded by the Kansas–Nebraska Bill which left it to each state to determine whether it would be a slave state or a free state. The battle, both intellectual and physical at times, would surely now be fought in the new territories lining up for statehood. And a new political grouping, the Republican Party, was being formed to oppose any extension of slavery. Abolitionists from New England streamed in to settle in the new territory of Kansas in a bid to populate it in sufficient numbers to vote for it to become a free state. But pro-slavery Missourians merely had to step across the state line. It was a turbulent time and the state was dubbed Bleeding Kansas. To Sojourner it was a race to win people over to her belief that the state should be free; to Garrison and controversial abolitionist Captain John Brown violence was inevitable. In the end, in spite of the geographical disadvantage they faced, the abolitionists prevailed in Kansas.

With Pillsbury as her co-speaker, she toured Indiana, Illinois, Ohio and Michigan. Tempers were frayed — eggs became stones — and the South rebelled.

For the first part of the war Sojourner kept on speaking. Many in the North opposed the war; some even secretly supported the South. These were clearly the most dangerous engagements she was to take on and she returned to Michigan exhausted. But she did not rest long and soon determined to help in the war effort.

She began by raising funds and gifts. On Thanksgiving Day she hosted a feast for the First Michigan Regiment of Colored Soldiers in training at Camp Ward, Detroit. She also composed the lyrics for a new song called *The Valiant Soldiers* for the regiment to be sung to the tune of *John Brown's Body*:

We are the valiant soldiers who've 'listed for the war;
We are fighting for the Union, we are fighting for the law;
We can shoot a rebel farther than a white man ever saw,
As we go marching on...

Look there above the center, where the flag is waving bright;
We are going out of slavery, we are bound for freedom's light!
We mean to show Jeff Davis how the Africans can fight,
As we go marching on...

Father Abraham has spoken, and the message has been sent;
The prison doors have opened, and out the prisoners went
To join the sable army of African descent,
As we go marching on...

Sojourner decided to go to Washington, DC, to see the Abraham Lincoln, the first openly anti-slavery head of state. She felt she might learn from him where her talents were most needed. She was now famous everywhere thanks to Harriet Beecher Stowe's profile of her, which had just appeared. She spoke to larger and larger audiences as she journeyed to Washington.

On meeting Lincoln, she is supposed to have said that she had never heard of him until he ran for president, to which he reputedly replied, "Well, I heard of you, years and years before I ever thought of being president. Your name was well known in the Middle West."

She was appalled at the condition of the freedmen in the DC area. Now approaching 70, Sojourner Truth threw herself into work with the National Freedmen's Relief Association at Freedmen's Village and at the Freedmen's Hospital. She also fought the streetcar companies in Washington, DC over white conductors' poor treatment of black people after the president ordered the vehicles to be desegregated. When a conductor hit her so hard that she dislocated her shoulder, the National Freedmen's Relief Association sued for assault and battery on her behalf. They won the case and the conductor was sacked within a week. After that, black people were treated somewhat better when they boarded a streetcar.

The sheer size of the problem Sojourner faced led her to think of equally big solutions. Handouts of clothing and food were not long-term solutions. This theme recurred often in her speeches: "They [the freedmen] are living on the government ... and it does not benefit them at all. It just degrades them worse and worse." Her idea was to give the freedmen land in the West, and to campaign for this she once again became an itinerant speaker, collecting many thousands of signatures for her petition. Her message was that the freedmen needed a hand up not a handout.

For seven years she pursued her campaign, visiting Congressmen, Senators and even President Ulysses Grant, but it failed. As she neared 80 she began to develop a broader interest in women's rights. Aged 81 she attended the thirtieth anniversary meeting of the Women's Rights Convention in Rochester, New York and undertook speaking engagements in 36 Michigan towns and cities. Her book was updated and continued to sell.

But in 1879 Sojourner began to hear reports that tens of thousands of freedmen and their families were marching from the South into Kansas to create new lives for themselves. She headed west, again paying her way by selling her photo and her song sheets. Once there she urged the newly arrived black people not to settle in the cities but to use the Homestead Act and claim their own land.

She died at home in Battle Creek on November 26, 1883. All her living children and grandchildren had by then moved to the area. Intriguingly, her headstone claims she died "aged about 105 years," rather than about 86. Probably, given that there was no birth certificate, it was a simple mistake.

Sojourner was a giant, physically, mentally and as an orator. She worked as hard for the freedom of her people as it was humanly possible to do. She had an astonishing purpose and an unshakeable core belief in liberty. That slavery ended is in part thanks to Sojourner Truth.

CHAPTER 7. HARRIET BEECHER STOWE

"The time has come when even a woman or a child who can speak a word for
freedom and humanity is bound to speak." — Harriet Beecher Stowe, 1851

Novelist and Abolitionist
June 14, 1811–July 1, 1896

HARTFORD, CONNECTICUT

Twenty-one-year-old Harriet Beecher had little experience of slavery, having
grown up in New England. But that changed when her family, whose patriarch
was the fiery preacher Lyman Beecher, moved to Cincinnati, Ohio in 1832. He
was to take up the post as president of the Lane Theological Seminary, recently
launched to educate Presbyterian ministers.

Ohio had abolished slavery in 1802 but did not welcome black immigrants.
Just across the Ohio River was Kentucky, a slave state, with men and women
desperate to cross the border. Ohio was all that stood between them and freedom in Canada. As a result Cincinnati was a city on the edge. Racial tensions
ran high and Harriet was now living at the start of one of many Underground
Railroads that conducted escaping slaves to safety via a network of secret routes
and safe houses.

The family helped to hide runaway slaves, permitting Harriet to learn first-hand about their ill treatment by their white masters and their struggle for freedom. In February 1834, while Lyman Beecher was absent, a star Lane student Theodore Weld, who was to become a leading light in the abolitionist movement (Chapter 5), launched an 18-day debate on slavery. All the students were against it but were unsure as to the solution. For nine days they discussed simply abolishing the institution and emancipating all slaves as soon as possible. Then for another nine days they discussed colonization, the idea of sending all black people back to Africa. At the end they took a vote. The students voted overwhelmingly for immediate abolition. Lane's trustees, outraged at this radicalism and wanting to quash discussion, banned all future meetings and outlawed all societies of abolitionists. Weld and fellow reformer Henry Stanton, who would later marry women's rights campaigner Elizabeth Cady (Chapter 8), walked out and enrolled at Oberlin College near Cleveland, taking most of the other students with them.

These experiences in Ohio laid the foundation for one of the most influential novels of all time, *Uncle Tom's Cabin*, which Harriet wrote under her married name of HARRIET BEECHER STOWE, and initially published in serial form in 1851 and 1852. She was moved by the plight of the slaves she encountered and read about, but what galvanized her into writing her fervently anti-slavery novel was the Fugitive Slave Act of 1850, which made it illegal to help or hide escaped slaves. They had to be returned to their master, however brutal he might have been.

The book was an extraordinary publishing phenomenon, both in the US and internationally. It was banned in the South where owning a copy could incur a ten-year prison sentence. It spawned theatrical adaptations and later movies; indeed it spawned a whole Uncle Tom industry and its characters' names entered common parlance. Uncle Tom became a universal term for a black person who remained unerringly loyal to white people, while we still talk about people or trends that "grow like Topsy" after the slave girl in the book who replied, "I s'pect I growed" when asked who made her. The book goaded pro-slavery "anti-Tom" literary responses from the South, including *Aunt Phillis' Cabin: or, Southern Life As It Is* by Mary Henderson Eastman. While the literary merit of Harriet Beecher Stowe's book has been debated hotly over the years, there can be no doubt that *Uncle Tom's Cabin* brought the issue of slavery to a worldwide audience and gave added impetus to the campaign to abolish it. Claims have even been made that the novel acted as a catalyst to the Civil War.

Its author was born in Litchfield, Connecticut, to Lyman Beecher and his first wife Roxana Foote, who died of tuberculosis when Harriet was only four. It was a large family, with Lyman's first two wives bearing 13 children over 22 years. All of his seven boys followed him as ministers, Harriet's brother Henry Ward Beecher becoming an even more famous preacher than his father. Theirs was an intellectual family in which even the daughters went on to make a mark on the history of the United States. Harriet's eldest sister Catharine Esther Beecher became a celebrated educator, while her younger half-sister Isabella Beecher Hooker became a prominent leader in the suffragette movement.

Harriet attended Litchfield Female Academy until her father moved to Boston with his second wife. At that point she enrolled at the Hartford Female Seminary, a progressive school founded by sister Catharine. It was one of the few establishments at the time which offered girls an education that extended beyond the skills that would fit them for marriage and society. Harriet learned a range of academic subjects including Italian, French, Latin, logic, ethics, mathematics and composition, which would stand her in good stead in her later career as a writer. At the age of 16, Harriet herself became a teacher at the seminary while continuing with her own studies and, when the Beecher family moved to Cincinnati, the two sisters founded the Western Female Institute there.

There had been fears that Harriet was getting beyond marriageable age and was too "intellectual," but in 1836 she married a Lane faculty member Professor Calvin Ellis Stowe, a widower. Together they had seven children, with one dying in infancy. But her husband was poorly paid and Harriet soon realized that his salary was not going to be sufficient, so she began to organize her time and her finances so that she could write for a period every day. After winning a writing competition run by the *Western Monthly Magazine*, she became a frequent magazine contributor.

By early 1850, the Stowe family went to Brunswick, Maine, where Bowdoin College, Professor Stowe's alma mater, had lured him back to teach. Harriet took the opportunity to stop and visit her brother Edward in Boston. She had already published *Uncle Sam's Emancipation* in 1845, a short story about a slave who with a Quaker's help persuades his master to liberate him, and Edward's wife Isabella Porter Jones encouraged Harriet to write more on the evils of slavery. Her sister-in-law is reported to have said, "If I could use a pen like you Hatty, I would write something that would show the entire world what an accursed thing slavery is."

A year later Harriet wrote to the editor of *The National Era* offering *Uncle Tom's Cabin* in installments, and it commenced in June 1851. She originally envisaged a few sketches but the project mushroomed. It came out on March 20, 1852, as a book of more than 500 pages and would be the best-selling novel of its time. Overall, only *The Bible* sold more copies in the nineteenth century.

Sales exploded. The paper mills, printers and bookbinders could not keep up with demand. In the English-speaking world it was selling at a rate of 150,000 copies a month. Harriet Beecher Stowe was admired and fêted in the North but hated and infamous in the South. And she did well from sales of the book: US royalties for April to June were $10,000 ($250,000 today). However, there was no international copyright law and there were probably no UK royalties in spite of its huge popularity there.

All three sisters and two of her brothers went to Maine to help Harriet cope. Catharine tried to negotiate a better deal for her sister from the publisher, while Isabella became her correspondence secretary. She found herself drafting replies to kings and queens one moment, then opening a vicious tirade from a slave owner the next. One reportedly enclosed an ear he'd hacked off one of his slaves.

Uncle Tom's Cabin, usually classed as a novel in the nineteenth-century "sentimental" style, has everything — adventure, pathos, a profoundly Christian message of the possibilities offered by redemption, and the themes of moral strength conferred by motherhood and the power of the family. But above all it is about the evils of slavery. Kindly white slave owners are forced to sell their noble slaves; there are escapes and river crossings; a drowning girl is saved; there are shootouts with bounty hunters, religious conversion, a knifing, whippings, and broken promises. Harriet's own voice can often be heard, especially in the overtly religious passages which read like sermons. The book threw up weighty ethical questions: If slavery is violent, is it right to use violence to topple it? Is it acceptable to break the law if you are fighting evil?

Its anti-slavery, pro-liberty message flew around the world. *Uncle Tom's Cabin* was translated into virtually every language on earth. It is reported to be the first American novel in Chinese. It was smuggled into Russia as a Yiddish translation in order to escape censorship. At home, it was so popular that in Boston alone in the year it was published, 300 baby girls were named Eva after Harriet's angelic white female protagonist.

Harriet Beecher Stowe's sisters also helped her collate material for *A Key to Uncle Tom's Cabin*, which came out a year later. It gave the story behind the novel, revealing the sources she drew on when writing it and aiming to counter criticism from supporters of slavery that the book contained glaring inaccuracies.

At around the same time, the Beecher Stowe family moved to Andover, Massachusetts where Calvin Ellis Stowe had accepted an important chair at the town's Theological Seminary, which came with a generous salary and free house. Harriet, well briefed by anti-slavery campaigners Frederick Douglass and William Lloyd Garrison, undertook the first of three major tours of Europe accompanied by her husband and her brother Charles who read aloud her speeches for her.

A travel book, *Sunny Memories of Foreign Lands*, followed, as did another slave novel, *Dred*, in 1856. *Dred* was panned but her name guaranteed sales. She was to write 17 more novels over the next two decades but nothing ever came close in popularity or influence to *Uncle Tom's Cabin*. In 1862 she visited Washington, DC to make sure for herself that Lincoln would free the slaves. She had tea with the President who reputedly said, "So this is the little lady who made this big war." However, this account of the meeting was written much later and other sources question that Lincoln even knew who she was.

Meanwhile, Harriet's sister Isabella had purchased a substantial piece of land called Nook Farm close to Hartford, Connecticut. She subdivided it, slowly selling off lots and creating a community of intellectuals and authors including Samuel Clemens who is better known as Mark Twain, the creator of *Tom Sawyer* and *Huckleberry Finn*. Calvin Stowe, by now retired, and Harriet had a large house built there on some four to five acres. They were to spend the rest of their lives at Nook Farm, wintering at Mandarin, Florida. Calvin Ellis Stowe died in 1886 and Harriet Beecher Stowe in 1896.

Harriet's observation that "women are the real architects of society" was certainly true in her family's case. As the nineteenth century unfolded, the baton passed inexorably from Catharine the educator and writer, to Harriet the best-selling novelist, to Isabella the suffragist. But the jewel in the Beecher crown was surely *Uncle Tom's Cabin*. As Charles Francis Adams Sr., the US ambassador to the UK from 1861 to 1868 and son of John Quincy Adams and therefore Abigail's grandson, said: "*Uncle Tom's Cabin*...exercised...a more immediate, considerable and dramatic world-influence than any other book ever provided." Leo Tolstoy praised it and it is credited with influencing other protest literature, including the writings of English social campaigner Caroline Norton, who succeeded in changing British law on the custody of children and the right of married women to inherit property and go to law.

Harriet Beecher Stowe understood perfectly that loud protest and tenacity could bring about change. "Never give up, for that is just the place and time that the tide will turn," she once advised.

CHAPTER 8. ELIZABETH CADY STANTON

"I obstinately refused to 'obey' one with whom I supposed I was entering an equal relation." — Elizabeth Cady Stanton

Advocate for Women's Liberties
November 12, 1815–October 26, 1902

SENECA FALLS, NEW YORK

Elizabeth Cady was eleven when her brother Eleazar died at the age of twenty. He was the only son in the family of eleven children to reach adulthood and her father, a lawyer, was wracked with grief.

"Oh, my daughter, I wish you were a boy!" he lamented.

"I will try to be all my brother was," she replied.

From then on, she was determined to excel. She worked hard at Greek and mathematics; she rode horses competitively, played chess, and participated in legal debating, or what we now call moot court. And she devoured her father's law library. While buried in a book there one day, she overheard her father talking with a client, a recently widowed lady. Enjoying no property rights, the widow had seen her late husband's estate pass to her son, who was now treating her unkindly. She wanted to know what she could do. Elizabeth's father replied that there was nothing she could do. Elizabeth was outraged. Her response was to threaten to cut out of his legal books every law that discriminated against women. Daniel Cady sat his daughter down and explained that the only way to change the law would be to go to Albany, the state capital, and lobby. She was clearly too young to do that but it was an early lesson to her in the importance of correctly targeted public protest in changing laws and systems.

ELIZABETH CADY STANTON, as she was to become, was the towering figure for women's liberties in America in the second half of the nineteenth century. From the right of women to own property to coeducation, from inheritance to child custody and more lenient divorce laws, from the abolition of slavery to universal suffrage — she campaigned on them all. She was highly intelligent and an accomplished speaker and writer. If Abigail Adams's clarion call of "Remember the Ladies" (Chapter 4) ever had an echo in the following century, then it surely was in the work of Elizabeth Cady Stanton.

Her father Daniel Cady grew up on a farm and began his career as an apprentice cobbler. Blinded in one eye in a workshop accident, he tried teaching instead before studying law. He began practicing in Johnstown, New York at the age of 26, marrying Elizabeth's mother Margaret Livingston two years later. She was 12 years his junior and several inches taller, the daughter of the patriot Colonel James Livingston who unmasked his fellow Continental Army officer, Colonel Benedict Arnold, as a turncoat.

An early indication of where Elizabeth might have developed her ideas on women's rights is contained in a minor incident involving her mother. When Margaret's church needed a new vicar, she insisted the ladies be given a vote.

Elizabeth was well educated at local Johnstown schools before going to a revolutionary new seminary for women in Troy, New York. It was run by Emma Hart Willard who was daring to give young women the kind of education previously enjoyed only by young men.

In her early twenties Elizabeth met an agent of the American Anti-Slavery Society, a close friend of Theodore Weld (Chapter 5) named Henry Stanton. Her father did not approve of the match, seeing Henry Stanton as little more than a panhandler. It seems likely that none of her family was present at the marriage in Johnstown on May 1, 1840, and the minister had problems with her refusal to "obey" her husband. She also refused to sign herself as Mrs. H. or Mrs. Henry Stanton, and always styled herself Elizabeth Cady Stanton or E Cady Stanton. Her critics later seized on this and relentlessly called her Mrs. Henry Stanton in their outpourings.

Just 11 days after their wedding, the couple sailed from New York City to England on an unorthodox honeymoon — the World Anti-Slavery Convention in London. Landing in England in early June, they joined other American delegates, many of them women, in a central London hotel.

The Convention opened on June 12 and immediately plunged into a long and furious debate about where to sit these American women. It was frowned on for women to take part in public or political life at that time. However, some of the participants argued that as accredited representatives who had fought for the cause, they must be seated. To others, including members of the clergy, it was equally obvious that it would be inappropriate for the women to sit with the men. Still others were more politically strategic: it was going to be hard enough to defeat slavery without taking on women's rights as well.

Elizabeth was stunned. Surely these were enlightened people who believed in freedom and were fighting slavery. How could they contemplate effectively excluding women from a forum that was devoted to discussing liberty?

Eventually Elizabeth and the other wives and delegates were permitted to stay but had to sit in a separate gallery, screened off from general view. When eminent abolitionist William Lloyd Garrison arrived later, he insisted on joining them.

Elizabeth was angry that she could not see the leading social reformer Lucretia Mott when she stood up to speak. It was the bond created that day in the Freemasons' Hall on Great Queen Street in London, England, between the young newly married Elizabeth Cady Stanton and Lucretia Mott, two decades older, that led to the founding of the US women's rights movement.

"We resolved to hold a convention as soon as we returned home, and form a society to advocate the rights of women," Elizabeth wrote later.

But their plan wasn't realized for another eight years. First the Stantons were to move back to Johnstown, where they lived with Elizabeth's parents while her husband studied law. By 1847, Elizabeth and Henry Stanton were living in Seneca Falls, New York, he practicing law and she raising three boys. Two more boys and two more girls were to follow in the 1850s. While she enjoyed motherhood, she felt unfulfilled and isolated in Seneca Falls.

However, she was now only a few miles away from Lucretia Mott, which whom she had kept up a correspondence. This led them finally to return to the idea they had hatched in London — the organization of the first public women's rights meeting in the United States. The Seneca Falls Women's Rights Convention took place on July 19 and 20, 1848. Elizabeth wrote *A Declaration of Rights and Sentiments* for the occasion.

This Declaration fully embraced the philosophy and cleverly used the language of Thomas Jefferson's July 4, 1776, Declaration of Independence. It was unashamedly pro-liberty: "We hold these truths to be self-evident: that all men and women are created equal; that they are endowed by their Creator with certain inalienable rights; that among these are life, liberty, and the pursuit of happiness."

It was wide in its scope. It covered women's suffrage, it accused men of making women "if married, in the eye of the law, civilly dead," it railed against the denial of property rights to women, "even to the wages she earns," and against spousal abuse ("chastisement"). Divorce, taxation of single women, monopolies reserving professions for men, unequal education, and different moral standards for men and women were all tackled in crisp, simple yet stirring language. She asserted that men had "usurped the prerogative of Jehovah himself by assigning roles to women when that job belongs to her conscience and her God."

She summarized: "He has endeavored, in every way that he could, to destroy her confidence in her own powers, to lessen her self-respect, and to make her willing to lead a dependent and abject life."

She insisted that women should "have immediate admission to all the rights and privileges which belong to them as citizens of the United States." To this end she pledged to form a speaker bureau, publish, raise petitions, lobby and harness "the pulpit and the press," and to follow the meeting in Seneca Falls with women's conventions all over the country.

The women and men who were present spent two days debating the issues and the strategies needed for change, and in the end about 60 men and 40 women signed Elizabeth's Declaration. This meeting led to her becoming one of the leading figures in the women's rights movement in America.

Two things happened: first, other women organized similar meetings and always started proceedings by reading the Declaration; second, she became much in demand as a speaker and writer. She could do little speaking given her young family, but she did a great deal of writing.

Then onto the scene came Susan Brownell Anthony, a house guest of Amelia Bloomer, the local postmistress who popularized "bloomers." Elizabeth herself enthusiastically adopted the loose trousers gathered at the ankle and topped by a short dress or skirt.

Susan Brownell Anthony was a typical Quaker of the early 1850s, a passionate believer in temperance and the abolition of slavery. Temperance was a women's rights issue, because the wives of drunkards had no rights, no recourse, and were unable to stop their husbands squandering the family money on drink. Slavery was a women's issue too; slaves were disenfranchised in a similar way to women, being unable to vote or own property or avail themselves of other rights accorded only to white men.

Susan had two great advantages: she was unmarried and so free to travel and she was a superb organizer. For over 50 years she and Elizabeth Cady Stanton worked together — and often fought too. Certainly until Elizabeth's seven children were older, the division of labor was clear. Elizabeth was the philosopher, strategist, article writer and speech coach, all of which she could do at home. Susan raised the money, gave Elizabeth's speeches for her and ran petition drives.

The second half of the nineteenth century seethed with abolitionists tackling the slavery issue, suffragists campaigning for votes for women and advocates of temperance. There were organizational and philosophical links between the three. For example, suffragists helped the North in the Civil War, knowing that it could help their own cause. There was no manual showing how to bring about social change, particularly for women. Instead there was a vast, messy debate not just on the issues but also about strategies and tactics.

Elizabeth Cady Stanton and Susan Brownell Anthony argued often and long. Were they better off running a single issue group promoting suffrage or a multi-issue umbrella sheltering suffrage, slavery and other campaigns? Should they be focusing on education for the long term or on short-term political ends? Were they gradualists, taking one step at a time (Susan's preferred approach) or great leapers, challenging people with big bold reforms (Elizabeth's view)? They also debated whether they should be operating at state or federal level, whether the frontier or the East was more fertile for change and whether alliances with other groups were useful or not.

There were many, including Henry Stanton, who felt that issues had to be prioritized according to the likelihood of victory. This put slavery at the top and votes for women at the bottom. His was a pragmatic call but Elizabeth disagreed with him on this, as she did on many other political and ideological issues.

Elizabeth tried everything from ballot initiatives to newspapers, from speeches to running for office and the courts. She formed organizations and when she was too radical for some tastes, they would splinter creating yet more groups. She spent months at a time on the stump campaigning for women's rights during the 1870s in the Midwest and in the frontier states and territories. She felt there was a greater appreciation for women out there. Wyoming, while still a territory, had given women the vote in 1869, just over half a century before the Nineteenth Amendment granted universal suffrage in 1920. Colorado adopted female suffrage in 1893, Utah in 1895 and Idaho in 1896.

Some of the debates were really brutal. Having abandoned campaigning during the Civil War, believing that women's rights would not have top priority at a time when slavery and secession were the key issues, Elizabeth violently opposed the passage of the Fourteenth and Fifteenth Amendments to the US Constitution added in 1868 and 1870. These gave black men citizenship and voting rights but did not include white or black women. Her uncompromising all-or-nothing attitude repeatedly led to arguments with gradualists who believed that change could only come about in stages, but it successfully highlighted the issues with clarity and consistency.

Despite health problems, Elizabeth continued the struggle throughout the 1870s and 1880s. She was a celebrity and in demand. She started a six-volume history of the suffragette movement in 1880, a huge undertaking which would span 42 years and a number of co-authors. The final volume came out in 1922, some twenty years after her death. To help sales she wrote to friends asking them to donate copies to the libraries of their local colleges and/or alma maters and she was very angry when Vassar and Harvard returned their sets.

Her 1892 speech, *The Solitude of Self*, delivered to the National American Woman Suffrage Association (NAWSA), the House Committee on the Judiciary, and the Senate Committee on Woman Suffrage marvelously bookends the 1848 Declaration. It is her resignation speech after serving as president of NAWSA and its predecessor for twenty years and is a powerful plea for individual responsibility and self-sovereignty: "The strongest reason for giving woman all the opportunities for higher education, for the full development of her faculties, her forces of mind and body; for giving her the most enlarged freedom of thought and action; a complete emancipation from all forms of bondage, of custom, dependence, superstition; from all the crippling influences of fear — is the solitude and personal responsibility of her own individual life."

The 77-year-old Elizabeth Cady Stanton delivered a masterpiece of eloquence and reason, culminating in a great pro-liberty rhetorical question: "Who, I ask you, can take, dare take on himself the rights, the duties, the responsibilities of another human soul?"

But it was far from being her final word. In 1895 she struck back at the clergy who had consistently preached against female suffrage and women's rights with publication of *The Woman's Bible*, in which she now marshaled arguments to reinterpret all the many passages of the Bible which had been used against her over the past five decades. It was a runaway bestseller both in the US and overseas. Now living in a New York City apartment, she marked the fiftieth anniversary of the Seneca Falls Declaration with her 1898 autobiography *Eighty Years and More*.

Her very last article was in October 1902. In it she pressed for divorce reform. Her last two letters came a few days afterwards. She wrote to President Theodore Roosevelt and First Lady Edith Roosevelt urging them to endorse a Constitutional Amendment in favor of female suffrage. When she died just days later, by her casket stood the desk on which she'd written the Seneca Falls Declaration and on it her family placed the first three volumes of her *History of Woman Suffrage*.

To Lucretia Mott she was "a pioneer," and to Susan B. Anthony she was the source who had to be consulted — whatever the issue. While Susan usually pulled the trigger, Elizabeth supplied the powder, the bullets and the rifling. To abolitionist and equal rights campaigner Frederick Douglass, Elizabeth Cady

Stanton was a master of logic while to William Lloyd Garrison she was a fearless woman who poured everything into her causes. And Wendell Phillips openly admitted that he stole from her work for his speeches. She corresponded with the philosopher John Stuart Mill and met the British MP John Bright, who did so much for free trade. She bestrode the debate on liberty for women throughout the latter half of the nineteenth century and did much of the groundwork that resulted in women across the US enjoying the right to vote on an equal footing with men 18 years after her death.

CHAPTER 9. CLARA BARTON

"I shall never do a man's work for less than a man's pay."

— Clara Barton

Founder, American Red Cross
December 25, 1821–April 12, 1912

WASHINGTON, DISTRICT OF COLUMBIA

Today the American Red Cross supplies more than 40 per cent of the blood and blood products used in the US to heal and help the sick and injured. It sends instant relief to 70,000 disasters in the US every year from home fires to hurricanes, and is part of a global humanitarian network reaching 100 million people in need across the world. As this new edition was in the final stages of preparation, Hurricane Sandy hit New Jersey, New York, and many other states with a record setting vengeance. The American Red Cross was immediately on the scene with thousands of its volunteers pouring in with all kinds of relief from food, water, and blankets to shelter and medical services. And to thank for it we have one small woman with a shy smile whose life was often blighted with depression but who emerges as a towering figure of the nineteenth and early twentieth centuries.

This vast organization built on care, compassion, and selflessness has its foundation in the work that CLARISSA HARLOWE BARTON performed as an individual. Frequently during the Civil War and later overseas, Clarissa — known as Clara — Barton risked life and limb to bring aid, succor, and relief to people stricken by war and misfortune. After creating the American Red Cross almost single-handedly, she often funded it out of her own pocket. In an era when the federal government rightly and resolutely refused public sustenance, she showed time and time again that private aid could be very effectively pinpointed to ameliorate lives and solve problems.

Clara Barton was the fifth of five children born to Stephen and Sarah Barton in North Oxford, Massachusetts. Theirs was a well-to-do Puritan family that did not vaunt its wealth. After a girl, born in 1804, Sarah delivered two boys and a second girl by 1810. When Clara came along a good 11 years later in 1821, she was to grow up in a home atmosphere that was pro-abolition, pro-suffrage and pro-education. Boys rather than girls would be her preferred companions.

Clara's schooling started when she was only three, with her elder sister Dorothea, already a teacher, playing a big role in her education. The little girl was already showing a sharp intellect and was able to spell nine-letter words. Very studious, she too became a teacher aged 18 after spells as a nurse for an injured brother and as a factory worker at her family's mill.

She worked hard, following the example of her mother who rose at 3 am. It was Clara herself who wrote that her mother "always did two days' work in one." And Clara was also imbued with the family tradition of philanthropy (it was recorded her father gave away $500 a year — $10,000 in today's money) and during breaks in the school year, evenings and weekends she engaged in voluntary work, including tutoring children and helping poor families. She also tended the sick in a smallpox outbreak. As a teacher her approach to discipline was unusual for that era. She reportedly dispensed corporal punishment only once in a decade. Later she said of that incident: "Child that I was I did not know that the surest test of discipline is its absence." She became an educational troubleshooter, moving from school to school. The Board assigned her wherever there was perceived to be the biggest problems.

After a decade of teaching she suffered the indignity of a new headmaster being appointed at more than twice her salary to run New Jersey's first free public school which she had set up. Stung, Clara moved south to Washington, DC and soon picked up a plum role as a clerk in the Patent Office paying nearly two and a half times the salary of the head who been brought in over her. This time she was earning the same as her male colleagues. She was a woman in a man's world, being one of only four or five female employees in the federal government. Ultimately, though, holding a man's job when men had the vote and women did not in the capital of political patronage was never going to be a long-term proposition.

The start of the Civil War in 1861 brought Clara Barton a new focus. Having been raised to be pro-abolition, she was firmly on the side of the North. And being based in Washington, DC she was within just a few miles of early battles in northern Virginia and western Maryland and saw the wounded making their way to the capital.

On her own initiative, she began making forays out to the battlefields by train or wagon or on horseback taking with her large quantities of medical supplies, clothing, food, and water, even brandy, wine, and tobacco. To begin with these came by way of gifts or monetary donations from the North but Clara quickly gained such a reputation for her relief work in extraordinarily difficult conditions that she could be considered an early example of a public-private partnership. Certainly she was a private entity performing what we might normally expect of the public sector — and doing it more quickly and efficiently, and less expensively!

She hacked at the government's red tape, which often frustrated her attempts to release supplies and gain access to the battlefields, managing to deliver tons of material to field hospitals close to the battle lines and distribute them to desperate surgeons. This diminutive teacher who suffered periods of the darkest depression — described in her diaries as "thin black snakes" of unhappiness — became a fundraising and logistical mastermind. She was able pull together supplies and guide them so close to the battlefront that she often came under fire. Not content with being a deliverywoman, she cared for the wounded and dying, and earned herself a reputation as "the Angel of the Battlefield."

As the War wore on, she moved from battlefield to battlefield, not always initially welcomed by everybody. Armies tend to be very rigid and rule-driven and this gadfly of a lady answerable only to herself irritated many in command. As the army of the North became better organized, her work met increasing official resistance. But she was becoming very famous, the need for her services was immense, and she was rarely idle. Often it seemed that her depression galvanized her to take on new, ever more ambitious projects which, remarkably, she was always able to realize however mentally frail she felt. She even ventured as far south as Charleston, SC for the siege of Fort Wagner in the summer of 1863 where, led by the 54th Massachusetts Volunteer Infantry, an African-American regiment, the North captured this important port. The movie *Glory* starring Matthew Broderick, Denzel Washington, and Morgan Freeman depicts the story of this battle and was nominated for and won three Oscars.

Far from scaling down her humanitarian activities with the end of the Civil War, she threw herself into three new ventures.

The first was to create a bureau in Annapolis, Maryland to help families discover what had happened to their sons. The second was to create a cemetery at Andersonville, Georgia, for 13,000 Union soldiers; most were identified from hospital records but 400 remained unknown. The third was to contract to do a series of lecture tours in the North and Mid West speaking about the war, her work, and her thoughts about the future. Her lecture fee of $100 in 1867 would represent $1,500 today; she spoke up to 14 times a month. She financed her missing soldiers' bureau, now moved from Annapolis to Washington, DC, and was becoming well established financially, often funding her activities out of her own resources. Moreover, she never charged charities and waived her fee for veterans.

A woman speaking in public was still a novelty. Partly because of that and partly because of her subject matter, she filled the lecture halls. As a strong woman who felt deeply that a woman should and could have equal status with men, she was often pressed to lend her name to women's issues but this was not her way. Clara's strategy was to press forward on all fronts rather than become focused on just one. She firmly believed that putting all your eggs in the basket of suffragism — obtaining the vote for women — was wrong and felt that economic rather than political advancement for women to be just as, if not more, important and broader based.

With the cemetery open (she was invited to raise the flag), correspondence to her bureau down to a trickle, and her mental health precarious following her war experiences and her public speaking tours, her doctor advised a long European vacation.

It was on this 1869 trip to Scotland, England, Paris and Geneva that she discovered an organization called the Red Cross founded in Switzerland in 1866. Its symbol, a red cross on a white background, was the inversion of the Swiss flag, which featured a white cross on a red background. In fact, the Red Cross had heard of her presence and sought her out at her hotel. It was at this meeting that she first learned about the Treaty of Geneva signed by 32 countries and dealing with Clara's first concern, the treatment of the wounded in times of war. However, the USA had refused to sign up three times, ostensibly because Secretary of State William H. Seward felt that the USA voluntarily did everything provided for in the treaty. However, the real issue was that America really never signed treaties except to end wars. This was because its foreign policy was guided by the Monroe Doctrine, the declaration by President James Monroe in December 1823, that the United States would not tolerate a European nation colonizing an independent nation in North or South America. Any such intervention in the western hemisphere would be considered a hostile act by the United States. There would, it was hoped, perhaps be a way for Clara to bring the Americans round. Their signing the treaty would give the necessary legal standing for the founding of the American Red Cross.

While visiting Louise, Grand Duchess of Baden and founder of the German Red Cross, in 1871 during the Franco–Prussian War, Clara heard that the city of Strasbourg had finally fallen following a two-month siege. She rushed there and plunged right in, running a soup kitchen. However she quickly decided that what was really needed to lift people was paying jobs. Donations of money and fabric were solicited from Germany, the UK and the USA and within months she had over 200 women at home or in workshops making clothes. They received a weekly wage for this work. It was a hand-up, not a hand-out, and Clara could see how much better this was than dishing out soup, which simply increased dependency.

Returning to the US, she suffered a mental and physical collapse. She finally moved to a sanatorium close to Dansville in upstate New York, and after some months was sufficiently recovered to buy and move to a house in the nearby town while continuing to be watched over by her doctors. It was in this small town that, prompted by yet another war in Europe and the need to shake off her demons by once again losing herself in activity, she wrote to the International Red Cross in Geneva. She asked if she could become its American agent and, if so, what she had to do.

They enthusiastically embraced this so-called "Florence Nightingale of the Civil War" after the British nurse of the Crimean War and advised publicity and fundraising. But, most important of all, the International Red Cross wanted Clara Barton to obtain senatorial approval of the Treaty of Geneva and a Presidential signature inscribed on it.

Over the next five years she made repeated trips to Washington, DC dealing with three different administrations. Clara cleverly trumped the objections about interfering in foreign affairs by stating that her Red Cross would not only deliver aid at a time of war but also in the far more likely event of domestic emergencies such as floods or fire. She also formed an organization which started to establish branches, the first opening in Dansville.

It was not at all plain sailing. Other women disaffected with Clara's autocratic style had set up Blue Anchor to build lifeguard stations on America's coasts. They felt they should have some stake in the American Red Cross. In response, Clara cultivated her own influential contacts, enlarged her own organization, sharpening its focus and mission.

A huge and deadly fire in Michigan in September 1881 saw Clara's new organization in action for the first time. Two male agents were dispatched and the fledgling new branches led by Dansville raised some $10,000 (today $220,000) to purchase much-needed clothing, food, tools, bedding and household items. She also made cash grants to families affected by the fire, which killed as many as 500 people.

Following disappointment with the Hayes administration, Clara, ever persistent, made real progress with Republican President Garfield, a man elected with the overwhelming support of Civil War veterans who revered the feisty humanitarian. Unfortunately he was assassinated but in December 1881 in Vice-President Arthur's annual message to Congress he supported the signing of the Treaty of Geneva. The United States finally signed it in March 1882.

Flooding rivers in the South and Mid West gave the new official American Red Cross the chance to prove itself. In 1882 and 1883 the Mississippi broke its banks followed in 1884 by the Ohio. Funds raised went from $8,000 to $18,000 to $175,000 which today would be roughly equivalent to $200,000, $400,000 and $4.2million, making a total of $4.8million. In representing the United States in Geneva at the Third International Conference of the Red Cross, Clara Barton became the first ever female US diplomat. She was not just welcomed but fêted. As she continued to build the American Red Cross her philosophy regarding the difference between philanthropy and charity hardened. She favored a short sharp intervention at the time of disaster — a hand-out or emergency relief. Then she wanted to withdraw and move out lest that charitable impulse create dependency and stifle entrepreneurship, personal initiative and responsibility. In its place she favored strategic philanthropy — the concept of a hand-up offering practical help and education. The Johnstown (Pennsylvania) or "great" flood of 1889 was a severe test, but her five months there in person with her staff and volunteers and some $250,000 (today $6 million) took the Red Cross to new levels.

Other droughts, hurricanes, bank-bursting rivers and floods followed and as the philanthropist, who never married, entered her eighth decade she had a large suite of offices and reception rooms in Washington, DC, a warehouse in nearby Glen Echo, Maryland, and a large ship at sea loaded with grain for Russian peasants whose crops had failed.

Ever dynamic even as old age approached, she was pleased with the fruits of her efforts. Describing a year-long operation to save and rebuild Sea Islands, South Carolina, after a devastating hurricane in 1894, she said, "It is probable that there are few instances on record, where a movement toward relief of such magnitude, commenced under circumstances so new, so unexpected, so unprepared and so adverse, was ever carried on for such a length of time and closed with results so entirely satisfactory to both those served and those serving, as this disaster."

At 75 she was in Turkey, organizing four missions of food and medical supplies into Armenia by mule, horse, and camel. Over a five-month period some $116,000 in privately contributed aid (today worth $3million) was distributed.

With the building of a trolley line between Glen Echo and DC, Clara closed her Washington house and relocated out to her store house, creating offices and living space. As she did so, Cuban resistance to Spanish rule was reaching new heights of violence and there were cries throughout the press for Red Cross involvement.

Without an instruction from President McKinley, Clara was reluctant to act as the Spanish, who were signatories to the Treaty of Geneva, had said they would welcome her only as a private citizen. McKinley proposed a fundraising relief committee, that supplies be shipped in care of the US consul general in Cuba, and that Clara be on the ground in charge of distribution. She agreed.

She went no less than three times, and did her best in conditions that brought back memories of the Civil War. Battlefield hospitals were organized and aided, thousands of tons of supplies distributed, and all manner of civil society institutions created, from orphanages to hospitals. It was very tough physically. Clara had never seen such suffering — people were herded into camps surrounded with barbed wire and armed guards, there was a drought and the crops had failed. Many people, including children, died. It was also tough politically as many in the US Army despised her band of volunteers. However, on seeing the results of Clara's work, they often changed their minds.

She was a real heroine to many from feminists to veterans. But her strengths lay in logistics, lobbying and motivating people at the battlefront, and not in accounting or reporting or good governance of a charity. She often dipped into her own pocket to fund the Red Cross and would set out on relief expeditions with little in the bank. But questions were raised about her accounting and lack of receipts, an area that was not Clara's strength. Factional infighting ensued, as so often happens with charitable concerns where property rights are blurred. On May 14, 1904, Clara Barton resigned from the organization she had created two decades before.

But this departure, painful as it was to her, hardly signaled her retirement. She threw herself into work for the National First Aid Association based in Boston, Massachusetts, which pioneered first aid kits — it was the Red Cross at the micro level — only to find it taken over by the now politically well-connected American Red Cross as soon as it began to show results. It claimed it owned the property rights to the idea as Clara had first tried it out as president of that organization.

It was a poignant end to her brilliant career, yet even today it remains doubtful that any woman or man ever did as much as Clara Barton to relieve war- or catastrophe-induced suffering.

Chapter 10. Harriet Tubman

"There's two things I got a right to, and these are death or liberty. One or the other I mean to have." — Harriet Tubman

Slave, Underground Railroad Conductor, Abolitionist and Spy
Winter 1822–March 10, 1913

AUBURN, NEW YORK

"I think slavery is the next thing to hell," HARRIET TUBMAN once remarked. She knew better than most, having been born into slavery as Araminta "Minty" Ross in Dorchester County, Maryland, on the Eastern shore of the Chesapeake Bay, south of Baltimore. Her parents Ben and Rit held responsible positions within the business and home of widower Anthony Thompson. But their circumstances were far from stable. While Ben belonged to Mr. Thompson, Rit and her children were owned by his stepson and ward Edward Brodess, soon to turn 21 and inherit. When Brodess came of age, he moved to the small farm that had been left to him some ten miles away across inhospitable territory, taking Rit and her children along with other slaves he owned, thus splitting up the family.

Brodess was not at all successful and slaves were soon being sold off or hired out. Rit fought to keep her family intact, once hiding Minty's youngest brother Moses for a month when a man from Georgia expressed an interest in buying him. When finally Brodess and his potential client tracked the boy down, Rit confronted them, saying, "You are after my son; but the first man that comes into my house, I will split his head open." The pair retreated and the sale never took place, but Minty learnt something valuable: that resistance can work.

And resistance was certainly the adult Harriet Tubman's stock in trade. She was a five-foot-tall powerhouse, physically strong from years in the fields as a slave and mentally strong in her commitment to liberty. She went from slave to escapee to organizer of the Underground Railroad that conducted slaves to freedom along a network of secret routes. Driven by her own wretched experiences, she became a campaigner for abolition, an army scout and spy, and a social worker. "I grew up like a neglected weed...ignorant of liberty, having no experience of it," she recounted many years later. "Now I've been free I know what a dreadful condition slavery is. I have seen hundreds of escaped slaves, but I never saw one who was willing to go back and be a slave."

Aged six, Minty was hired out as a house and field slave. She received frequent whippings for the slightest error, leaving permanent scars. At age 13 she was unfortunate enough to be present when an overseer, thinking one of his male slaves was about to run away, hurled a large metal weight at him. It missed the slave and hit Minty on the forehead. This left her with brain damage that often caused her to nod off even in the middle of a conversation, only to reawaken as if nothing untoward had happened.

But the blow to her head did nothing to dampen her entrepreneurship. When she was twenty, she suggested to her owner's stepbrother, to whom she had been hired out, that he should let her manage her own time. Her rationale was that if she were free to do so, she could make a profit for him, at the same time putting money by for herself. He agreed.

She met and fell in love with John Tubman, a free mulatto, and they married in about 1844. However, Minty, now Minty Tubman, was still owned by Edward Brodess. A complex web of rights and payments governed this "market."

Two events now conspired to make her future look uncertain. First, she paid a local attorney a few dollars to check back on the wills of her mother's past owners and discovered that Rit, now 64, should have been manumitted (freed) on her forty-fifth birthday. Second, Edward Brodess died. The combination of these two events soon led to a law suit as various factions of the wider Brodess family squabbled over the principal asset — Minty's family. Brodess's widow was furious with Minty, whose action in hiring the attorney had made this legal attack possible. Minty in turn fully realized that she was at risk of being sold to a slave trader for a couple hundred dollars and being shipped further south.

Minty decided to take control of her own destiny. She slipped away one Saturday evening, knowing that she would not be missed until Monday morning.

She took with her two brothers but the men squabbled between themselves, and after only a few hours all three turned back. It turned out to be a mistake, as that very Monday brought the news they had feared: Minty would be sold. So she fled north alone on foot, armed with one piece of information, the address of a safe house. From there she could move on to another safe house, and so on every night until she reached Philadelphia, 100 miles from her starting point in Dorchester County. Most such homes were owned by white Quakers and Methodists who were strongly opposed to slavery.

The route was teeming with bounty hunters eager to catch runaway slaves and pick up rewards of up to $100, sometimes more, per head. Minty walked most of the way with the occasional ride in the back of a horse-drawn farm wagon, traveling by night when her skin color and slave clothes could not easily be spotted. Her route was mostly off road, through woods, along creeks and across wetlands, always following the stars. By day she rested at the next safe house. Later, in a biography written by Sarah Hopkins Bradford, she recalled the moment in 1849 when she reached Pennsylvania: "I had crossed the line. I was free, but there was no one to welcome me to the land of freedom. I was a stranger in a strange land."

And as she entered Philadelphia she gave herself a new name. She was now Harriet Tubman.

Harriet took work as a servant, saving as much as she could so that she could help the rest of her family escape. At the same time, the US Congress was debating the Compromise of 1850. This was an extraordinarily complex packet of five Acts. At the heart of this legislation was western expansion, and with it the admittance of new states into the union. The Southern states feared, rightly, that as more such slave-free states were added, so the balance of power in Congress would shift against them. Harriet was chiefly interested in one aspect of the Compromise, the Fugitive Slave Act. This mandated that all US citizens had to help in the return of fugitive slaves to their rightful owners, moving the touchdown line from the southern border of Pennsylvania right up to the frontier with Canada. But this Act, as with so much government legislation, had unintended consequences. It advanced the abolitionist cause by years as citizens in the North and the West were outraged, believing that the South was using the federal government to impose measures they wanted no part in. The penalties for not taking action to return a fugitive were severe — a $1,000 fine and six months in prison. It turned mildly interested citizens into ardent activists.

Harriet was becoming more and more involved in developing the lines of safe houses and other routes out of the South. This network, which became known as the Underground Railroad, now extended as far north as Canada. She developed lines of information, raised funds from as far away as the UK and Ireland,

and devised strategy and tactics. She also went back to Dorchester County for her husband only to discover that he had taken a new wife. Instead she took 11 other slaves all the way to the Niagara Falls, crossing into Canada.

For the next few years she repeated this operation about a dozen times. She would work all spring, summer and fall and save hard. Then when the long winter nights came, she would head out of Philadelphia to Baltimore and down the Eastern shore of the Chesapeake Bay. Winter was also auction season, an unsettled and worrying time for the slave community, when a master or mistress might decide to put slaves up for sale. It was the time they were most motivated to take flight.

By the mid 1850s Harriet had helped at least 50 people from slavery to liberty. As she put it later in the opening line of her speeches in favor of women's suffrage: "I was the conductor on the Underground Railroad for eight years...I never ran my train off the track and I never lost a passenger." Her codename on the Underground Railroad was "Moses," a nickname that stuck once the wider world heard it via the press. No one knows exactly how many trips she made or how many people she rescued from bondage, though her memorial in Auburn, New York, where she later lived, claims it was as many as 300.

What is certain is that she was indirectly responsible for the escape of many other slaves. Her success encouraged a large number to try their luck and her advice proved invaluable to still more. Large groups of up to 30 at a time were on the march. They reached Canada in such numbers that racial tensions between black and Irish people sprang to the surface over jobs.

By 1857 Harriet had rescued all but three members of her family who had not been sold on to the deep South. Those helped to flee included her parents. Her father Ben had become a free man and succeeded in buying and manumitting her mother Rit, but both were under threat for aiding fugitives. Harriet got them both out to Canada and now had the responsibility of providing for a couple in their eighth decade.

There were many trials for Harriet and other abolitionists who helped man the Underground Railroad, from the harsh winter weather in Canada, the destination of most of the slaves, to the efforts of the state to close down the Railroad. In one case a member was sentenced in Maryland to ten years in prison for owning a copy of Harriet Beecher Stowe's incendiary anti-slavery novel, *Uncle Tom's Cabin* (Chapter 7). The book was banned in the South.

Harriet could neither read nor write but she could speak and sing. Her celebrity status grew and she was in demand as a performer, speaking against slavery, telling stories and singing songs. The controversial abolitionist Captain John Brown sought her out hoping that she might help in recruiting for the army of 100,000 men he planned to raise in order to invade the South and free the slaves. In common with Harriet, he was a fugitive. In his case, it was because of his armed resistance to slavery in Kansas. And, like her, he lived between safe houses, raising money for his cause. His big idea collapsed a year later when his raid on the Federal Armory at Harpers Ferry in Virginia — now West Virginia — went awry and he was captured, tried and hanged. The marching song of the Union army, the "Battle Hymn of the Republic" which later became known as "John Brown's Body," is thought to have been named after him.

In 1859 the US Senator and potential 1860 Republican Party presidential candidate William H. Seward sold to Harriet on generous terms a house and outbuilding on seven acres in Auburn, New York, close to Owasco Lake. The area was well known to her as it was on the Underground Railroad route. But it must have been a somewhat risky transaction for both parties, as Harriet was not only a fugitive but also a thief, having "stolen" slaves from their masters. In effect, Seward was aiding and abetting her. She moved her parents down to Auburn from Canada and took to the road spreading her abolitionist message and raising the money she now needed to pay the loan on the property.

Harriet was close to 40 when Abraham Lincoln, having beaten Seward to the Republican nomination, became President. But to her the new President was a moderate and she did not stop campaigning. Later when Sojourner Truth (Chapter 6) asked Harriet to accompany her on a visit to meet Lincoln, Harriet had no hesitation in refusing. It was her protest against the President's policy of paying white soldiers twice the amount he was paying blacks.

She was a prominent member of the 1860 group of abolitionists and fugitives who scuffled with government agents to free fugitive slave Charles Nalle in Troy, New York, where he was being held under the Fugitive Slave Act. She worked the crowd up, gaining their support, before intervening personally on Nalle's behalf. She then whisked him away to Canada and freedom.

Harriet again headed south on a mission to bring out her last remaining relatives — her sister Rachel and her children Angerine, 13, and Ben, 11. It turned out to be her most dangerous raid yet. When she arrived, she found her sister had just died. The Underground Railroad was in disarray as many of its members had been arrested or had fled or were simply too fearful to carry on. She failed to rescue either Angerine or Ben but did manage to lead a young family of five to freedom in spite of appalling weather, spies, and unreliable lines of intelligence.

With the advent of the Civil War, Harriet's life took another dramatic twist. Governor John Andrew of Massachusetts formed the New England Freedmen's Aid Society and called for volunteers to be shipped south to the Charleston, South Carolina, area. Harriet leapt at the chance, at first working as an army nurse by day and running a food and drink business by night. Then Thomas Wentworth Higginson, one of the Secret Six, the group of influential men who had funded John Brown, was appointed to lead the first black regiment being formed at nearby Camp Saxton. The Six all knew of and admired Harriet Tubman, and Higginson must have been astonished when she knocked on his door.

In fact, Harriet was not merely a nurse by day and entrepreneur by night; she was also quietly building a list of men who could be trusted and who knew the rivers and tricky tidal flows well enough to pilot boats inland. She was also sending out spies along the rivers and developing lines of communication. On June 1, 1863, at 9 p.m., Harriet and her chief pilot boarded the *John Adams*, a ferryboat turned gunboat, with a similar boat, the *Harriet A Wood*, astern.

The 300 troops who boarded with them were all from the black regiment under the command of the pro-abolition Colonel James Montgomery. Their mission was to steal up the Combahee River overnight, surprise rebel farmers at dawn, liberate their slaves and destroy enemy infrastructure. Montgomery, a controversial figure, scorned the ordinary rules of warfare, and was given to looting and burning the communities he raided.

The raid was a huge success. Some 750 slaves were liberated, a major river crossing was destroyed and everything in sight was torched, causing tens of millions of dollars' worth of damage. And not a single soldier was lost. Harriet was widely praised for her role, in particular the way in which she successfully relayed instructions to the slaves that on hearing a certain signal they were to drop everything to run to the riverbank. She had also calmed the fleeing slaves in the ensuing chaos. It is probably too much to say she led the raid, as some newspapers claimed, but she certainly was a key figure in the planning, intelligence gathering, communications and execution. Most of the able-bodied men among the 750 liberated signed up for Montgomery's regiment. For the rest, the women, children, the infirm and elderly, Harriet helped to look after them and smooth their path to liberty.

Harriet served as a nurse during the assault on Fort Wagner in the summer of 1863, the first time a black regiment fought side by side with white regiments. Her side, the Union Army, suffered a heavy defeat. (The story of the 54th Massachusetts Voluntary Infantry was retold in the 1989 movie *Glory* by Matthew Broderick, Denzel Washington, Cary Elwes, and Morgan Freeman.) She then became responsible for interviewing all the black people who crossed over from rebel territory in order both to help them as best she could to resettle and to debrief them as to the location, numbers and defenses of the opposing army.

With the war over, Harriet returned to Auburn and her house on its seven acres. Hundreds of thousands of people, including many members of her wider family, were on the move across the United States, with slaves now free to go where they chose. The make-up of her household changed daily at times. A

25-year-old boarder named Nelson Davis moved in and soon married Harriet, who was then 47, her first, estranged husband having been shot dead.

The battle to free slaves may have been over, but Harriet was far from idle. Denied a proper salary for her work during the war and unable to depend on her husband, who was slowly dying of TB, she relied on her entrepreneurial talents, taking in lodgers and growing crops on her small landholding. In addition, her first biography came out and she raised money for the South despite being under financial pressure herself.

She also took up suffragism. A white woman is reported to have asked her if she believed that women should have the vote. Harriet answered: "I suffered enough to believe it." She spoke at the first meeting of the National Association of Colored Women.

Her poverty eventually was eased after she finally received both her nurse's pay and a widow's pension following the death of her husband. Seward died and his son forgave the outstanding debt on her home.

Harriet Tubman's final project was to raise the funds and build on her land the Harriet Tubman Home for aged and infirm black people. It opened in 1908 and she died there in 1913.

The story of Harriet Tubman is astonishing, exhilarating and inspiring. Born a slave, she became respected and admired by a host of leading Americans of the day. Her courage and stamina in pursuit of liberty are breathtaking. The social reformer and statesman Frederick Douglass summed up her contribution when he said to her in 1868: "Excepting John Brown I know of no one who has willingly encountered more perils and hardships to serve our enslaved people than you have."

Chapter 11. Bina West Miller

"There is nothing unusual about success. I only carried out my idea. Too many people fail because they are afraid of other people's opinions. This is especially true of women. The only thing to do is go ahead." — Bina West Miller, quoted on the website of the Woman's Life Insurance Society.

Businesswoman
1867–April 18, 1954

PORT HURON, MICHIGAN

Bina West was seething. The young teacher from rural Michigan had been full of hope for two promising students, a sister and brother. Tragically, their mother had died and their father was forced to split them up and place them with foster families in separate cities. As if all that wasn't bad enough, Bina had just learnt that the children's new families had sent them out to work. The girl had been hired out as a domestic servant while the boy would be cleaning out livery stables. Their education was over. Bina was struck by the sheer injustice of their situation. If their father had died, the family would still have been together and the children in school, simply because he enjoyed life insurance through his all-male fraternal society. In the late nineteenth century, the vast majority of women had no such access to personal insurance cover. But what could she do about it? Bina felt frustrated, but most of all she was angry. She resolved somehow to do something that would protect women and their families.

Sabina May West, known as Bina and later by her married name, BINA WEST MILLER, was the first of five children born to Alfred J West of Columbus Township, St Clair County, Michigan and Elizabeth J Conant, a direct descendant of Roger Conant, the founder of Salem, Massachusetts. Before meeting his wife, Alfred had been a sailor on the Great Lakes and served in the 36th Illinois Regiment during the Civil War, receiving an honorable discharge after being badly injured by an enemy shell. He became an entrepreneur, building up a portfolio of interlinked businesses ranging from real estate to lumber and farming. He was away a lot, which drew Bina close to Elizabeth. However, they were well provided for and, as Alfred was an avid book collector, they had a good library on which to draw at a time when rural Michigan had no public or traveling libraries.

Bina's intelligence was evident. She graduated from Capac High School aged 16 and trained as a teacher at St Clair County Normal School, becoming certified aged 18. By the time she was twenty she was an assistant principal and had been elected onto the Board of County School Examiners. This made her one of the very first women to hold elected public office in Michigan.

Clearly she could easily have enjoyed a stellar career as an educator but while she was still in her early twenties a different path opened up to her.

Her damascene moment came late on a summer afternoon in June 1891, not long after the foster children episode that had so moved and angered her. She was riding in a horse-drawn buggy over the roads of St Clair County, Michigan with her Aunt Nellie on their way back from a picnic organized by an all-male fraternal benefit society. She had listened to several inspiring speeches extolling the advantages of membership of such a group. It promised social and self-improvement, along with practical benefits such as life and disability insurance, but only for its male members. Suddenly, Bina knew what she would do to help families. Turning to her aunt, she confided in her that such societies were "the greatest thing I ever heard of. I will make this my life's work. There is a great need and I know I can fill it." The need was to provide insurance for women.

Life insurance provided by joint-stock companies had come to the US as early as the 1750s followed by mutual life insurance companies in the 1840s — mutuals are companies owned not by the stockholders but by policyholders. But the policies of both such companies were out of the reach of the average person. The solution for many came in the shape of the fraternal benefit societies that were formed in 1860s and spread like wildfire. They offered insurance funded through collections in order to offer a service previously available only to the wealthy.

This was no new concept. While it came to the US from the friendly society movement in the UK, it had ancient roots, including the Roman guilds, which were associations of craftsmen. Bina threw herself into the study of what was formally named the Fraternal Beneficial Society System, which still exists today, helping both members and the community.

Bina's organization was to be run by women and to provide for women. It aimed to overcome the view that women were uninsurable because pregnancy and childbirth led to unacceptable mortality risks. Later in life Bina recalled her desire to form an organization that "would permanently ameliorate and improve the conditions under which women and children lived."

She began immediately after her revelation on the road back to Columbus Township on June 25, 1891 by helping to found the women's auxiliary of an existing male fraternal order, the Knights of the Maccabees, in Capac, Michigan. This was a bold new development as such auxiliaries had met with ferocious opposition from men and had only recently been allowed. Bina threw herself into the work of the auxiliary, which served her local area and by August she was already a delegate to a statewide meeting of auxiliary officers. She so impressed Major Nathan S. Boynton, the COO of the Knights of the Maccabees, that he offered her a job based in Port Huron overseeing the setting up of new auxiliaries right across Michigan. It would involve a great deal of traveling throughout the state hiring local staff and recruiting new members.

She went home to discuss the offer with her parents. She had the unwavering support of her mother Elizabeth, who succeeded in winning over her husband. He was deeply concerned about his 24-year-old unmarried daughter traveling alone all over Michigan. Bina started her new job in September and by the fall of 1891 she could, according to Keith L. Yates, who charted her legacy in his 1992 book *An Enduring Heritage*, "do nothing but think, talk, and dream of the plan."

By October she was crisscrossing the state either by train or horse drawn buggy on poor roads. Her strategy from day one was to contact the head of the male fraternal society in a particular town and to ask to talk to its members about how a women's auxiliary could benefit their female relatives. If successful (and she nearly always was) she would parlay this meeting into a second one with the women. A poor public speaker to begin with, she gradually became more at ease talking to groups and actually came to enjoy speaking from the pulpit in churches. She is quoted in Yates' book as saying, "I came, I saw, I conquered. I feel a sense of victory and greater confidence in my own ability." Often so many women turned up to the first meeting with their husbands, fathers or brothers that a second one was not needed.

Initially Bina received no salary. Her contract was commission only, her earnings based on her success in recruiting members and setting up auxiliaries. She had little to worry about. By the summer of 1892 she had established 146 new groups and recruited 3,433 new members.

What Bina West was offering was far more than a financial transaction. The auxiliaries or chapters of what became known as the Woman's Benefit Association (WBA) — today called the Woman's Life Insurance Society — met often, usually monthly. They elected officers, developed dress codes and rituals, held social gatherings around the year and more generally supported each other and their communities, offering practical help in times of need. Women, who in the nineteenth century had few rights or prospects for personal growth, now had access to education and other opportunities to expand their talents and horizons.

At this point, in the summer of 1892, only Michigan and New York had such women's groups in place but Ohio was following fast behind and was courting Bina to run its affairs. But an even bigger opportunity beckoned. News of these early women's groups had spread throughout the country and the "parent" male fraternal order, the Knights of the Maccabees, was concerned about two matters. The first was how to cope with the surging demand for women's benefits and the second was how to ensure uniformity across the different state-based organizations. Their solution was to form a national coordinating office with Bina as full-time COO. In today's language, she would be company secretary and head of sales and marketing. It would be her responsibility to keep growing New York, Michigan and Ohio, ensuring they all followed the same procedures and guidelines, and to spread the business model to the other 41 states that existed at that time. There was a lot to do.

With her savings and a $500 loan (worth $12,000 today) Bina opened the new national office, based as before in Port Huron, Michigan, and busied herself devising forms, prospectuses and rules. She began to foray out to create more branches and recruit more members. The $500 loaned on November 12, 1892 was repaid in full on February 13, 1893. While Bina began to travel more, visiting Illinois, Missouri, Connecticut and Tennessee, she also recruited local agents in other states. By March 1893 she had a full-time personal assistant and her salary was now $1,200 per annum — equivalent to about $30,000 today.

The association really started to prove its worth in September 1893, when four women members died. All four widowers were promptly accorded substantial payouts. The first of the four women had been paying dues for only four months but her husband received his check in under three weeks. It was enough to allow him to keep his family together. A little over two years since her fury at the fate of her two pupils, who lost their education at the same time as losing their mother, Bina was having a life-changing impact on families across America. As membership soared, that impact could soon be seen on a daily basis.

Bina undertook longer and longer trips to recruit members and start new branches in response to the letters pouring into Port Huron. Her train was the one on which a generation earlier a young Thomas Edison had sold newspapers.

In 1894 she traveled by rail as far as California, setting up new chapters in Los Angeles, San Bernardino, Riverside, Pasadena, Santa Ana and the San Francisco Bay area. By day she would travel or run training meetings for local staff and volunteer officers and by night she would lecture to groups ranging from a few score to several hundred. She was even able to command audiences of several thousand.

New states, including Pennsylvania, Illinois and Wisconsin, were added and by the end of 1894 the association was active in 18 states and Canadian provinces. As the head of such a quickly growing force, Bina was invited to represent the WBA at meetings of both the National Council of Women and the National Fraternal Congress of America. At the latter she would meet her future husband George W. Miller, an attorney, whom she married in 1929.

While numbers soared, so did problems. There were local branch jurisdictional fights to be arbitrated. A bank holding the funds a local branch had just collected failed. Another branch asked to pay no dues for a year as all its farmer members had been devastated by drought. Some women lied on their application form, often about their age, or misled the examining physician about a pre-existing condition.

To the fights Bina brought sanity and peace; to the failing bank and drought-devastated farmers she brought compassion and an amnesty; and to the liars and cheats she was, it is safe to say, no nonsense.

At the Association's first biennial review in 1895 Bina's leading role was confirmed but now she had a new nominal boss in the form of Lillian M Hollister, who had headed the Michigan WBA for the past two years. Hollister's new role allowed for Bina to take her first vacation since leading the organization and to serve as its official delegate to meetings in the US and Canada.

Lillian's early career mirrored Bina's. She had finished high school and then trained as a teacher, qualifying in her teens. And now together the two women formed a remarkable double act, leading the group to spectacular new heights. Bina and Lillian headed the WBA from 1895 to 1911, when Lillian was forced to resign because of failing health. They took it from a few thousand members to 160,000; assets went from a few thousand to $5 million ($115 million today); and the insurance fund available to indemnify members rose from the low single millions to $110 million, or $2.5 billion today.

The WBA was speedy and effective, even when required on a grand scale. On April 18, 1906 a huge earthquake hit the San Francisco Bay area. Fifty-two people died and 28,000 buildings collapsed. Without waiting for any claims, Bina wired the local rep $1,000, the equivalent to $25,000 today. Each member was asked to help and a further $125,000 in today's money was quickly raised. Across the Bay in Oakland, members set up soup kitchens and places to sleep for the hundreds streaming out of San Francisco. Two members had died and their families were quickly paid. Another 121 members were indemnified after losing their homes and belongings.

But it was not all plain sailing. One early plan was to have the members and branches collect funds to improve rooms in local hospitals. However it was discovered that this did not secure special treatment, rates or even access for members, so this was replaced by a medical plan and other combined health and burial insurance plans.

Following Lillian's retirement, Bina was enthusiastically and unanimously elected to replace her as both titular and operational head of the WBA at a meeting on July 12, 1911; less than a month later Lillian died.

Bina West Miller's achievements go far beyond that of a pioneering businesswoman, not least her contribution to women's suffrage. She made speeches throughout the US and Canada, even traveling to Europe and the Near East, calling for women to be given the right to vote. The right of American women to vote was enshrined in the Constitution in 1920.

In 1925 she became the first woman president of the National Fraternal Congress of America and as a Republican served on presidential commissions and advisory councils. She was selected to make one of the nominating speeches for Herbert Hoover in 1928, the same year as she was voted Michigan's top businesswoman in a *Detroit Free Press* poll. The Associated Press once called her "one of the five greatest women in America."

Bina continued to lead the WBA until May 1948 when aged 81 she resigned after more than half a century at the helm. She wanted to make way for younger blood. The staff now numbered 125; there were some 225,000 members; $120 million of insurance was in force (the equivalent of $1.1 billion today); there were assets of $55 million ($485 million at today's prices) and an annual surplus of $4 million (around $35 million now). It is recorded that in its first decade alone, the WBA paid out the equivalent of $50 million today in death and disability benefits. It was an extraordinary achievement.

She died six years later in Evanston, Illinois on April 18, 1954 after a short illness. Her entry at The Michigan Women's Historical Center and Hall of Fame concludes: "Miller was chief executive officer of the Women's Benefit Association for more than 56 years. Her years of service stand as testimony to her lifelong commitment to improve women's status in society by providing financial security along with opportunities for social and community involvement and self-improvement."

The Woman's Life Insurance Society is still operating in Port Huron. At the end of 2009 it had 263 chapters.

CHAPTER 12. MADAM C. J. WALKER

"There is no royal flower-strewn path to success. And if there is, I have not found it for if I have accomplished anything in life it is because I have been willing to work hard." — Madam C. J. Walker

Entrepreneur
December 23, 1867–May 25, 1919

INDIANAPOLIS, INDIANA

She went from plain Sarah Breedlove, the daughter of slaves, to millionaire beautician, philanthropist and social activist MADAM C. J. WALKER. It was an astonishing transformation for a woman of her humble beginnings.

Sarah was the first member of her slave family to be born free but her early life was far from easy. As she said many years later, "I got my start from giving myself a start." Sarah came into the world in a cabin in the chaotic, ravaged South in Delta, Louisiana on December 23, 1867, and almost as soon as she could walk she was working in the cotton fields. She later claimed to have spent only three months in school learning the three Rs. What she did learn was mostly taught at Sunday school.

Her mother died when she was six and her father remarried, but a year after that, he too was dead. Sarah was adopted by her older married sister Louvenia but her brother-in-law, whom she later described as "cruel," was not happy with the arrangement.

As soon as she could, she bolted into the arms of Moses McWilliams. She was 14 when she married, a mother at 17 and a widow at 20. Sarah had but one option: to head with her daughter Lelia (who later renamed herself A'Lelia) to St. Louis where her three brothers lived. They were, by the standards of most black people towards the end of the nineteenth century, doing relatively well as self-employed barbers.

Sarah took a room in a rough area and started to work as a washerwoman. The work was hard but it brought in a very necessary $1.50 per day. One account even puts her in the $12-a-week bracket (that would translate to $284 a week today). Lelia was enrolled in school and Sarah involved herself deeply in St. Paul's African Methodist Episcopal church, observing how middle-class blacks dressed, spoke and behaved. She was determined to better herself.

Marrying John Davis in 1894 did little to advance this aim. Davis was often unemployed, a gambling alcoholic who beat her and kept a mistress called Susie. Somehow Sarah and Lelia survived and in 1901 Lelia graduated from L'Ouverture Elementary School, aged 16 and nearly six feet tall. Sarah had saved up and was able to send Lelia to Knoxville College, Tennessee, in the fall of 1902, paying the equivalent of $200 per month for her daughter's ongoing education.

With Lelia in Knoxville and John Davis away with Susie, Sarah began seeing Charles Joseph (C.J.) Walker, a successful newsman who sold subscriptions and advertising. He seemed very much a cut above Davis, with his charm, taste for fine clothes and talent for self-promotion. Sarah began to focus on her own education, going to night school. She also made sure she improved her wardrobe and demeanor, and threw herself into church and community projects. These included volunteering at St. Paul's Mite Missionary Society and, after reading a newspaper article, organizing a collection of money and groceries to help an elderly man struggling to take care of his blind sister and invalid wife.

Things were looking up but there was a problem that she just didn't seem able to cure: her hair had been falling out for a decade. Sarah described her appearance as "frightful." As her great-great-granddaughter A'Leila Bundles wrote in her biography of Sarah, *On Her Own Ground*: "The complaint was a common one for the era, due usually to a combination of infrequent washing, illness, high fever, scalp disease, low-protein diets and damaging hair treatments."

People paid little attention to hair hygiene at the turn of the twentieth century, and black women experimented relentlessly with methods that would alter the natural texture of their hair to make it straighter, longer and easier to style. They used soap, goose fat and oils, as well as harsh chemical straightening agents. But these treatments also made it drier and prone to thinning. There were many products on the market with names such as *Kink-No-More*, prompting serious debates in the black and white press about the restorative and straightening claims of some. Sometimes newspaper publishers refused point blank to run adverts for certain treatments.

As she prepared to marry again, Sarah became very involved in this industry. A businesswoman named Annie Pope-Turnbo had set up in her neighborhood offering hair treatments. She and Sarah became friends and when a job as a hairdresser was offered at twice her earnings as a washerwoman, Sarah jumped at it.

She loved her new work, and the pleasure it brought to her customers reinforced that feeling. Sarah left St. Louis in July 1905, taking the railroad a thousand miles west to Denver where her sister-in-law Lucy Crockett Breedlove — her brother's wife — lived with her four daughters. She took with her a large supply of Annie Pope-Turnbo's product and set up as a sales agent for her.

Once in Denver, Sarah embarked on two careers: the first as a cook for an upmarket rooming house at $685 a month in today's money and the second selling the hair products. Sarah soon met a leading pharmacist named Edmund L. Scholtz, who owned the Scholtz Drug Company. One story has him rooming where she was the cook; another has him approaching her when she was looking around his shop. He analyzed the product and suggested refinements to the formula that stood to make her a lot more money.

She saved hard from her cook's salary and by November she was once again doing laundry two days a week, while spending the other five selling her improved hair formula. This she mixed by the tubful in a tiny attic. Sarah, ever conscious of the need to better herself and to establish useful social connections, also joined every black group she could. CJ joined her before Christmas and they married in early 1906, in spite of the fact that she was still married to John Davis. He was later to make a claim on her estate when she died. She styled herself Madam C. J. Walker, imitating Annie Pope-Turnbo, who called herself Madam Poro.

Her relationship with Annie Pope-Turnbo soured. Annie claimed that Sarah had stolen her product. Sarah maintained that the formula was hers alone. Her story was that her prayers to God to cure her thinning hair had been answered when a "big black man" had come to her in a series of dreams and given her the formula for a new product. She had even, she said, had to import ingredients from Africa. The product had worked not only on her, but on her family, her friends, and her neighbors too. And so she had marketed it. Sarah's version with its references to "God," "a big black man" and "Africa" hit a lot of hot buttons in her market. She had shown herself to have an astute command of marketing that would stand her in good stead and leave her former boss, herself to become one of America's most successful black women, in the shade.

The split between Annie and Sarah spilled out into the black press. Annie put out advertisements warning "BEWARE OF IMITATIONS," specifically targeting Sarah's products. Undeterred and armed with "Madam Walker's Wonderful Hair Grower," Sarah began performing treatments and running instructional courses, while CJ established himself in a variety of roles from realtor to impresario. Madam Walker's publicity included photos of herself with a good head of hair and the claim that only two years earlier she had been close to bald. Another showed her before and after her "wonderful discovery." As business boomed, Lelia joined her mother, working on marketing, training and distribution strategies.

While Sarah went off on a sales trip through the southern states, Lelia kept the business running in Denver. Annie Pope-Turnbo was unhappy and established a new salon in the same street in direct open competition. It can have been no coincidence that Sarah came back from the South and announced that the Denver market was way too small — there were, she felt, not enough blacks there. So she closed up and moved back to St. Louis. By this time she wanted to form an army of agents who would become economically independent. For Sarah, her business was not just a beauty product but a way to economic empowerment for black women in a market economy. She was very determined about this.

In 1907, Madam C. J. Walker's turnover was growing to quite a respectable level. Her road trips across America, especially in the South where the vast majority of blacks lived, had convinced her that she had really hit on a gold mine of possibilities. Handling the growing tsunami of mail orders while on the road had become burdensome, nigh on impossible and the business was soon on the move again. She selected Pittsburgh as a temporary new headquarters because of its excellent railroad connections.

Her turnover rose doubling in 1908 and soaring another 33% in 1909. In three years since leaving Denver she had trained hundreds of agents as well as treating hundreds of women herself. Her story, her personal example, the possibility of enhanced beauty and the chance to make some serious money had black women (nearly all of whom had a low-status job such as domestic servant or washerwoman) beating down her door. However, once more, Pittsburgh did not have a sufficiently large and vibrant black community for Sarah and she was soon looking to move yet again.

Early 1910 saw Sarah struggling with two problems. First, C.J. seemed incapable of keeping up with her and she was sure he was stealing from the company. Second, she was falling in love with Indianapolis. Located as it was at the crossroads of America, it seemed perfect for her manufacturing and distribution plans. As the year ended, her turnover had jumped yet again to very substantial levels. She had bought a house in Indianapolis and extended it, and she had put up collateral to launch the C.J. Walker Manufacturing Company of Indiana. At the same time, her marriage to CJ was on the rocks and Sarah finally instructed her lawyers to act in 1912. She was, however, happy to keep his name.

Money for Sarah was not an end in itself. It allowed her to become an active philanthropist for black causes. Her philosophy was self-respect through self-support. She started attending the conventions of the National Association of Colored Women and the National Negro Business League; she made strategic donations and she spoke at civil rights leader Booker T. Washington's Tuskegee Institute.

Business continued to boom as she trained more and more agents. By early 1913, she was well on the way to a $1 million turnover (roughly equivalent to $20 million today) and firmly believed in a philosophy of entrepreneurial, bottom-up, self-help-driven economic development. She looked ahead to the future, diversifying her portfolio of investments so that should her business falter, her income would not. She also needed to resolve the potential succession crisis posed to her business by Lelia's childlessness. Together the two women decided that Lelia, now married and known as Lelia Walker Robinson, should adopt Fairy Mae Bryant, a young black girl they knew who had a beautiful head of hair. Her father had died suddenly, leaving behind a large family. Mae's mother was initially uncertain, but on the promise of ongoing education, training in the business and open contact with her blood family, she agreed. Mae became heir to what promised to be the largest black fortune in history if the business continued to grow.

Madam C. J. Walker was constantly traveling. A sales drive to the Caribbean and Central America was followed by months at a time spent visiting both coasts in 1914 and 1915. Mae began to come too, and Walker's sales pitches became not only explanations of hair care and the use of her products, but also lessons in African-American entrepreneurship illustrated by photographic slides. While on the west coast, she learnt of the sudden death of Booker T. Washington; her attorney represented her at the funeral.

No sooner had Madam Walker returned to Indianapolis than she announced that she would relocate to New York City. The corporate headquarters, however, would remain in Indianapolis.

She felt that only New York could provide the right base to indulge all her philanthropic interests. In recent times there had been a veritable explosion of parties and testimonial dinners. She also sponsored a dinner to pay off the balance of the mortgage of a home for former slaves who had no pensions and she wrote a big check herself. Her charitable work also included helping the Daytona Normal and Industrial Institute for Negro Girls, the YMCA, as well as many other schools, orphanages and homes for the elderly. The local paper *Freeman* ran a front page story regretting her loss to the city. Her business was "a monument to negro thrift and industry throughout America."

The thrust of her business of recruiting sales agents moved away from hair care to economic opportunity and empowerment for those willing to work hard.

Her black female agents made up to $650 per week at today's rates at a time when a low-skilled white man was on around $180.

Madam Walker was welcomed fulsomely to Harlem where her daughter Lelia had constructed a salon at 108/110 West 136th Street to surpass those of Helena Rubinstein and Elizabeth Arden. One report noted Sarah's six figure income and 10,000 agents.

While Madam Walker had made some philanthropic donations, some motivated as much by business concerns as by an urge to do good, she now struggled with constant demands for handouts. Her relocation to New York brought her onto the radar of the fledgling National Association for the Advancement of Colored People (NAACP) and she donated $5,000 ($60,000 in today's money) to its anti-lynching drive. It was the largest donation in the NAACP's history so far and testament to her wealth. A local white newspaper in Louisiana called her the "World's Richest Negress." She had come a long way from the cotton fields and the laundry.

She now dreamed of forging her 10,000 troops into an army of women whose economic development would lead social change. Key to this would be a training program for black schools and vocational colleges. Forced to rest for six weeks in Hot Springs, Arkansas by fatigue from traveling and post-traumatic stress after a near-fatal train crash, she drew up plans both to build a mansion close to John D. Rockefeller at Irvington-on-Hudson and to have her training program adopted. She planned to invest $100 — about $2,000 today — in equipment in each school or college and place one of her agents on the faculty. The school would purchase supplies from her and there was to be a profit-sharing deal.

When she became a millionaire shortly before World War I, she was the first woman ever to reach such a milestone on her own initiative and without inheritance or the use of force, according to *The Guinness Book of Records.*

Her dynamism knew no bounds. In 1917, Philadelphia was chosen by Madam Walker as the venue for the first ever national meeting of her agents. More than 200 turned up representing nearly all 48 states. The focus was on business and female entrepreneurship, but the issue of widespread lynchings of black people was also aired and the women sent a collective telegram to President Wilson protesting his seeming lack of interest in the subject. The following week, in New York, Madam Walker was elected president of a new trade association representing the hair care industry, and only two weeks after that she was made vice president at large of the National Equal Rights League.

Throughout the fall she drove out daily to Irvington to inspect the progress on her new 30-room mansion. She confided to her closest friends that she had worked so hard for all of her life that the time for some rest had come. But her health had started to deteriorate and she was packed off to a sanatorium for an indefinite stay. Finding it unbearable, she checked out and just a few weeks later was back at work, celebrating her fiftieth birthday and Christmas in quick succession.

America's entry into World War I prompted huge debate in the black community. Many asked why they should fight while the President failed to stop lynching. However, Madam Walker and Lelia were soon heavily involved in the war effort, sitting on many committees.

Well aware that her health was failing, Madam Walker undertook one last long road trip which took in Pennsylvania, Ohio, Indiana, Illinois, Missouri, Kansas and Iowa. Not only did she continue recruiting agents and promoting her products but she also toured forts and military camps as a member of the Circle for Negro War Relief. Addressing black soldiers, she would acknowledge the arguments of those who questioned their involvement but each time she repudiated them: "Let me say to you that this [is] our home...All we have is here, and the time will come, and it is not far distant, until we must and will receive every protection guaranteed to every American citizen under the American Constitution." People who knew her well or who had heard her speak before noted how much each speech took out of her, but she was still able to motivate big crowds and command standing ovations lasting several minutes.

The war was causing major disruption to her business, in particular to the supply of the tins in which she sold her products. But she pressed on, developing a new business model that we all would recognize today as a franchise — the Madam C. J. Walker Parlors.

She continued to attend black conventions. A few years earlier she had been a quiet spectator, but now she was fêted. And at her second convention for her agents, this time in Chicago, she took pleasure in sending President Wilson another telegram. This time she and the other delegates were able to commend him for his newly announced tough stand on lynching.

The summer of 1918 also saw her move into her opulent Irvington-on-Hudson mansion, but it was never designed purely as a home. It was also a meeting place where leading lights in early twentieth-century society would gather to discuss key policy issues of the day. The famous Italian tenor Enrico Caruso, who was invited there, christened the house Villa Lewaro, a contraction of Le(lia) Wa(lker) Ro(binson).

The end of 1918 saw turnover at $4 million and with the end of the war, Madam Walker was confident she could double that figure in 1919 as her line of products expanded. Such was her standing in the black community that there was talk of her attending the Paris Peace Conference at Versailles as one of six Negro observers. However, members of the administration feared that "the negro question" might be raised and embarrass President Wilson, so no passports were issued to a long list of black people including Madam Walker. But as a true patriot, she was on the streets as part of the mayor's welcoming committee to greet the return of the Atlantic Fleet and Harlem's own 369th Hellfighters of the Provisional 93rd Division, for whom she threw open her villa for two weeks. The Hellfighters had fought with the French rather than fellow Americans and had never conceded an inch of ground in spite of 191 days of bombardment, the longest of the war. The French had heaped honors on them. Now it was Madam Walker's turn.

On a short spring business trip to the Midwest, her health became so bad she was confined to bed. A private Pullman car was arranged and she was accompanied by a doctor and nurse to Irvington. A few weeks later, on Sunday May 25, 1919, she passed away. Lelia and Mae were trapped in Panama City on a sales trip. The funeral service took place on the following Friday without them. Police guided a line of thousands through Irvington. Lelia returned 24 hours later and the actual burial was the following Tuesday.

Her death as the wealthiest woman in history made news all over the world. While Lelia was the main beneficiary of her will, many bequests also went to black schools and colleges. In 1998 she became the twenty-first person commemorated by the USPS in its Black Heritage Series of stamps and to this day the Madam Walker Theatre Center in Indianapolis, Indiana, puts on the annual Madam Walker Spirit Awards for Entrepreneurs.

Like her exact contemporary Bina West Miller (Chapter 11), she was overtly one thing but covertly another. Bina was ostensibly concerned with insurance but had a richer, deeper agenda of solidarity. Sarah was superficially in the business of beauty, while her real mission was one of advancement through entrepreneurship.

CHAPTER 13. LAURA INGALLS WILDER AND ROSE WILDER LANE

"The consequences of dishonesty were excessively painful... If your word were not as good as your bond, your bond was no good and you were worthless... It is impossible to get something for nothing." — Rose Wilder Lane in her 1935 novel, *Old Home Town*.

Laura Ingalls Wilder
Author
February 7, 1867–February 10, 1957

MANSFIELD, MISSOURI

Rose Wilder Lane
Journalist, Author, Philosopher
December 5, 1886–October 30, 1968

DANBURY, CONNECTICUT

LAURA INGALLS WILDER and her daughter ROSE WILDER LANE together created the "Little House" series of books which stressed personal responsibility and traditional values. Since the 1930s these books have been translated into 50 languages and read by so many children that they have a claim to being among the most popular series of children's books ever written. And if there were ever any danger of sales flagging after the authors both passed on, then the legendary actor Michael Landon took care of that when he produced, wrote and starred in the *Little House on the Prairie* television series which still shows around the world today.

Laura was the nominal author but Rose took the Wilder legacy further still. In addition to quietly helping her mother shape the "Little House" books, she was a published journalist and author in her own right. Aside from her fiction works, she wrote *The Discovery of Freedom: Man's Struggle Against Authority*, in which she made the case for individual initiative and action over the ideas and systems imposed by a central authority. With Ayn Rand (Chapter 20), Isabel Paterson (Chapter 15) and Taylor Caldwell (Chapter 18), Rose kick-started a post-World War II renaissance in thinking about liberty.

Laura Elizabeth Ingalls was born in Wisconsin, the second of four daughters of Charles Ingalls and his wife Caroline. In common with James Warren, the husband of Mercy Otis Warren (Chapter 2), she was descended from Richard Warren, a passenger on the Mayflower. This made Laura the second cousin four times (generations) removed to Mercy's husband, something she might not have known.

Her father was a restless character keen to try everything, and the family moved from Wisconsin to Kansas, before going back to Wisconsin and on to Minnesota and Iowa. Finally, when Laura was 12, they moved to the Dakota Territory and a town named De Smet, where Charles Ingalls established a land claim and worked for the railroad. It was her experiences over these years which led to the "Little House" series. While they are of course fiction, they have a clear factual basis, which gives them a fascinating realism. Today De Swet in East-central South Dakota markets itself as Laura's "Little Town on the Prairie," organizes a Laura pageant and uses 1-866-LAURASD as its tourist free phone line.

Once they were settled in De Swet, Laura began attending school. At age 15 she was a teacher, which helped the family finances, and at age 18 she married 28-year-old Almanzo Wilder, a local homesteader with 320 acres. Fifteen months later Rose was born but the family went through some torrid years. Almanzo was left with partial paralysis after a bout of diphtheria; a second baby, a son, died at birth; fire destroyed their home and outbuildings; and the region suffered a series of droughts. It was hard but all of it eventually provided excellent material for the books.

The family regrouped for a spell, first at Almanzo's parents' farm in Minnesota and then in Florida, but they were soon installed in a small home back in De Smet. Rose went to school and her parents took hourly paid jobs to make ends meet, Almanzo doing odd jobs and Laura sewing buttonholes at a local dressmaker's shop. A final move came when Rose was eight years old. The family traveled some 700 miles south to Mansfield in Missouri, which today markets itself as "Where the Little House Books were Written." This city of 1,500 or so residents claims to attract thousands of "Little House" fans every year, a phenomenon that began while Laura was still alive.

They settled in 40 acres, building Rocky Ridge Farm and eventually expanding to 200 acres of mixed arable and livestock, including chickens, dairy cattle and apple trees. The farmhouse they built is preserved to this day.

It is very hard today to imagine the commitment, vision and sheer hard work involved, especially given that Almanzo was weakened physically. The deposit used up their small savings and the land was covered with trees and stones. The former were chopped up and sold in town at 50 cents a wagon-load, while the latter were cleared. By the late 1890s, Laura and Almanzo and Rose were living in the town. Almanzo had a sales job and Laura was taking in boarders and running a food business. Any spare time and cash went into Rocky Ridge and they were so astonishingly confident of the future that they planted apple trees, which take a minimum of seven years to start to produce a crop.

Almanzo's parents visited at this time and were apparently sufficiently impressed by their son's dedication to the Rocky Ridge project that they purchased the house Laura and Almanzo had been renting and gave it to them. No longer having to pay rent relieved the financial burden and the family were eventually able to move to Rocky Ridge for good; the sale of the house in Mansfield provided yet more working capital.

Finally, when Laura was in her mid-forties and Almanzo his mid-fifties, the couple began to enjoy the fruits of their labor. They built a new 10-roomed home that stands to this day and the farm was well diversified to protect it from any sudden problems or downturn. Rose was pursuing her own career as a journalist, and it was possibly her example that encouraged Laura to start writing a regular column for a local rural newspaper from 1911 to 1925. She wrote about farming and life on the prairie. Laura also became an agent for a company that made small loans to farmers.

Accounts of Rose's education vary markedly. However, Mansfield does seem to have brought comparative stability to her learning and she discovered the literary greats such as Austen, Dickens and Gibbon thanks to McGuffey's Readers, the famous series of phonics-based, conservative, Presbyterian text books that educated tens of millions and are still used today outside of public schools in, for example, the home-school movement. Much later Rose was to act as a biographer for Henry Ford, who described McGuffey's Readers as his "alma mater."

She went 700 miles south to live in Crowley, southern Louisiana with her Aunt Eliza (Jane Wilder Thayer) to attend high school, and graduated top of her year in 1904.

By 1905 Rose was the night telegraphist for Western Union in Kansas City, Missouri, selecting the graveyard shift so she could read. By 1908 she held a similar job in San Francisco, where she met and married salesman Gillette Lane in March 1909. She became pregnant but complications developed. She lost the baby during or shortly after the birth and was never to conceive again. She and Lane traveled all over the US, holding many jobs. Rose continued to read widely and began to realize that she and Gillette had little in common, in particular intellectually, and she became very depressed. After returning to California, they broke up but not before his friends in journalism had helped her to gain a position on the left-leaning *San Francisco Bulletin*.

At the *Bulletin* she prospered as an editor and a writer with her own photo and byline. She was a socialist who embraced communism following the Russian Revolution. In 1920 the Red Cross hired her to tour Europe writing reports on its relief work for donors and potential donors. It was on an extended visit to the Soviet Union that she had her damascene moment, realizing how antithetical communism was to liberty. She later wrote in her 1939 monograph, *Give Me Liberty*: "I came out of the Soviet Union no longer a communist, because I believed in personal freedom. Like all Americans, I took for granted the individual liberty to which I had been born. It seemed as necessary and as inevitable as the air I breathed; it seemed the natural element in which human beings lived. The thought that I might lose it had never remotely occurred to me. And I could not conceive that multitudes of human beings would ever willingly live without it."

She was angry with herself for having been so stupid.

Back in New York City, Rose became a highly-paid freelance journalist and, in addition to the biography of Henry Ford, also recorded the lives of Herbert Hoover, Charlie Chaplin and writer Jack London. But she often journeyed back to Rocky Ridge.

She did well in the stock market and her parents followed her example and invested their retirement savings with Rose's broker. However the crash of 1929 and ensuing Great Depression put paid to thoughts of retirement. Rose suddenly found herself supporting her 63-year-old mother and 73-year-old father.

But Laura was not without ideas of her own as to how to ameliorate their circumstances. In 1930 she gave Rose a manuscript based on her early years. It is unclear how great Rose's input into her mother's writing actually was, but at the very least she advised her mother. She may even, drawing on her professional experience of ghostwriting and editing the work of well-known people, have rewritten and edited it, as well as cajoling more detail from Laura. *Little House in the Big Woods* by Laura Ingalls Wilder (Rose had no desire to be credited for her role) came out in 1932.

Over the next decade it was followed by *Farmer Boy, Little House on the Prairie, On the Banks of Plum Creek, By the Shores of Silver Lake, The Long Winter, Little Town on the Prairie,* and *These Happy Golden Years. The First Four Years,* in which Rose featured as "Baby Rose," was the last in the series and did not appear until the 1970s, after their deaths. It was the only title in the series on which Rose did not collaborate. But to both women, these were not just good stories of the wild frontier. They wanted their readers to understand the core principles of the early settlers and to apply them to their lives.

The books emphasized family values and the need for resilience and resourcefulness, rather than depending on others. It stressed the importance of religious belief and education, the joy of giving and the simple things in life. It was no coincidence that General MacArthur suggested translating the books into German and Japanese just after World War II.

For eight decades now the Little House books have never been out of print. The TV series has run in 100 countries and contracts already in place guarantee it will continue to run at least through 2025. Boxed DVD sets of the 48 most popular episodes or even the whole 200-plus episodes are still actively promoted. It was President Ronald Reagan's favorite TV program.

The royalties from the books meant that the stock market losses of 1929 were soon a distant unpleasant memory to the Wilders. The 1930s and 1940s also saw Rose at her personal best as an author in her own right as her novels such as *Let the Hurricane Roar* (later *Young Pioneers*) and *Free Land* did for adults what *Little House* had done for children.

While Rose established a home at Danbury, Connecticut, Almanzo and Laura lived on at Rocky Ridge Farm until their deaths, Almanzo in 1949 at the age of 92 and Laura in 1957 aged 90. They were constantly amazed at the volume of mail they received and the car loads of visitors wanting to meet "Laura." On her death Rocky Ridge Farm was turned into a museum and tourist attraction with Rose donating money to set it up and family heirlooms to fill it, as well as covenanting an annual sum to keep it going.

After the 1930s Rose turned increasingly to writing about politics, economics and philosophy, arguing for limited government intervention in the lives of citizens. An early article, *Credo,* for the *Saturday Evening Post,* was republished by Leonard Read (then head of the Los Angeles Chamber of Commerce but soon to found the Foundation for Economic Education or FEE) as *Give Me Liberty.* In it she explained her philosophy of life and liberty: "I began slowly to understand the nature of man and man's situation on this planet. I understood at last that every human being is free; that I am endowed by the Creator with inalienable liberty as I am endowed with life; that my freedom is inseparable from my life, since freedom is the individual's self-controlling nature. My freedom is my control of my own life-energy, for the uses of which I, alone, am therefore responsible."

In another piece for the Federal Writers Project, set up to support writers during the Great Depression, she argued: "Individualism, *laissez faire* and the slightly restrained anarchy of capitalism offer the best opportunities for the development of the human spirit."

Rose Wilder Lane devoted nearly all her time and energy throughout 1942 to her great classic *The Discovery of Freedom: Man's Struggle Against Authority*, which came out in early 1943 with a print run of a mere one thousand. It was not reprinted until 1972, four years after her passing, largely because she had spent so many years editing and re-editing it in a bid to make it perfect. But in the meantime, it was the kind of book that was passed around, each copy being read by many people. The ideas it contained were to have an immense impact on American libertarian thought.

She argued that allowing individuals to have free rein over their creativity could result in a civilization infinitely superior to that offered by overly prescriptive governments. She cited examples from history and condemned communism, fascism and even the New Deal, the series of programs introduced in response to the Great Depression. Revolutions, she argued, just meant that one controlling group was replaced by another, and that individual freedom never had a chance.

To Rose there had been in history three major attempts at freedom, the first led by Abraham, the second by Mohammed and the third by George Washington. The chapter on Mohammed today circulates as a free-standing monograph from the Minaret Institute, an Islamic think tank based in Bethesda MD, "to draw people's attention to the positive role that Islam has played in the establishment of human rights, especially of individual conscience," as Muslim scholar Dr Imad-ad-Dean Ahmad writes in the introduction.

This wide-ranging philosophical work covers property rights, human rights, the Constitution, the right to vote, democracy, republicanism and the Industrial Revolution. Libertarian businessman Robert LeFevre, who founded the Freedom School, set up to teach his philosophy of freedom and free-market economics, called *The Discovery of Freedom* "one of the most influential books of the twentieth century."

From 1942 to 1945 Rose wrote a weekly column for the *Pittsburgh Courier* which had a circulation of 270,000 throughout the US — it was the best read black newspaper of the era. Historians David T. Beito and Linda Royster Beito recently wrote: "No libertarian has ever more creatively weaved together laissez-faire and anti racism than Lane." They conclude their study of her columns in "selling laissez-faire anti racism to the black masses" as follows: "Her work for this newspaper represented the most ambitious effort of any author during this period to promote laissez-faire ideas to a black audience. Through her columns, she often proved creative in linking her philosophical beliefs to current issues of major concern to her readers, including segregation, civil disobedience, entrepreneurship, and the struggle for liberty, both overseas and at home."

For the rest of her life Rose dedicated herself to the promotion of liberty through the Freedom School, the free-market William Volker Fund and her editorship of the National Economic Council's *Review of Books*. She was very much a talent scout for the Volker Fund and was involved in its National Book Foundation. Books that she liked would be reviewed in a quarterly newsletter circulated to librarians all over the US. If librarians liked the sound of any of the titles, all they had to do was to return a postcard and a free copy would be sent to them.

It is thought that Rose Wilder Lane was the first person to talk about the "libertarian movement."

In the late 1950s she was the sole beneficiary of Laura's will and so inherited the rights to the "Little House" series. She continued to write and in 1965, aged 79, she toured the Vietnam war zone as an accredited correspondent for *Woman's Day*.

Childless, Rose Wilder Lane took many young people under her wing over the decades, often paying for their education. Chief among these was Roger MacBride, son of one of her editors at *Reader's Digest*, whom she described as her "adopted grandson." He in turn called her "Gramma." While she didn't pay for his studies at Princeton and Harvard Law School, the prelude to a legal career in Vermont, she did very much school him in the principles of liberty. He in turn became her heir as well as her attorney and business manager and contributed to building the Little House brand, including acting as producer of the TV series under Landon, the overall executive producer.

It was surely her philosophy that informed MacBride's political gesture in 1972. He was by now a Republican Party member of the Electoral College. He had written a book about the Electoral College and knew he was not bound to vote for Richard Nixon, who was up for re-election, and his Vice President Spiro Agnew. He became a "faithless elector" and instead cast his vote for the Libertarian Party's John Hospers and Tonie Nathan. He went on to become that party's presidential candidate in 1976, flying himself around the US in his own plane, *No Force One*.

MacBride added extensively to Rose's oeuvre after her death in 1968. He reissued *The Discovery of Freedom* and published a correspondence between Rose and businessman Jasper Crane as *The Lady and the Tycoon*, as well as *Rose Wilder Lane: Her Story*.

He also built on Laura and Rose's literary legacy, crafting a whole new series of books on the *Little House* model, based on the life of Rose up to age 17. They were *Little House on Rocky Ridge, Little Farm in the Ozarks, In the Land of the Big Red Apple, On the Other Side of the Hill, Little Town in the Ozarks, New Dawn on Rocky Ridge, On the Banks of the Bayou* and *Bachelor Girl.*

He died at the age of 65 in March 1995 and five of the eight Rocky Ridge books appeared posthumously. David Boaz of the libertarian think tank the Cato Institute described him as the last surviving link back to the best of the so-called Old Right. This included not only Rose, but Isabel Paterson (Chapter 15), Albert Jay Nock, H.L .Mencken and Howard Buffett.

The "Little House" phenomenon grew up thanks to the three-way collaboration: Laura Ingalls Wilder's memories, notes and creativity, Rose's quiet work making the very best out of them and MacBride's business acumen and adherence to principles of liberty. These were the very principles that Laura had first suggested in her tales of the frontier and that Rose consolidated and developed in her own writings.

Chapter 14. Alice Paul

"I never doubted that equal rights was the right direction. Most reforms, most problems are complicated. But to me there is nothing complicated about ordinary equality." — Alice Paul in a 1972 interview.

Campaigner for Women's Suffrage
January 11, 1885–July 9, 1977

WASHINGTON, DISTRICT OF COLUMBIA

It was March 3, 1913, the day before Woodrow Wilson's first inauguration. ALICE STOKES PAUL, a campaigner for votes for women better known in the UK than in her native America, had chosen that date for her march deliberately, knowing that it would garner maximum publicity for her cause. The route along Pennsylvania Avenue in Washington, DC, was also chosen carefully — many political people would be in the capital that day and the eyes of the world would be on it.

A march in itself was a bold gesture in the US, where the campaign for female suffrage was much less militant than across the Atlantic, and Alice had spent two months organizing it down to the last detail. She had rented space at 1420 F Street, began raising funds, and called on Police Chief Richard Sylvester to request a parade permit. Among the aspects that had appalled Sylvester about Alice's plan was the thought of two parades in two days, but after a month of lobbying by the wives of prominent men organized by Alice he relented and all the necessary permits were issued. But just in case there was order to be restored, he laid on a mounted army detachment.

Alice's march took the form of a pageant. The key message of the parade was a demand for a constitutional amendment. It was led by women on horseback followed by bands, floats, more women on horseback, and finally between 5,000 and 10,000 marchers. Many wore uniforms or capes to represent different aspects of American society, for example nurses, farmers or teachers. Alice wore her academic gown. There was even a section of male supporters in the long line of marchers.

But that did not stop the crowd, mostly men, from jeering, jostling, and ridiculing the parade. Some women were tripped and pushed. The unruly mob surged forward, making it almost impossible for the parade to continue. The marchers were reduced to single file. Police Chief Sylvester ordered the cavalry to charge in a bid to control the crowd.

There were over 100 injuries and Alice's followers finished up bruised, battered, shaken, and ashamed of their countrymen.

But suddenly Alice, until now a journalistic oddity in the US for her suffragette activities in England, had become a major figure in the US. Her every move and utterance now had to be recorded. Seven hard years later in 1920 the Nineteenth Amendment was passed and women across America had the vote. After many decades of campaigning by Elizabeth Cady Stanton (Chapter 8), Susan B. Anthony and other women who believed in the intrinsic justice of universal, rather than male, suffrage, Alice Paul was able to overcome a mountain of ideological opposition, scorn, vested interests, violence, and hatred, in order to change history.

Alice Paul grew up in comfortable circumstances on a farm of more than 150 acres. Her father William Paul was also a local bank president. But the family was Quaker and lived simply. The Quaker movement had since its earliest times given more respect, authority and responsibilities to women than was generally the case elsewhere in society. Quaker men and women had also been leaders in the fight for abolition and were prominent among the ranks of the earliest suffragettes. Alice's own family had 60 years earlier known prominent Quaker suffragette Lucretia Mott and her parents had always supported female enfranchisement.

Alice had access to many books, which she devoured, and she excelled at her local school before entering the Quaker-founded co-educational Swarthmore College in 1901. Her maternal grandfather William Parry had helped found it and her mother Tasie Parry had been among the earliest female graduates.

Having flirted with biology as her undergraduate major (chosen because it was the only subject she had not yet studied), she then tried social work at the New York School of Philanthropy. However, she quickly rejected that because she felt that it did not and simply could never change anything. She felt she had to fix the causes and not the results. A year studying sociology, politics and economics at the University of Pennsylvania was much more to her taste and her evident academic prowess led to a Quaker scholarship to Woodbrooke near Birmingham in England, a center founded by the British Quaker and chocolate manufacturer George Cadbury.

Several times a week she bicycled to the campus of the University of Birmingham where she was reportedly the first ever female student in its Commerce Department, a faculty that was briefly to gain a reputation to match the University of Chicago Economics Department. In a corridor in December 1907 she spotted an advert for a public lecture on campus by leading British campaigner for female suffrage Christabel Pankhurst. Alice was intrigued and wanted to hear what she had to say. Christabel Pankhurst was the daughter of Emmeline Pankhurst, the leader of the suffragette movement in England which believed in "deeds not words." In fact the whole family was steeped in the cause, from Christabel's late father Richard to her sisters Sylvia and Adela.

Hearing the controversial Christabel was Alice's Damascene moment. There were two lectures, the first so badly disrupted — the speaker was shouted down by a baying crowd of male students — that a second had to be organized. This time the university president ordered the entire student body both to attend and to listen without disturbance as he took the chair himself. Effectively Alice experienced two awakenings: the first was to the sheer hostility the subject engendered and the second was to the exact detail of Christabel's message, one that triggered something within her, something that was to guide her life for at least the next 13 years.

She moved to London to attend the London School of Economics and Political Science (LSE) and to become involved with the Women's Social and Political Union (WSPU), a Pankhurst initiative which was on the more militant end of the continuum. Indeed two words had emerged in England by then. If you were a suffragist you believed in votes for women but, female or male, you were welcome in polite society and could be relied on to act with decorum. On the other hand if you were a suffragette then you went on marches, threw bricks through windows, set mail boxes on fire and took part in other acts of civil — and more usually criminal — disobedience. The suffragettes believed that gentle lobbying would achieve nothing.

Becoming involved in a campaign of direct action, appealed very much to Alice and so she became a suffragette not a suffragist. This was an interesting decision for a Quaker, given the latter's commitment to pacifism. And as a WSPU volunteer Alice graduated from selling its newspaper, *Votes for Women*, to street corner soapbox public speaking. It was then that she learned the Pankhurst strategy of change: even if some members of one political party supported female suffrage, the women would fight the entire party if not all of them did. This has strong echoes in British politics today where anti-European Union (EU) candidates fight sitting MPs who are just as anti-EU as they are. The idea is to force dissenters within a party to put pressure on colleagues and make the whole party of one mind.

It was also at this time, in June 1908, that Alice was first arrested — she would be arrested seven times in total. Two hundred suffragettes, denied a meeting with Prime Minister Asquith, charged repeatedly at a six-deep line of 3,000 police officers, including many on horseback, outside Parliament at Westminster in the center of London. The women wore thick winter clothing to protect their bodies and fortunately nobody was killed. However, some members of the group were old and frail and their protest had been pre-arranged with the police; Emmeline led the elderly ladies to a senior officer and as expected slapped him twice in the face on behalf of all of them. They were all then escorted away.

It was there in Westminster that Alice drank in the Pankhurst modus operandi of shock tactics and maximum publicity. When, for example, the Post Office, a monopoly, advertised that it would deliver anything anywhere, two suffragettes paid to be delivered to 10 Downing Street, home of the Prime Minister. A doorman refused delivery calling them "dead letters." But actions like this kept the issue in the press. As did the new strategy of hunger strikes in which Alice participated when she was imprisoned on three occasions. Her screams on being force fed — the authorities' response to hunger-striking suffragettes — were heard throughout the building.

She went home, landing in the US on January 20, 1910, nine days after her twenty-fifth birthday.

She had achieved minor press notoriety in the US for her activities in London but now she became a huge draw for suffragists and suffragettes who wanted to hear about her experiences. Alice was soon giving speeches in cities such as New York and Philadelphia, though often there were more questions about force feeding than votes for women. When she was quizzed on the British custom of throwing stones through windows, she replied that they were only government windows paid out of taxes and not private ones.

While she continued her academic interests living on a stipend from her parents, she immersed herself in studying the history of the US suffrage movement. In the UK there were two approaches: the militant and the conservative. In the US even mild heckling was heavily condemned but here too there were also two approaches: one was to seek the vote state by state while the other was to press at the federal level for an amendment to the Constitution.

Alice came to the conclusion that fighting state by state was impossible. Only four states had to date given women the vote and all were in the sparsely populated West. It was taking decades to make advances as each state had different, usually very complex rules about constitutional change. None of the big states and none of the founding 13 had enfranchised women. She much preferred the federal route, using as her example the Fifteenth Amendment to enfranchise black men.

To this end she attended the annual convention of the National Woman Suffrage Association (NAWSA) in Philadelphia in late November 1912. Her goal was to secure a position of autonomy in Washington, DC where she could develop her own ideas and strategies, and she was successful in being appointed chair of the then moribund NAWSA Congressional Committee (the condition being that she would raise 100 per cent of the budget). Her first goal was a march — about the most militant measure NAWSA would condone — on March 3, 1913.

Woodrow Wilson couldn't fail to notice her. Not only had he discovered that the poor turnout to greet his arrival at the rail station in Washington on the eve of his inauguration was due to Alice's controversial pageant, but the violence it engendered hit the headlines. She quickly met the new President Woodrow Wilson three times but to no avail. She also organized a second peaceful march and saw a suffrage amendment to the federal Constitution introduced but languish with little support.

Inevitably, perhaps, internal tensions were mounting within NAWSA as young militant Alice in DC followed her own strategy and became a public figure, while older, more conservative leaders at the head office in New York City were not much in tune with her. Back in the UK, the Pankhursts planned a US fundraising trip while escalating their levels of violence. Alice welcomed both. NAWSA head office was dismayed.

She caused further consternation when she adopted the Pankhurst electoral strategy proposing that in the western Congressional districts where women had the vote, all Democrats (who were in power) be opposed in close races as long as their national leadership refused to support female enfranchisement. Even Democrats who supported votes for women would be opposed and, Alice hoped, unseated as long as "the party in power" was opposed. It was a clever phrase implying clearly that Alice would do the same to a Republican President, but new battle lines had been drawn. Alice left NAWSA and established her own Congressional Union to fight for the amendment.

She quickly raised the funds needed to deploy her female agents in the nine western enfranchised states. They enjoyed few victories but they clearly they touched a nerve. Ever with an eye on publicity Alice arranged for a woman who enjoyed the vote in California to be driven from coast to coast by other women collecting signatures for a petition, arriving in DC as Congress met. It's useful to remember that in 1915 hardly anybody had driven coast to coast, let alone a group of women. And among those who welcomed its arrival in DC was Margaret Wilson, daughter of the President. Airplanes with women on board dropped leaflets over cities and trainloads of women were sent out campaigning.

Alice felt that Wilson prevaricated on the issue. He would go from a flat refusal to recognize votes for women as a national issue, through a states' rights position, to announcing he would vote yes in his adopted state of New Jersey. Overall it was clear he thought matters of trade and war to be more important.

Taking her strategy one step forward Alice launched the National Woman's Party (NWP) in July 1916 — 25 per cent of Electoral College votes were controlled by states where women now had the vote. The math was becoming interesting. Could she become a President-maker? Throughout the 1916 General Election her women fanned out across the Mid West to the West campaigning for a constitutional amendment. Wilson won a second term but at the same time anti-suffrage Democrats in the House suffered and were no longer in the majority.

Alice now decided to use the little over two months' delay before Wilson's second inauguration to post "silent sentinels" at the gates to the White House. These sentinels were women armed with often outrageous banners — or at least for the times — demanding votes for all women. This was unprecedented, the furor was enormous and the debate raged across the entire country.

It was a very hard winter-long fight with no quarter given. It was cold. Finding volunteers to cover the operation was tough. Wilson's offer to them of warmth in a room in the White House was rejected. Fundraising was also difficult as many thought this action went well beyond the pale. American involvement in the war in Europe loomed.

Over in the UK the Pankhursts had stopped their pro-suffrage actions as soon as World War I was declared and had turned their organization into one which wholeheartedly supported victory. Suffragettes now accosted young men on the street who were not in uniform and presented them with white feathers to mark their cowardice.

In the US, Alice struggled with this strategy and decided otherwise. She knew enough history to recall that during the Civil War American women in the North had been asked to drop their demands for female suffrage, focus on the immediate, and anticipate reward post victory. Their hopes were never realized.

Black men had been rewarded with the vote via the Fifteenth Amendment, passed immediately after that war, but the case for white women had, if anything, gone backward.

Alice was not about to repeat the mistakes of the past.

Tensions rose within the NWP. There were attacks from her more conservative NAWSA opponents and from the administration.

It all broke into open war on June 20, 1917, when a Russian delegation was due at the White House and the "silent sentinel" banners provocatively pointed out that the United States was not a democracy and that, unlike Russia where women were enfranchised, American women had no right to vote. Wilson, the banners proclaimed, was the main obstacle.

While other American women were throwing themselves into the war effort the suffragettes continued to battle for their cause. Both the public and the authorities took violent umbrage. Alice and her banners polarized America. Confrontations between the suffragettes and the public escalated with the police often simply looking on while thousands of government office workers, servicemen and visitors attacked the women and destroyed their banners. There was, it seemed, no middle ground and for a while the police and the courts had no idea how to handle the matter.

At first the ladies would be held for a few hours and then released, but as the summer of 1917 wore on, the penalties became more draconian. Where first they might be sentenced to three days, if they were tried at all, soon they were receiving sentences of 60 days. However, this sentence was considered so harsh that President Wilson pardoned the 16 ladies involved after just three days.

Behind the scenes, a deal was done. While 60 days was deemed excessive, 30 days would not trigger another pardon. And conditions in the local jail were appalling.

One exception to the 30-day sentence was made in the case of Alice herself, who was given a suspended term and then promptly rearrested, garnering her seven months. She was held in a cell in the psychiatric unit, the windows were boarded up, and she was force fed three times a day after adopting the tactics she knew so well from her time in England and starting a hunger strike. She was, however, not to complete her term as over 30 of her ladies launched a major picket, were arrested and jailed, and promptly joined Alice on hunger strike. The system could not cope with force feeding so many, and after eight days every single suffragette was released.

The dynamics, the politics, of female enfranchisement were changing. Some 12 states now allowed women to vote and Canada was about to do so, too. Sensing an opportunity, the Republican Party was embracing suffragism. This in turn made President Wilson think hard. Had those Silent Sentinels with their banners gotten through to him? Had perhaps his daughter Margaret, coached by Alice, played a persuasive role? Or did he just want this issue to go away so he could focus on his main interest of foreign policy?

For a federal amendment to succeed, it had to go through three stages: winning a two-thirds majority in both the House and the Senate, and finally a simple majority in three quarters (36) of the states in existence then.

With Wilson's support and heavy lobbying by Alice's team, the so-called Susan B. Anthony Amendment (named for the prominent women's rights campaigner of the previous century) came before the House, needing 274 "ayes" and receiving exactly that number. It was then on to the Senate, where Alice was told she was 11 votes short. One by one, senators not fully pledged to support the amendment were visited by her ladies. One moved to the aye column simply because he had been waiting for a lead from the President. Another moved against his personal beliefs because his constituents wanted it. A third said he would do so only if his state legislature passed a positive motion — a week later it did, thanks to Alice's army. By the summer of 1918, 11 had become three. By this time NAWSA in New York City had come fully on board, adding its weight and contacts. The magic number was 64, and the estimates ranged from 63 to 67 depending on the source. Despite a last minute plea by President Wilson, who was by now desperate to focus on war and imminent peace, it failed by two votes on October 1, 1918.

Alice's army of ladies now unleashed a barrage of protests on the 34 senators who had voted against the amendment. The Silent Sentinels moved from the White House to Capitol Hill. One last route was left to try — the lame duck Congress that would meet after the November 1918 elections — or Alice and her followers would have to start again with the new Congress in mind.

January saw an explosion of pickets, pageants, bonfires, and more arrests, including Alice. Many of her stalwarts were arrested multiple times and over 150 were jailed.

They ran out of time. However, as the Sixty-sixth Congress met, President Wilson cabled his support from Paris and the amendment quickly cleared the House by a wide margin. The same happened in the Senate, though the margin was a lot narrower. Now Alice faced the final lap — ratification by the states. This was a major operation. Some states rushed to ratify within days while others dragged their feet, and yet more states, in the West, where women had long voted, sat on their hands.

By the end of 1919, Alice could count 22 of the 36 states she needed, and in early 1920 she was looking at 31.

It was a close vote in many states and Alice's army worked tirelessly to barrage local politicians with letters and telegrams. In Charleston, West Virginia, the Senate was deadlocked at 14 to 14 with one member on vacation in California. They stayed in session for six days while he was brought home at a cost of thousands of dollars in a series of trains, some hired just for him. The thirty-fourth state became the thirty-fourth to approve the amendment. Washington became the thirty-fifth and by August it was all down to Tennessee, where approval cruised through the Senate and squeaked by the House, 49 to 47. A tie would have meant defeat so one man, one vote, made all the difference. The Nineteenth Amendment was on its way for registration by the Secretary of State in Washington, DC.

The story of Alice Paul is truly inspirational. She was a genius at strategy, tactics, fund-raising and publicity. She was deeply principled: when judges ordered a fine or jail, you went to prison and you went on hunger strike. She never gave up. When asked by an interviewer why she had dedicated her life to the struggle for female suffrage, she credited her upbringing on a farm. Her mother had always said, "When you put your hand to the plow, you don't put it down until you get to the end of the row." Alice Paul was also a great leader: after a meeting with her followers, one lady wrote, they felt twice as tall and able to accomplish anything.

Chapter 15. Isabel Paterson

"If there were just one gift you could choose, but nothing barred, what would it be? We wish you then your own wish; you name it. Ours is liberty, now and forever." — Isabel Paterson

Writer, Mentor, and Political Theorist
January 22, 1886–January 10, 1961

NEW YORK, NEW YORK

ISABEL MARY PATERSON was born Isabel Mary Bowler and grew up in the Wild West at the end of the nineteenth century. Incredibly to us, perhaps, she called it "rather dull." Instead, she dreamed of adventures in Australia.

Mary, as she was known as a girl, was one of nine children. She was born in Tehkummah on the Canadian island of Grand Manitoulin, Lake Huron. Her father Francis Bowler owned and operated a grist mill there, grinding grains into various products. But he was not successful and her childhood was spent on the move as the family went rapidly down the economic ladder. The Bowlers moved first to Newberry in Northern Michigan, then to Utah (yet to become a state) and finally to Canada's Northwest Territories (not yet a province).

As Isabel Paterson suggested, the West of the late nineteenth century was probably less wild than we imagine. This was borne out by the book, *The Not So Wild, Wild West* by Terry L. Anderson and Peter J Hill, which opens with a man on the frontier ditching his gun in a river because it was so cumbersome and unnecessary. In *The Culture of Violence in the American West* the economist Thomas J. DiLorenzo shows how good the "land clubs, cattlemen's associations, mining camps, and wagon trains" were at keeping order. But life was certainly very tough. As a child Mary helped the hay pitchers, made soap and took care of the livestock. She also knew how to fix a log cabin, cook bear meat and make her own clothes. Frank Bowler, being a far cry from the industrious entrepreneur farmer that characterized the era, let much of the farm work fall to his wife Margaret and to Mary herself, who was very dependable. Later in life she often blamed the conditions in which she grew up for her unique shape — or perhaps shapelessness and cited malnutrition for the uneven growth that left her with a head that was too large; square, narrow shoulders; and short legs, though none of this was apparently visible to her contemporaries or evident in pictures.

Mary was a precocious child, talking in short simple sentences aged just one and reading aged three. How, why and when children read was to be a life-long interest and she strongly favored the phonic method. However, professional teachers disagreed with her belief that reading was something every child could and should learn at home well before they started school. In fact, she often inspired debate and controversy for her ideas that were sometimes considered old-fashioned but which were actually often very ahead of their time. She is considered, for example, one of the founders of the modern libertarian movement, and her beliefs and writings were highly influential.

In Utah, aged around seven, Isabel spent one month in school before leaving, with permission, on the grounds that she knew far more than her teacher. The teacher wanted to read a story about a little red hen when Isabel wanted to discuss William Jennings Bryan and the silver question. Later, in Canada, she attended school for two years but seems to have been left to her own devices as she pursued her own advanced reading course. These two brief flirtations with school were the sum total of her formal education.

In her late teens, she decided it was time to move out and make her own way in life, not least to escape her family's grinding poverty. At one point they had even been forced to live in tents. She did a range of jobs in Montana and North Dakota, including waiting tables, and along the way she picked up some secretarial and accounting skills. Perhaps because of her limited formal education and the fact that she had had to do hard farm work from a young age, she believed strongly in the importance of being a self-starter.

By 1905, Isabel Bowler was working in Calgary, Alberta, for R. B. Bennett, an attorney for the Canadian Pacific Railway. He was to become Canada's Prime Minister from 1930 to 1935, and while he and Isabel shared many political views, he was a conservative and she more of a unilateral free trader. Later, as premier, Bennett would embrace a pro-British Empire tariff system, imposing no tariffs within the Empire but high tariffs between Canada and the US, an illogical strategy given that the US was Canada's closest and biggest trading neighbor.

Isabel Mary Bowler became Isabel Paterson on April 13, 1910, when at the age of 24 she married a traveling salesman turned local realtor named Kenneth Paterson. Little is known about the marriage, except that within a very few weeks Isabel had moved to Spokane, Washington, without him. By 1918, she had apparently lost all knowledge of his whereabouts.

Isabel continued to be a voracious reader as a young woman. She had also shown an early interest in writing. As a girl she had scribbled out her own stories and columns, some of which were published in newspapers. Now at a party in Spokane, the newly arrived Mrs. Paterson was offered a job as secretary to the publisher of the *Inland Herald*. She took the job but so intimidated her new boss with her superior command of English that he quickly moved her to the editorial department.

Within months she could see that the *Inland Herald* was headed for the rocks, and she moved to Vancouver where she was soon writing her own column for the *Vancouver World*. This is where she first really began to spread her wings, flagging up individualist ideas about the economy, regulation, international relations and women. She discussed, for example, the changing nature of the relationship between the female head of a family and her female servants, presaging in early 1911 changes that would come to pass decades later. For example, she chided ladies with servants for having the attitude that these girls should be grateful for their jobs, stating that gratitude had no part in a business contract. She soon left the *Vancouver World* for the *Province* and after less than two years there she moved to New York City.

She had barely gotten her East Coast bearings when she read of an air show to be held on election day November 5, 1912, on Staten Island. The finale late in the afternoon was to be an attempt by one Harry Bingham Brown to set a new height record for a plane with a passenger on board. Always keen to try something new, she volunteered to be that passenger and flew to over 5,000 feet, one mile high, seated next to Harry. Together they set the new record. The crowds cheered wildly as they landed back safely in the gathering dusk.

Her career too was ready to take off. She became a novelist, literary critic, columnist and mentor of young thinkers, including Rose Wilder Lane (Chapter 13), and Ayn Rand (Chapter 20). This triumvirate has been described as the "founding mothers" of American libertarianism. And the men she influenced read like a roll call of foremost pro-liberty thinkers: Leonard Read, who founded the Foundation for Economic Education (FEE), America's first libertarian think tank; businessman and Republican representative Howard Buffett; William F.

Buckley, who founded the political magazine *National Review*; libertarian news-paperman R. C. Hoiles; and political philosopher Frank Meyer.

At the same time as taking on a range of New York-based journalistic assignments, including interviews with artists, she worked on promoting her first two novels to publishers. *The Shadow Riders* came out in 1916 and *The Magpie's Nest* in 1917; both are autobiographical, rooted in the Canadian west and contain a pro-free trade message. *The Shadow Riders* has an almost wistful, dreamlike quality as the heroine returns to the Calgary she once fled but this time as wife of a senior businessman and politician. Again she is laying the basis for Ayn Rand's ideas about political economy with her businessman who is tempted to pay a bribe because he wants the satisfaction of building a new tram line and fleet of vehicles for his city. He declines to pay it, but the episode throws up a whole series of questions about the relationship between the state and free enterprise, particularly the state and bigger businesses.

Isabel Paterson's big break came in 1922 when Burton Rascoe, literary editor of the *Chicago Tribune*, moved to the *New York Tribune*. The writer Alta May Coleman persuaded him to meet Isabel. He was determined to dislike her, feeling he had been railroaded into seeing her with a view to publishing and possibly hiring her. But he discovered that she hated the idea that she should be rewarded on connections rather than talent. Ironically, this prompted him to hire her after all and she became his secretary. But Pascoe was soon replaced by Stuart Pratt Sherman, who died shortly afterwards. Amid the fallout, the newly renamed *Herald Tribune* now had a Sunday book section and Isabel had the job she would hold for 25 years: writer of the famous *Turns with a Bookworm* column.

She wrote 1,800 words a week about books and their authors, publishers and editors (some 2.34 million words) and became a redoubtable literary critic. Many of those who read this weekly epistle to book buyers loved her directness and freedom-based opinions, including her opposition to prohibition. Many loathed her, too, but there was no denying her huge following. Publishers did all they could to keep any book they thought she might savage out of her hands. On the other hand, if she liked a work and felt it was not selling well enough, then she would demand her readers go out and buy it.

As her column took off, so did her own fiction with an historical trilogy of *The Singing Season* (1924), *The Fourth Queen* (1926) and *The Road of the Gods* (1930). They are set respectively in fourteenth-century Spain at the Court of Henry II, sixteenth- and seventeenth-century England at the court of Elizabeth I, and first-century-BC Germany. Once again, free trade is a theme in all three and despite going against the tide of opinion of the times, the books sold well enough to turn a profit.

They were followed by *Never Ask The End* (1933) and *The Golden Vanity* (1934), which did much to stabilize her finances after the Crash of 1929.

The late 1920s and 1930s saw Paterson's radical individualism become much more political. During this period, in 1928, she became a US citizen just in time to vote against Hoover, whose idea that he could guide the economy and plan the future she dismissed as ridiculous. She believed it would lead to a huge waste of resources. She railed against prostitution laws which saw women arrested but never their clients. Like Clare Boothe Luce (Chapter 19), she was appalled by the Smoot-Hawley Act that imposed high tariffs on imported goods, and like the writer Willa Cather, she recalled the Depression of the 1890s. In that instance President Grover Cleveland had intervened very little and the economy had recovered much faster than in the 1930s. She also felt the Fed had made a very bad mistake, pursuing monetary policy that was too soft at times and too harsh at others.

The 1930s were a decade-long education in economics as Isabel read widely and debated vociferously. It was the decade of J. M. Keynes and his *General Theory of Employment, Interest and Money*, which advocated state intervention in a time of recession, and the decade of the New Deal which acted out these theories. The proper role and size and scope of government were the number one topics of the era yet, as a leading public intellectual, Isabel was almost a lone voice in her praise of individualism over collectivism. She also attacked both Russian communism and German/Italian fascism. To her they were limbs of the same tree; they were not left and right, they were both simply totalitarian, using the power of the state to crush the individual. Whichever way you looked at them, they both added up to "serfdom," a word she used often in the decade before F. A. Hayek published his epic book *The Road to Serfdom* (see Chapters 16 and 24).

With the money from her book sales, Isabel chose a piece of land near Stamford, Connecticut, which she could easily access by train from New York City. She selected a builder and gave him a budget. This was to be her retreat from the big city until the early 1940s when the rise in local property values — and consequently in taxes — encouraged her to move to Ridgefield, a more rural spot in the same state.

Believers in a *laissez-faire* approach to economics in the 1930s and 1940s were a small, isolated group. There was not the infrastructure of think tanks, publishers, publications — with the sole exception of *Reader's Digest* — or colleges. Nor were there the range of radio and TV programs and stations that flourish today. There was Albert Jay Nock, the editor, writer and publisher; there was Garet Garrett the great novelist, social and economic critic, political theorist and financial journalist; H. L. Mencken the critic; Felix Morley of *Human Events* and finally Frank Chodorov, the writer and publisher. Matching these five men, all born in the 1870s and 1880s, were four women: Isabel herself, Willa Cather, Rose Wilder Lane and writer Suzanne La Follette. Later they were joined by a fifth woman, a very young Ayn Rand, and then a sixth in Taylor Caldwell. It was a lonely path they trod.

Isabel was to influence at least four of the five, in particular Ayn Rand, who discussed ideas of immense importance literally sitting at the older woman's feet both in her New York office and her house in Connecticut. Ayn constantly quizzed her host — sometimes through the night — about economics, politics, history, legal theory and morals. They called each other "sister."

With the approach of the 1940 presidential election, Isabel cast her vote for Republican candidate Willkie, not so much because she approved of his middle-of-the-road platform but rather because she feared a third term of Roosevelt and his policies of big government intervention. In this she was joined by Ayn Rand and Clare Boothe Luce. Isabel never voted again.

Among the authors she continued to promote was the English engineer-turned-novelist Neville Shute. He had arrived at disillusionment with government control of business by a curious route. In the 1920s, the British government had decided that airships represented the future of transportation. It announced two contracts for prototypes: one was awarded to the public sector, the Royal Airship Works, to build the R101, and the other to a private sector company, the Airship Guarantee Company, to build R100. Shute was the chief calculator, or engineer, on the privately constructed R100. It was faster, lighter and more economical than the public R101. It also carried a bigger payload. So which one did the government select? The R101. And what happened next? It crashed on its maiden voyage, killing 48 out of the 54 on board. The British government responded by ordering the privately built R100 to be destroyed too. It was sheer vandalism and a crass attempt by politicians to cover their backs.

Shute's reaction was to write well over twenty novels, many of them with an engineering or aviation theme, many with a frontier element and many propounding anti-government and pro-free enterprise views. While he is mostly remembered for *On The Beach* (1957), which became Stanley Kramer's 1959 nuclear war apocalypse movie starring Gregory Peck and Ava Gardner, this is atypical of his output. Isabel must have loved the engineering and aviation focus, as well as the hard-working, problem-solving characters that rely on themselves, not others, and certainly not the state. *Ruined City* and *A Town Like Alice* would have struck a particular chord. Both are stories of hardship, even time in jail, but entrepreneurship plays an important role and at the end of the day there is in both novels a series of successful businesses and thriving communities.

The early 1940s saw Isabel and Ayn in a close race to see their books published, and Isabel Paterson's *The God of the Machine* and Ayn Rand's *The Foun-*

tainhead appeared within days of each other in May 1943; Rand however won the race.

The God of the Machine was clearly important for its time. Ayn Rand commented that it "does for Capitalists what *Das Kapital* does for the Reds and what *The Bible* does for the Christians." This is just one of many extravagant endorsements of Isabel's book. Albert Jay Nock proclaimed that Isabel Paterson, along with Rose Wilder Lane, whose *The Discovery of Freedom* was also published in 1943, had shown men how to think. He wrote that "they make us male writers look like Confederate money" — in other words, useless. And to journalist John Chamberlain, reading *The God of the Machine* was akin to being hit by a "ton of bricks."

But *The God of the Machine* is far from being an easy read. It weaves a free-market view of economics with history from the fourth-century BC through to modern times. Political and legal theory and religion feature, as do constant references to engineering, which is used as a metaphor for political economy. At the time her book attracted mixed reviews. However, among the handful of individualists of the time it became a fundamental part of the canon. Only 6,000 copies were published and the book was soon out of print, so it circulated from hand to hand, like samizdat copies of Hayek and Friedman behind the Iron Curtain. It was initially not reprinted for commercial reasons and did not reappear until 1964.

It was to be Isabel Paterson's last published book but it was by no means the end of her influence.

She mentioned Rose Wilder Lane's *The Discovery of Freedom* but once in her column, reflecting acerbically that the author wanted to live forever to see how history turned out. When Rose Wilder Lane challenged her as to why her work only merited one cursory comment, Isabel retorted that if Rose insisted on more, she would write a column detailing what was wrong with the book! The put-down silenced the author. In contrast, she sang the praises of her friend Ayn Rand's *The Fountainhead* on 14 occasions in 1943; more endorsements followed later. After a slow start her one-woman public relations drive for Ayn Rand's fictional treatise on individualism resulted in a rise in sales, particularly in the heartland where Isabel's most loyal readers lived.

Many of those Isabel Paterson influenced tried to help her. H. M. Griffith wanted her to teach at a university; R. C. Hoiles bought her book by the hundreds, many boxes at a time; and Howard Buffett gave her moral support. But, always a difficult character, she refused all offers and would quarrel with anybody in a flash.

However, she continued to spark ideas. In late summer 1943 in a telephone conversation with Ayn Rand, the latter conceived the idea of a country's best minds going on strike. This led to Rand's seminal novel, *Atlas Shrugged*, which had a huge influence on Americans. But the two women fell out spectacularly in 1948 when Isabel was the guest of Ayn at her Southern California home. Paterson was in a poor frame of mind as she sensed that her time at the *Herald Tribune* would soon be up (she was axed in January 1949). And her former pupil Ayn Rand had become emboldened by the sales success of *The Fountainhead* and the upcoming movie version. Their argument centered on religion — Ayn Rand was a staunch atheist — but Ayn also accused Isabel of stealing her ideas.

In retirement, Isabel refused to take any social security money. She wanted to remain free of the state. She had some savings and some rental property income and a modest company pension. In the 1950s, she became quite active in the property market.

However, massive schisms with former friends persisted. Leonard Read at FEE had been brewing plans for a monthly journal, *The Freeman*, for a number of years. Isabel wanted it not only to preach but also to live capitalism. To her this meant surviving on subscriptions and advertising, and eschewing donations. All the others involved, which included John Chamberlain, wanted to find wealthy donors to subsidize it, which infuriated Isabel. Eventually, the donor money ran out and *The Freeman* was sold for $1 to Leonard Read. Chamberlain also somehow incurred her wrath by writing a *Freeman* article naming Isabel Paterson as one of the five greatest living individualist women. The others were Rose Wilder Lane (Chapter 13), Ayn Rand (Chapter 20), Vivien Kellems (Chapter 17) and Taylor Caldwell (Chapter 18).

Rose Wilder Lane's friend, the Du Pont executive Jasper Crane, had, like Hoiles, been buying box loads of *The God of the Machine* and supported *The Freeman* with grants. He wanted to buy yet more copies to give away, but the idea that her book and the magazine were being turned into charitable ventures was anathema to her. She was brutal and uncompromising in her view that businessmen had no understanding of why it was necessary to defend the market order of capitalism and how it should best be done.

The last five years of her life were dominated by William F. Buckley's launch of the *National Review*. He welcomed many but by no means all from the right, from traditionalists and anti-communists through to some libertarians, and spent an extraordinary amount of time, ink and postage trying to recruit Isabel to his stable of writers. Now in her seventies, she did write for him occasionally but angry encounters were never far away. When the writer Whittaker Chambers reviewed Ayn Rand's *Atlas Shrugged* under the headline "Big Sister Is Watching You," and criticized it for being a "remarkably silly book," Isabel felt Ayn should take out a libel suit, though Ayn didn't follow her advice. Shortly before she died, she had a furious row with Buckley over her view that businessmen were often the very worst enemies a market economy could have. In Isabel Paterson's obituary, Buckley described her as "intolerably impolite, impossibly arrogant, obstinately vindictive."

In her remaining months, however, she reached out to many old friends, before dying in Northern New Jersey on January 10, 1961, revered, in spite of her abrasiveness, by all who love liberty.

Chapter 16. Lila Wallace

"Many wives could have wrecked an enterprise like this. I think Lila made the *Digest* possible." — DeWitt Wallace

Magazine Publisher and Philanthropist
December 25, 1889–May 7, 1984

PLEASANTVILLE, NEW YORK

It was 1921 and Lila Bell Acheson had just married. She was 33 years old, which made her a late starter in the matrimony stakes in those days. Not only was she looking forward to a life with her new husband DeWitt Wallace, but she was eager to find out how a major mailing promoting their new business idea had performed while they had been away on their honeymoon in the Pocono Mountains of northeastern Pennsylvania.

They had spent long hours in the New York Public Library selecting and condensing articles from other publications for a new magazine they called *Reader's Digest* and they had sent out letters to friends and other names soliciting subscriptions. And then they had set off for a romantic 14 days as newlyweds.

But when the couple returned to Greenwich Village, they discovered that the mailing had flopped. Their plans lay in tatters. DeWitt Wallace wanted to throw in the towel, but she, the new LILA ACHESON WALLACE, had other plans. Who could predict that her vision would create the world's most-read magazine and with it a multi-brand media and marketing company?

Born on Christmas Day 1889 in Manitoba, Canada, where her mother was visiting her own mother, Lila moved around all over the Midwest and the South as a child, as her Presbyterian minister father accepted one job after another. She finally graduated in 1917 from the University of Oregon, Eugene, after stops in North Dakota, Minnesota, Illinois, Tennessee and Tacoma, Washington. It took her a mere two and a half years to complete the four-year course. She then taught high school for two years and helped run a YWCA summer home.

It was while living in Tacoma a decade earlier that Lila had met her future husband. DeWitt Wallace was attending Berkeley and had rekindled his friendship with Lila's brother, Barclay Acheson, who was at the nearby San Francisco Presbyterian Seminary. Both men had previously attended Macalester College, where DeWitt's father taught. They took the steamship from San Francisco to Portland for Christmas 1910. However Lila was already engaged and DeWitt had to content himself with a date with one of her four sisters, Bessie Jane. But a bond clearly formed; for the next year DeWitt used Lila as a convenient PO Box and forwarding agent for his mail.

Over the next ten years their paths diverged but provided, nonetheless, the foundations for what was to become one of the greatest and most influential publishing successes of all time. Barclay became a minister and married into money, while DeWitt dropped out of Berkeley and stumbled from job to job all over the US. No work ever lasted for long, but often provided experience in sales and publishing which was to prove useful later. In one post with a publishing firm that specialized in agriculture he proposed, wrote, and sold 100,000 copies of *Getting the Most Out of Farming*, which was essentially a *Reader's Digest*-style guide for farmers. It listed a variety of agricultural publications and provided a synopsis of each. And it was on a sales trip, lying awake during the night under the Montana skies, that the idea of a more general digest of the best writing, writing that would appeal to everyone, popped into his mind.

He also spent time in the army fighting in France during World War I, being invalided out with shrapnel wounds. This gave him the opportunity to refine his idea and he spent his convalescence reading and condensing articles in the Minneapolis Library in St. Paul. He produced the first dummy issue of *Reader's Digest*, had 500 printed and spent the whole of 1920 circulating copies, but publishers and investors were unimpressed.

Lila became what today we would call a cross between a human resources manager and a customer service representative for the YWCA. During the war, the Y developed a program to help women, and Lila organized recreational centers for those who worked. She set up social centers in munitions factories and other industrial plants. In one, in Pompton Lakes, New Jersey, hot meals were served to night-shift workers for the first time. But mostly, Lila was involved in organizing classes in homemaking, languages, music and the arts, perhaps sowing the seed which grew into her later philanthropic interests. She also campaigned for factory owners to open schools and recreational centers for their migrant workers, organizing meetings and making speeches.

DeWitt picked up his friendship with Barclay Acheson once again and discovered, to his surprise, that Lila had never married. He sent her a tongue in cheek telegram: "Conditions among Women Workers in St. Paul Ghastly. Urge Immediate Investigation."

Within months she was in St. Paul to set up a new YWCA. She arrived on October 15, 1920, and DeWitt proposed the same day; she thought about it overnight and then accepted. At the same time she told him how excited she was about the *Reader's Digest* business idea. She clearly saw its potential early on. As she was to say later, "I knew right away that it was a gorgeous idea." From the start, she was marrying not just the man but his vision, a vision she understood and could help shape.

They had no money to marry or to invest in the Digest concept. Lila returned to New York City while DeWitt took a job in Pittsburgh, where a co-worker read the dummy copy of the magazine and came up with a piece of advice that was to prove invaluable: it should sell by subscription, not on the newsstand.

Armed with a family loan, DeWitt began highly targeted, personalized direct mailings mostly to lists of women. He offered a year's subscription for $3, which would convert to about $35 today. The response was encouraging. DeWitt moved to New York City in preparation for marriage in Pleasantville, New York, where Lila lived. They wed on October 15, 1921, a year to the day after his proposal, with Lila's brother Barclay, now a Presbyterian minister, officiating. Barclay had also invested in their project, providing another $100 for a big mailing of 10,000 letters.

When their high hopes for this mailing were dashed on their return from their honeymoon, Lila was undeterred. The idea may have been DeWitt's but she was the business brains, providing much of the impetus that would turn *Reader's Digest* into a global success story, while her husband concentrated on the editorial side of the enterprise. However, they both shared a belief in the importance of self-help and self-improvement. In Lila's case this came from her Presbyterian upbringing.

Lila kept her full-time YWCA job; she rented out half the tiny apartment they had taken underneath a Greenwich Village speakeasy at 1 Minetta Lane; and she persuaded Barclay to lend them the equivalent of about $60,000 in today's currency. This cash injection and some better direct-mail results gave the fledgling business the boost it needed and Volume 1 Number 1 appeared in February 1922. Lila and DeWitt Wallace were listed on its masthead as joint editors.

The first print run was 5,000 copies — the few copies that survive today now go for $500 plus each at auction.

The concept was to boil down about 30 already published pieces to as little as a quarter of their original length. Each article would be "of enduring value and interest." And from its earliest days *Reader's Digest* embraced anti-communism and conservatism with a libertarian free-market streak. For example, in July 1943, when Russia was an ally, the *Digest* went against the grain of the times with "We Must Face the Facts about Russia" by ex-communist Max Eastman.

It was tough, hard going and DeWitt often fell into depression. Lila always chivied him out of it. She was a natural optimist, providing the perfect antidote to his worrying and self-doubting tendencies. Just a few months on and they were out of New York and into a one-bed apartment and a tiny former stable as an office in Lila's old base of Pleasantville. Although they had 7,000 paying subscribers, Lila still had to work full time to keep the ship afloat for its first two years, but the day was fast approaching when she could devote herself full time to the *Digest*.

The direct mail that built the early subscriber lists was a cottage industry with elderly ladies handwriting and addressing envelopes to carefully selected targets. The percentage returns were astonishingly high and the print run for each issue was soon well over 10,000.

In 1923, Lila hit on a brilliant marketing idea. *Reader's Digest* was already sold on subscription only; why not build on that idea and offer a Christmas gift subscription? The response was overwhelming from the targeted women and small-town mid-America which lapped up the *Digest*. More staff was urgently needed and Lila played a major role in interviewing candidates. Both she and her husband expected high standards from staff, and were fanatical about time-keeping. By 1925, subscriptions had nearly quintupled.

Once newsstand subscriptions were added in 1929, the results were spectacular. By 1935, combined monthly sales hit 1.5 million copies. Lila and DeWitt were now very wealthy and were able to purchase more than 100 acres in Westchester County and build their dream house, High Winds.

As soon as it was completed, and with combined monthly circulation nudging two million copies, Lila and her team tackled the main problem caused by *Reader's Digest*'s exponential growth — office space. Staff members were now spread all over Pleasantville and in 1937 Lila and DeWitt bought close to 100 acres near Chappaqua, New York, not far from Pleasantville. Over the next two years Lila oversaw the construction of a new 90,000-square-foot Georgian-style headquarters, which included a heavily subsidized cafeteria. In that, there is evidence of Lila's years in human relations and social work in the factories. As a result, *Reader's Digest* became known as a great place to work. For example, when

Lila and DeWitt received a $70,000 windfall, they split it evenly between each of the 72 employees on $3,000 a year or less. In today's money those staff would have been earning under $37,000 and each would have received the equivalent of a $12,000 bonus.

But Lila paid attention to the aesthetic details of office life, too. She was responsible for ensuring that there was always a beautiful supply of fresh flowers from her garden and, with her sharp eye for art, she bought original paintings to adorn the offices. In time and under her supervision, the company built up a large collection of art, which included pieces by Marc Chagall, Monet and Van Gogh. When a part of it was sold in 1998, a representative of Sotheby's described the body of art as one of the most important corporate collections ever assembled. Lila was also to become the only woman on the board of directors of the New York Central Railroad, because, as the president put it, there was a need for "an intelligent women who could make top decisions — not only about the housekeeping of a railroad, but corporate decisions where a woman's viewpoint and intuitive sense would make a valuable contribution."

Increasingly, Lila was becoming interested in philanthropic causes. The couple had no children, but they had a lot of money. In 1938, Lila and DeWitt established the Reader's Digest Foundation to support youth and community projects. In the same year, buoyed by the magazine's continuing success, *Reader's Digest* opened its first international edition, in London, where a team produced a separate edition for the UK.

In 1940, the first foreign-language edition was launched — Spanish for the South American market. This hit one million copies per month and new offices were opened the world over from Sweden, Norway and Finland through to Cairo and even Tokyo. Troops fighting in World War II received 1.5 million copies and 50 more staff had to be hired just to cope with 8,000 daily address changes from members of the forces alone.

As war ended, the April 1945 issue was to have the most extraordinary long-run worldwide impact. It carried as its condensed book — the longer read which featured in every edition — F. A. Hayek's *The Road to Serfdom*, which had been published in the UK the previous March. Penned while Hayek sat at night above a Cambridge college as a fire lookout, it was a dire warning of the dangers of socialism and was dedicated to the "socialists of all parties."

But Lila and DeWitt didn't just condense this classic of political and economic thought and stick it in the back of the magazine — the usual position for that issue's extended read. Uniquely, they broke with editorial convention and placed it up front as the lead article. Its banner was, "One of the most important books of our generation."

Hayek himself said on more than one occasion: "I thought it impossible to edit *The Road to Serfdom* to just a few thousand words, so imagine my surprise and my delight when they did such a good job!"

The extract in *Reader's Digest* was influential beyond the founders' wildest dreams. It was this condensation that led a young British RAF officer named Antony Fisher to Hayek's office at the London School of Economics. Fisher told Hayek he was in total agreement with the *Digest* condensation and wanted to go into politics and "put it all right." Hayek counseled otherwise: set up an institute to make the case to the intellectual classes for a market-based society. Their influence would prevail and the politicians would follow, he argued.

Fisher made a fortune by factory farming chickens and in the mid 1950s he established the Institute of Economic Affairs in London, UK, to do just what Hayek had suggested. Two decades later it provided the intellectual underpinnings for what became known as "Thatcherism" and was copied the world over. Today there is a network of some 250 market-oriented think tanks in over 100 countries. Each can trace its roots back through Fisher's IEA to the *Digest*'s condensed version of *The Road to Serfdom*. Today, over 65 years later, that condensation is in twenty languages and is sold or downloaded by the tens of thousands every year.

That Lila-and-DeWitt-edited April 1945 issue was striking in a number of ways. First, it boasted a talent bank of nine senior editors and 19 roving editors plus 30 other editors. There was Max Eastman, the former organizer of the Men's League for Women's Suffrage. Then there was Fulton Oursler Sr., author of *The Greatest Story Ever Told*, which was anonymously dedicated to the Wallaces, "two people, man and wife, who in their lives personally and professionally exemplify the teachings of Jesus Christ more completely than any others I know." There was also William L. White, husband of Katherine White and confidante of Clare Boothe Luce (Chapter 19), and Burt MacBride, father of Roger — who, as a teenager, met Rose Wilder Lane (Chapter 13) who in turn became his "adoptive" grandmother. He was to bring *Little House on the Prairie* to TV.

Second, the entire issue gave huge support to the condensed *Serfdom* in the form of quotations, offers of reprints and a two-page *Newsweek* condensation alerting US citizens to the kind of economic order around the corner, the very kind Hayek was warning about. The article, by the then very famous economics commentator and journalist Ralph Roby, was entitled, "What is being planned for you," followed by the barbed question: "What becomes of the enterprise which has created a great nation when this program gets going?"

It contained a dire and prescient warning that Washington, DC, was planning restrictive measures ranging from a "planning agency" to control the economy to production quotas to ensure "full employment" to the permanent fixing and control of prices to the sinister-sounding "program of government expenditures and expansion of Government activities."

Another piece from the *Wall Street Journal* ends with three paragraphs that could have inspired Ayn Rand (Chapter 20) to write her great novel *Atlas Shrugged*: "Yes, those who are making these plans know exactly what they are doing. And make no mistake about whether they are smart. They are as smart, and clever, and ruthless, and determined, as any group in this country."

"One further point. Do not expect this program ever to be presented as a whole for consideration by Congress. It will be brought out part by part, each apparently designed merely to meet a particular problem of pressing proportions. And every part will be carefully labeled with an innocuous name and wrapped around and around with beautiful and innocent-sounding names especially prepared to cover up the real purpose and intent of the proposal.

"So if you happen to be a believer in individual enterprise and freedom, watch for the component parts of this program. And don't be misled by someone's telling you that we are just taking a small step toward 'industrial democracy' or a 'planned economy.' Rather remember that this same program when it was in effect in Italy was known as 'Fascism.' And today in Germany it goes under the name of 'Nazism.'"

There are another four articles of a broadly free-market flavor, making the Wallaces' sympathies very clear. One example, "Can we break the building blockade?" by Robert Lasch, condensed from the *Atlantic Monthly*, has a succinct tag line: "Must a great postwar housing program be hamstrung by restrictive and obsolete building codes kept in force by pressure groups?"

One paragraph provides inspiration for Digest contributor Henry Hazlitt's brilliant bestseller, *Economics in One Lesson* (1946): "Union glazers frequently refuse to install windows fully fabricated at the mill. Painters rule out the use of spray guns, or even the use of brushes exceeding a certain width. In New York, lathers refused to install metal lath and metal rods which were not cut and bent, at extra expense, on the job. When prefabricated pipe of fitted lengths was delivered to a job with threads already cut, Houston plumbers demanded the right to cut off the threads and rethread the pipe at the site."

The story of the Houston plumbers duly appears on page 50 of the first edition of Hazlitt's book.

Over the years, *Reader's Digest* became a campaigning medium not only against communism and over-regulation, but also against tobacco and against slaughter on the roads and many other causes, giving the publication a solid status as a public-interest magazine. What an extraordinary publication Lila and DeWitt had created. But they didn't stop at magazines. The company condensed books — fiction and non-fiction — and sold them by direct marketing throughout the world. In time there were coffee table books, tapes, videos, CDs, and DVDs.

In 1973, the year after the magazine had celebrated its golden jubilee, the Wallaces stood down from the day-to-day running of the company they had created. To mark its 50 years, there was a white-tie banquet at the White House and President Richard Nixon presented the co-founders with the Medal of Freedom, the highest civilian honor in the United States.

The couple could now devote themselves to good causes. While DeWitt bestowed many quiet gifts on people and groups who needed money, Lila's philanthropy was more focused on the arts. She is estimated to have given away $60 million. Her beneficiaries included the Metropolitan Museum of Art, where she paid for a new wing and for a supply of fresh flowers to be placed in the Great Hall in perpetuity, the Juilliard School, the Metropolitan Opera and, in France, Monet's house and garden in Giverny. She also gave to the Sloan-Kettering Institute for Cancer Research and to many Presbyterian charities.

DeWitt passed away on Monday, March 30, 1981, with the Digest just shy of its sixtieth birthday and easily the most-read magazine in the world.

Lila followed him on Monday, May 7, 1984. Her death made front page news. Like Madam C. J. Walker (Chapter 12), she died the richest woman of her time in America.

Today the US circulation is eight million and readership is 38 million. Worldwide circulation is 17 million and readership is more than 100 million. Outside the US, including many former communist countries, such as Russia and the former Yugoslavia, nearly 70 million people read 52 different editions in 100 nations and 35 languages.

What an achievement and how she helped with her enthusiasm, her fundraising — especially that early loan that ignited the magazine's success — and her salary in the early years, her sacrifices, her human relations skills and her marketing ideas. It is not hyperbole to say that without her, *Reader's Digest* would not have become the phenomenon it did and the world would be less free today.

As former Defense Secretary Melvin R. Laird stated after her death, "Publishing, music, art, opera and the performing arts have lost a grand woman. Her contribution to all will be a living memorial to her for many, many decades."

CHAPTER 17. VIVIEN KELLEMS

"Of course I'm a publicity hound. Aren't all crusaders? How can you accomplish anything unless people know what you are trying to do? — Vivien Kellems, quoted in *Reader's Digest*, October 1975

Entrepreneur and Tax Protestor
June 7, 1896–January 25, 1975

WESTPORT, CONNECTICUT

VIVIEN KELLEMS was convinced the weight was falling off her. In the anxious two and a half hours she waited for the jury to deliberate on her case against the Internal Revenue Service (IRS), she lost two and a half pounds, she later claimed.

It was nearly 2.30pm on January 25, 1951, when word spread that the jury in New Haven's Federal District Court was ready to be seated. Everybody filed in and the clerk of the court asked: "Ladies and gentlemen of the jury, have you agreed upon a verdict?"

The foreman replied that they had and handed a piece of paper to the clerk, who read it without expression before handing it on to the judge. He in turn read the note, poker-faced, and instructed the clerk to "verify the Interrogatory and the verdict."

The clerk addressed the jury: was the plaintiff's failure both to withhold income taxes from her employees and to send such monies to the Collector "not willful"? The judge had that very morning, at the last moment, changed the wording.

But the jurors all responded that their verdict was indeed that Miss Kellems' action had not been willful. Yes, the defendant, the IRS, owed her thousands of dollars plus interest and costs worth about $75,000 in today's money.

Vivien's head spun. The legal terminology and the judge's last-minute rephrasing of the question had confused her. Before she could figure it out, her attorney whispered, "We've won!"

"We have?" she gasped.

Vivien was descended from John Kellam of Nottinghamshire, England. Fittingly this was the stomping ground of Robin Hood, whose arch enemy was the Sheriff of Nottingham, responsible for collecting taxes which Robin would steal and give back to the poor. Kellam landed in Virginia in 1636 and Kellam became Kellems at some point. His descendants married into many great local families and 11 of Vivien's ancestors fought in the Revolution. Her grandparents crossed the Midwest in covered wagons to Oregon and Vivien was born in Des Moines, Iowa on June 7, 1896, as her minister father completed his education at Drake University. She had six brothers and learnt to assert herself in a male-dominated environment from an early age. All seven siblings attended Oregon State University in Eugene, where the Reverend Kellems taught in a small theological college between Sunday sermons. Vivien was the only female member of her university debating team.

Vivien took a bachelor's degree in economics in 1918, followed by a master's. Then she spent a couple of years on PhD work at Columbia University, New York, where her special subject was taxation. This was followed by a stint at the University of Edinburgh, Scotland. When she took on the IRS much later, she knew what she was talking about.

In 1927 her brother Edgar invented a cable-grip that was far superior to anything then on the market. It had an incredible number of applications. Vivien thought it "an excellent idea" and wasted no time in setting up a small factory to manufacture it. She then hit the road, selling the device, used largely by power and electrical companies, throughout the Americas and Europe. She even promoted it as far away as Australia. The venture was soon employing some 75 people.

She later delighted in explaining to General MacArthur how the cable-grips operated in the gun turrets of the battleship *Missouri* and claimed that "during World War II we lifted all the shells...all the cables on battleships were secured permanently with our grips." She wrote: "The cable-grip business is fun, because something new is always popping up."

And that might well have been Vivien's career, her sole claim to fame, that she was the lady cable-grip entrepreneur who had a ball making a great product and being a good employer. But her love of America and "the brilliant men who wrote our Constitution" took her down a highly principled but dangerous route when she became a lone protestor against the way in which taxes were collected in the US.

It all started on February 13, 1948, when Vivien Kellems spoke to the Rotary Club in the ballroom of the Los Angeles Biltmore Hotel. It was packed. She could not eat lunch as "my tummy won't take it," as she later recounted in her book, *Toil, Taxes and Trouble*, and her knees were knocking so badly a friend had to assure her that the large podium would hide them. Finally she stood and addressed a thousand men.

What followed was a monumental speech that belied her nerves and marked the beginning of a campaign that she would wage until she died. She began with an attack on the Sixteenth Amendment to the Constitution, passed in 1913: "The Congress shall have power to lay and collect taxes on income from whatever source derived, without apportionment among the several States, and without regard to any census or enumeration."

Up to that point, she said, taxes had always been uniform and apportioned — imposed on the basis of state population — and the Founders had been very explicit about this. Why? "For one reason only. Our forefathers were determined to build a republic, with equal opportunity and equal responsibility for each and every one of us. They knew that the power to tax is the power to destroy, and they did not wish to have one group of citizens, or one part of the country, penalized for the unfair advantage of another."

George Mason University Law School professor Todd Zywicki comments: "The reason the 16th Amendment was enacted was because the Constitution only permitted a 'poll' tax as in a head or capitation tax. The Federal government wanted to tax incomes but this was struck down by the Supreme Court hence the 16th Amendment."

She saw the continued presence of this Amendment to the Constitution as violation of freedom, of citizens' right to privacy, as enshrined in the Fourth and Fifth Amendments. In taking money compulsorily from a person's pay check the IRS was infringing a person's privacy.

But this was just an *amuse bouche* or two before she tucked into the real red meat, namely "withholding," introduced in 1943 as a temporary wartime measure. Withholding is the process under which an employer does not pay an employee their agreed weekly wage in full but rather holds back certain amounts and then sends them to the IRS. Employers who did not do this risked fines and imprisonment. "This in free America," she said with sarcasm.

"This," she protested, "is the miserable system foisted upon the people of our country by New Deal zealots and arrogant communists who have wormed themselves into high places in Washington. This system is deliberately designed to make involuntary tax collectors of every employer and to impose involuntary tax servitude upon every employee."

She pointed out that it cost employers a great deal to do all the paperwork and forward these taxes. Should they not be paid for all this work? Vivien announced that her company had just distributed the weekly pay roll and that it had withheld taxes for the very last time. She was sure all her employees would pay income tax of their own volition, she said, but that if they did not then that was between them and the government, just as with their relationship with God. "I have no right to inject myself into either relationship," she declared.

"If High Tax Harry wants me to get that money for him, then he must appoint me an agent for the Internal Revenue Department, he must pay me a salary for my work, and he must reimburse me for my expenses incurred in collecting that tax. And I want a badge, too. I am not a tax collector and if an American citizen can be fined and thrown into prison for not collecting taxes from his workers, then let's know about it now."

She was throwing down the gauntlet to the authorities. And she didn't mince her words when referring to them: "Like all bullies and bloodsucking parasites, those mangy little bureaucrats down in Washington are at heart yellow cowards," she continued. "So no matter what they do, I'm standing on my rights until the court hands down its verdict."

Vivien's defiant speech openly condoned law-breaking and civil disobedience as a way of preserving or reclaiming freedom, invoking the protagonists of the Boston Tea Party: "Rather than pay a tax they threw the tea into the harbor." She likened withholding to the National Prohibition Act of 1919 that so many had flouted by making, selling and drinking their own liquor. "It is no more possible to enforce the income tax law than it was to enforce the prohibition law. We couldn't plug those liquor leaks and we can't plug these tax leaks."

When Vivien finally sat down, she received a standing ovation. Her speech was an extraordinarily passionate *tour de force*, a speech for the ages. The thousand men in the audience applauded until she stood again, her knees no longer knocking. And even then they carried on applauding. Her rhetoric, her arguments, her vehemence had struck a loud chord.

But in the end she acted alone, supported by her brother. Her goal was to force a test case before the Supreme Court so that she could openly challenge the constitutionality of the Sixteenth Amendment. She had many objections to the income tax, but the narrow point she felt she could force was on the supposedly temporary wartime policy of withholding. The plan was simple: as an employer she was simply going to stop doing it; the IRS would then sue and the matter would go to the justices in the nation's highest court as a test case. Or so she thought.

Her concerns were threefold. First, she objected to the way in which withholding made her and all other employers unpaid servants of the state who could be fined and even jailed for getting it wrong. Second, she felt that withholding at source blinded tens of millions of citizens to exactly how much Uncle Sam was stealing from them. Third, she was concerned about privacy, believing that the federal government was intruding on citizens' private lives through their income.

She sped back East to Connecticut and on the following Friday gathered her employees to explain why she was about to break the law by not withholding and not forwarding their taxes for them. "Paying taxes is a duty, a responsibility and, believe it or not, it used to actually be considered a privilege of citizenship," she told them. But she didn't exercise lots of other "duties, responsibilities and privileges" of being an American on their behalf, so why should she collect their taxes?

Vivien explained that from now on all their wages would be in their pay packets with the amount they should save for the taxman written on the outside. That amount would be written there every Friday; they would be told when the taxes were due; the relevant forms would be procured and they would have help filling them out. Vivien told them she would personally pay the charges for all postal money orders they would need and also cover the cost of the registered envelope to send in said orders.

According to her own book, *Toil, Taxes and Trouble*, she ended: "We'll do anything and everything to help you but we will not collect nor will we pay your taxes for you. Now I have gambled upon your loyalty and good citizenship. I hope you will pay your taxes. If you don't it will be unpleasant for you and it will be practically disastrous for me."

She walked out of the room. Her staff conferred. Many did not even have savings accounts, which risked complicating the issue. But it didn't hold them back them for long. As a temporary measure they appointed one man who would hold all that was due to Uncle Sam, while they thought the matter through. Vivien heard through the grapevine that her employees were stunned at how much money they were actually paying over. Within days they had all opened savings accounts.

Vivien had, she says in her book, always thought of withholding as a way "to lull the taxpayer to sleep, to deceive him and make him believe that not he, but someone else was paying the tax." It was "insidious" and a "narcotic," she believed, and a cynical ploy to hoodwink citizens. She was convinced that the men orchestrating withholding were well aware that if taxes were taken weekly from a pay packet, then in the end the individual concerned would pay little heed to it. "He would consider only the amount of money in his envelope as his pay. If he did feel any resentment it would be directed at the employer, not the government. That is what the government wanted and this is exactly what happened."

Vivien's strategy started to work immediately. Staff began approaching her, asking in surprise if they really paid such a lot in taxes. Was she sure the number on the outside of their envelope was correct? Soon they were taking a lot more interest in news and current affairs, noting how taxpayers' money was spent. Vivien had expected all this. What she had not expected, however, was that many of her staff "developed the savings habit and put more than the amount of taxes in their accounts."

She knew she had broken the law and she did not expect others to follow suit. However, she did come up with a totally legal strategy for other companies unwilling to pursue her policy of refusing to withhold. The aim of it was "to make every worker completely tax conscious and aware." The idea was to pay every worker in full at noon on Friday. They would enjoy a weighty pay packet for a few hours but then, as they left for the weekend, a "company collector standing right by the door or gate" would demand they hand back the social security, the income tax, the union dues, the unemployment and any other charges they had to pay. She hoped that if every employer detailed how employees' taxes were broken down, there would either be a revolution or severe contraction in federal spending.

This never happened. What did happen was that the following May, 1949, four men walked into Kellems Cable Grips Inc. at its headquarters in Connecticut. They were IRS agents. They demanded the books, pored over them for days, and interviewed all the staff one at a time, before finally saying all taxes were paid. The agent in charge of the operation even congratulated the company and its employees on the way they had "safeguarded the funds of the government." But when they left, they went straight to Vivien's bank and demanded $1,685.40 (close to $15,000 today).

The bank manager asked for proof that Kellems Cable Grips Inc. owed the money — to which the agent retorted that they needed no proof, as they were from the IRS.

The manager drew himself up. "That is all very well," he said, "but I have been in the banking business most of my life and I have never yet taken money out of a private account and handed it over to someone else unless there was some proof that the money was owed and that I had authority to pay it."

He refused to give them a cent without a court order or some other official document and said that he would consult his lawyers. The agent told him he had 24 hours.

However, Vivien told the bank manager to pay up.

Even though Vivien's staff had all paid their taxes in full, her "willful" failure to collect or account for these monies under the relevant regulations made her vulnerable to 100% penalties. The penalty for non-payment would have been a mere 50%. The sum demanded comprised $837.50 for taxes already paid (quibbling that they had been paid by her employees, not her, as the law stipulated), plus the 100% penalty and $10 in interest.

Having graced the front pages of newspapers all over the USA after her incendiary Rotary Club speech, she was there again, and the editorials were gradually moving her way. However, she realized that she might have made one tactical error — perhaps she had not collected enough evidence of payment and receipt thereof.

As the next quarter's deadline approached, Vivien did three things. First, she secured the permission of her staff to be photographed by the press as they filled in the forms, purchased the money orders and mailed it all off to the Collector. The photos were distributed all over the US. Next, she copied every single piece of paper and, finally, she paid for return receipts for every single envelope. This meant there were many layers of proof. She also wrote repeatedly to the President and the Treasury Secretary, demanding they make an example of her in the courts so as to create a test case. All such letters were ignored at worst, or received a perfunctory acknowledgement at best.

Then suddenly, in August 1949, IRS agents walked into her bank and demanded $6,100 — this would work out at about $60,000 today. It was pure penalty for not withholding; there was no mention this time about taxes and interest. To Vivien the only difference between these men and Jesse James was that the latter had a gun. As she later wrote in her autobiographical *Toil, Taxes and Trouble*: "No trial, no lawyer, no judge, no proof that the money was owed. They just walked in and took it. This, is in free America!"

As head of a modest company, Vivien could not take a hit of $6,100 and decided to go to court. Immediately the IRS threw up obstacles — it was clear they didn't want to open up their practices to scrutiny. The agent who had collected the original sum was no longer in office; this meant he could not be sued. So for that first amount Vivien would have to sue the government in the Federal Court before a judge, rather than a jury. On the other hand, the $6,100 had been collected by the current incumbent, so she was allowed a jury for that slice. The judge ruled that two trials would not be necessary — they could do it all in one go. He would rule on the case involving the smaller amount and the jury would come to a verdict on the larger sum.

The case was heard in a day, with the judge instructing the jury the next morning. Vivien read out her Los Angeles speech, to the fury of the IRS, and her attorney read out all her letters to the President and Treasury Secretary.

The whole case hinged on whether her deliberate and intentional breaking of the law on withholding in order to create a test case was willful or not. It was a highly principled case based on the Fourth Amendment (unreasonable search and seizure), the Fifth Amendment (just compensation for takings), Eighth Amendment (no excessive fines) and Thirteenth Amendment (neither slavery nor involuntary servitude).

After the jury had passed their verdict that Vivien's actions had been "not willful," she went over to thank them personally. All but one of them congratulated her.

She had won a moral victory on the larger amount, but the judge did not take the same view as the jury over the first and smaller sum. Two months after the first hearing, Vivien was back in court to hear him rule that her refusal to collect the $1,685.40 had indeed been willful.

And there it ended. Vivien never had her day in the Supreme Court to test the constitutional validity of the Sixteenth Amendment. She was not prepared to appeal and risk bankrupting her company as a result of legal costs and penalties. But neither did the IRS appeal against the $6,100 they had forfeit at the jury trial; it "had had enough" she wrote. But for her remaining 25 years Vivien continued to rail against the "hydra-headed monster" of tax law and demand that "all taxes should be visible."

"Every hidden tax must be abolished," she declared, "and when a tax is paid, it must be recognized as a tax, and the taxpayer must feel the unpleasant pinch of paying it."

She died an icon to all tax reformers and protestors and it is rumored that her last ten tax returns were sent in blank.

CHAPTER 18. TAYLOR CALDWELL

"If one of my children were a writer I'd say 'God help you. You'll need it'. There must be easier ways of making a living, such as working the salt mines."

Novelist
September 7, 1900–August 30, 1985

BUFFALO, NEW YORK

TAYLOR CALDWELL had a "tough" upbringing, as she put it herself in the title of her autobiography — *On Growing Up Tough*. Her family wasn't poor, but it believed in hard work and discipline.

She was born Janet Miriam Taylor Holland Caldwell in the Prestwich district of the large industrial city of Manchester in northwest England. Her family was middle class and she started at a private school aged four. Every moment of her time, seven days a week was accounted for. If she wasn't at her studies, there were fires to lay, dishes to wash, and clothes to mend and iron. On the weekend, church, Sunday school and more domestic tasks awaited. Punishment for any transgression was likely to be a beating from her parents or from the headteacher if she stepped out of line at school. By the time she left with her family for Buffalo, New York, at the age of seven, Janet had finished two years of Latin and one of French, possessed a good grasp of history and geography, and was already reading poetry, including Shakespeare's Sonnets.

She had also started writing essays and short stories, and even as a child won prizes for them.

By her own account, the young Janet Caldwell flourished in the authoritarian atmosphere of her family. In *On Growing Up Tough*, she outlined her belief that all children were born "rude and uncouth," even "reeking with Original Sin." She wrote: "A child starts out even in these 'loving' days by having no more a sense of decency and kindness and charity and reverence than did his caveman ancestor. These are things which must be taught by strict discipline, example and the power of a parent's good right arm."

In her later years, in the 1970s, she agonized about the "idiot child-psychiatrists" whose influence on social workers and teachers she saw as responsible for soaring crime rates among under 18-year-olds, and she thanked God her parents had been strict.

She wrote 42 novels and her autobiography, all of which reflected her conservative views. They sold over 100 million copies in many languages and her *This Side of Innocence* was the single best-selling work of fiction in 1946. *Time* magazine claimed there had been more books still but that she had destroyed 140 unpublished novels. As late as 1979, as she neared 80, she was able to sign a two-book publishing deal which would today be worth $11.375 million. For two decades, while Harold Robbins was the most popular male author on earth, she was the most popular female writer. When her *Captains and the Kings* and *Testimony of Two Men* were made into separate mini-series, it was the first and only time in US television history that one author had two such major productions airing in consecutive years. She was as famous as any movie or pop star.

Her success brought her wealth, and she claimed in *In Search of Taylor Caldwell*, a book by Jess Stearns, her friend, adviser and co-author in later years: "Anonymously, I have helped thousands. I have made one provision, however: No one is to be helped in any way with my money unless they have demonstrated guts, drive, ambition, and intelligence. It is a waste of money and effort to help those who show no desire to help themselves, and no self-respect."

Like Sojourner Truth (Chapter 6), she believed fervently in a hand up, not a handout, and her fictional heroes are often self-made immigrants.

Taylor Caldwell herself claimed descent from a ruggedly individualist Scots-English-Irish family. Her father Arthur was an illustrator on the left-leaning newspaper the *Manchester Guardian*, moving to Buffalo to take up a similar post. Her mother Anne was a housewife, looking after both the young girl and her younger brother Arthur Jr.

Her American school experience was chiefly characterized by boredom. While she found literature, history and languages easy (and it turned out was already writing enormously long novels), other subjects such as mathematics were a closed book. She could never learn to divide, struggling even as an adult. After leaving school, she started at a bindery at the age of 15, working ten hours a day. She awoke at 6AM to go to work and in the evening she went to night school, where she trained as a stenographer and court reporter. Ten o'clock at night would see her finally walking home.

Her father did not approve of her writings, but in 1913 her parents nonetheless mailed their 12-year-old daughter's first novel, *The Romance of Atlantis*, to her grandfather who worked for a publisher in Philadelphia. He promptly returned it, asking for it to be burned as it was clearly copied — no child of that age could possibly have written it! In the end, *The Romance of Atlantis* did not appear until 1975. And when she was 16, she received an old typewriter for Christmas.

World War I saw her in Washington, DC, working for the US Navy as a "yeomanette," where she met the first of her four husbands. William Fairfax Combs, reportedly a descendant of Lord Fairfax, was a construction engineer with dreams of making his fortune in the oil fields of Kentucky. At 19 she was married to Combs and living variously in a tent and a dilapidated 200-year-old cabin with their baby daughter Mary, known as Peggy. They had a mule, a cow and some chickens, and Janet became an expert rifle shot to augment their pot. In her autobiography she wrote in graphic detail about her grueling time in the remote and inhospitable Kentucky wilderness and the many skills she was forced to learn. She grew vegetables, cured ham and bacon, made cornbread, knitted, sewed, and planted and mixed herbal medicines. The family lived five miles from the nearest town, Benton — to which she walked once a week — and forty miles from the nearest railroad. For a long time all their efforts were concentrated on surviving, and she wrote not one word. Four years later they moved to Bowling Green, Kentucky, and Janet began walking the 12 miles a day to town and back to make $18 a week as a public stenographer.

But her husband never struck oil (his employer filed for bankruptcy, owing him over $1,000) and, disillusioned, Janet headed back home to Buffalo with her young daughter and $44 in her purse. As she stepped off the train, officials from the County Welfare department were there to meet her. They wanted to put mother and daughter into a shelter, and Peggy up for adoption. Fortunately, the Salvation Army intervened and faced down the authorities, including police officers, finding Janet a place to lodge and a job as a secretary. Her lodgings were $15 a week and her salary was $25. But soon she passed her court reporter exam, which allowed her to earn an improved $1,800 a year. This was an important stepping stone. She was able to send her husband the rail fare so that he could join her and used her new legal contacts to sue his former employer, settling for $800. She paid her way through SUNY College at Buffalo and was promoted to the staff of the Department of Justice.

It was the Great Depression and William Combs was unemployed for long spells. What little they had in common — mainly a dream of oil wealth — had disappeared. She divorced him in 1931 and married Marcus Reback, an older man and fellow Department of Justice employee.

It was at this time that she began serious work on what was to be her first published novel, *Dynasty of Death*, a door-stopping multi-generational epic of family businesses set in a fictional town on the Allegheny River north of Pittsburgh. She was still working on it five years later when her husband was briefly relocated to New York City, but this gave her the chance personally to hawk the manuscript around major publishers. While Macmillan turned it down, Lois Cole, a friendly editor there, was an enthusiastic supporter of the novel. She suggested the author try Maxwell Perkins at Scribner's and gave the book her strong personal endorsement.

Perkins was arguably the most famous editor in literary history, handling names such as Ernest Hemingway and F. Scott Fitzgerald. He liked the book and it came out in 1938. Janet Reback was launched as Taylor Caldwell. It was a deliberate marketing tactic and it certainly succeeded in getting her talked about when it emerged that Taylor was in fact a woman. More recently, the same tactic of obscuring the sex of a female author was used with Joanne Rowling, who became J. K. Rowling by adding K from in her grandma's name Kathleen.

Between 1940 and 1980 some 41 more novels were published — she hardly missed a year and if she did, there would be two titles the following year. American entrepreneurs with marked ethnic backgrounds strode across her pages and she often focused on the American Dream. Other novels used historical themes. On reading her oeuvre, the reader would meet Pericles, Cicero, Genghis Khan and Richelieu. Biblical figures featured too, including Judas Iscariot, St. Luke, St. Paul, St. John, Jesus and Mary of Magdala. In one novel, *Dialogues with the Devil* (1967), she even had Lucifer and the archangel Michael in correspondence with each other.

Underpinning all her writing was her political philosophy. She made no secret of it: for example in *A Pillar of Iron* (1965) she wrote, "Antonius heartily agreed with him [Cicero] that the budget should be balanced, that the Treasury should be refilled, that the public debt should be reduced, the arrogance of the generals should be tempered and controlled, that assistance to foreign lands should be curtailed lest Rome become bankrupt, that the mobs should be forced to work and not depend on government for subsistence, and that prudence and frugality should be put into practice as soon as possible..."

Taylor Caldwell gives us fiscal policy, civil service reform, cuts in aid to less developed countries, and welfare reform all in one sentence.

As Jess Stearn wrote in *In Search of Taylor Caldwell* (1974): "She was a conservative politically believing the spoils belonged to those who toiled for them. There were no free lunches. She abhorred the welfare philosophy that gave handouts to free-loaders, decrying rewards for indolence and incompetence."

Taylor was ignored or sneered at by left-wing intellectual book reviewers and dismissed as a low-brow storyteller all her writing life.

As the author, an avowed anti-communist, wrote in a letter to the FBI in 1957: "I am the only major best-selling novelist in the United States who is not tainted by 'liberalism' and Communism, and who has never belonged to a communist front. As a result, the press, which is mainly 'liberal,' has been furiously attacking me for years in their alleged 'reviews.'... In our bitterness, we are beginning to wonder what protection an anti-communist has in the United States now, had we been communists we'd have had the enthusiastic support of the press and would now be very wealthy."

However, in spite of these protestations, she was popular and successful, and it made her rich. When Marcus Reback reached the minimum pension age, he retired to become her business manager until he died in 1971. They had one child, a girl named Judith, known as Judy, who was born in 1932 but committed suicide in 1979 after a long legal battle with Taylor over Reback's will.

Time and again movie rights to Taylor Caldwell's blockbusters were sold, but all such projects faltered for many years because Hollywood simply could not digest the size and scope of her works. However the creation of the two TV mini-series in the late 1970s finally proved that it was possible to adapt her books successfully.

In 1972, she married William Everett Stancell, whom she had met on a cruise. It was his eighth marriage and her third. It was not a success and they divorced the next year. In February 1978 (by then approaching 80), she eloped to Mexico with a 60-year-old California realtor, Robert Prestie. They were formally married in a Catholic church, which struck many as odd given her twice-divorced status. Her explanation was that as her first three marriages had not taken place "in the eyes of the Church" — she had been married in civil ceremonies — it was permitted. She also planned to make the Church the biggest beneficiary of her will.

Taylor dedicated *Answer as a Man*, her last book, to Prestie in 1980. He doted on her, protecting her and bringing order to her confused financial affairs, including bizarre contracts with publishers which delayed royalty payments by many years so as to keep taxes away from what she dubbed the *InFernal* Revenue Service, which she hated with a vengeance.

As Taylor Caldwell entered her eighties she worked sporadically on a long-term project, a book on Mary of Magdala. She also proposed a brand new book on Saladin, reflecting her concern about the potential problems of an oil-fueled rise of Islam, something she had long warned about. As her health failed her in the mid-1980s, predictable squabbles erupted over her large estate and future earnings. This pitted her fourth husband Prestie against her only surviving daughter, Peggy, the offspring of her first marriage.

Taylor Caldwell was far more than the mere storyteller so disdained by left-wing literary luminaries. Walter E. Grinder, President of the Institute for Civil Society, writes that he "grew up with Ms. Caldwell" in an extended family where everyone read her books. In correspondence with the author he wrote: "There is a whole, magnificent world lying just beneath the surface of Caldwell's writings, a world that one would not know well unless one had been immersed in her writings. There are scores, if not hundreds, of little incidents and vignettes, all of which stand as lessons for how to lead one's life and how best to live well (and good) in the social (and political) world. There is what amounts to a morality play in nearly each and every one of her chapters. Her writings were used in our household as moral lessons for life. I don't think my experience was much different from probably hundreds of thousands of other kids growing up in America during the 1940s and 1950s." To Grinder she was a favorite author for those who favor liberty mainly because of her 1952 book *The Devil's Advocate* which tests one man's integrity against the power of the state.

It was this "extremely influential book .... of singular importance that solidified Caldwell in the hearts and minds" of those who are pro-liberty.

She had an enormous talent. So broad were her novels in their scope and vision that they were too much for Hollywood and, with their overlay of personal responsibility and free markets, too much for the critics. But for every critic she had hundreds of thousands of fans who rarely allowed her off the bestseller lists from the end of the 1930s to the 1980s. As every reader knew, because she never tried to hide or make any apology for it, she stood full-square for liberty and personal responsibility.

Chapter 19. Clare Boothe Luce

"I refuse the compliment that I think like a man. Thought has no sex; one either thinks or one does not." — Clare Boothe Luce

Writer, Editor, Politician, Diplomat
April 10, 1903 — October 9, 1987

NEW YORK, NEW YORK

It was 1929, the Depression had started and Clare Boothe Brokaw was newly divorced from her gin-drinking and increasingly aggressive husband, George T. Brokaw. She had accepted a relatively small settlement from the multi-millionaire and ensconced herself and her five-year-old daughter in an apartment at 444 East 52nd Street, New York City. So, aged 26 and a single mom, she was looking for work.

She decided to try journalism and started with one of her contacts, Condé Nast, the founder of the eponymous glossy magazine company. She asked him for a job at *Vogue* but he referred her to the editor, who told her to come back in a couple of months. When she returned a few weeks later, well before the deadline, both Nast and his editor were in Europe. Looking around, Clare found two empty desks vacated by caption writers on their honeymoon, so she sat down and started to work. When Nast returned, he reviewed her work and took her on. Popular legend has it that he thought the editor had given her a break and that *Vogue*'s editor thought Clare was her boss's appointment. Both were wrong, but it was early evidence of the determination and ingenuity of the woman who would become CLARE BOOTHE LUCE, whose illustrious career would span seven decades and different fields from foreign correspondent to playwright, from politician to ambassador, from a woman in a largely man's world to apologist for women, their rights and their opportunities.

Clare had succeeded in getting her foot in the door at Condé Nast, but her eyes were already set on *Vanity Fair*, another magazine in the stable. At her first interview with *Vanity Fair*'s editor, she was challenged to come back a week later with an impossible-sounding 100 story ideas. She did just that and was hired. On naïvely asking whether all 100 ideas were good ones, she was told that many were awful but that there were two excellent ones; and two in one week was double what she needed to produce.

Initially, she was not allowed to write for the magazine and had to content herself with screening vast piles of unsolicited articles. One day she took a piece on manners that she had penned herself, signed it with a pseudonym and slipped it in with three other pieces for onward transmission to the managing editor. Hers was accepted, the others were rejected. She'd made a point.

She came to run *Vanity Fair*'s famous Hall of Fame pages, adding a new section on people who should be sent to oblivion. An early character to be dispatched in this way was Senator Reed Smoot of the infamous Smoot-Hawley Tariff Act which raised the tariffs on imported goods to record levels. Clare called it "the most imbecile political feedbag in economic history," giving clear vent to her emerging free-market sympathies. When it came to the Hall of Fame entry on the publisher of *Time* and *Fortune*, one Henry Luce, she struggled. He claimed to have no interests other than work, leaving Clare complaining that the caption couldn't help but be dull.

By 1933 her *Vanity Fair* articles appeared as a collection called *Stuffed Shirts*. The very same year she became managing editor of the magazine. One of her very first features after assuming the post was a brutal parody of Henry Luce's *Time*.

Already her latent interest in politics had been stirred by the election of Franklin D. Roosevelt to the presidency in 1932. Her admiration for FDR was short lived as *Vanity Fair* subscribers and advertisers fled in the face of ongoing economic troubles. But it was her very brief time as a member of a committee, the Motion Picture Code Authority, set up to censor movies under the 1933 National Industrial Recovery Act, which was a defining moment in her political life. She realized that "the fatal flaw" in the New Deal was its element of "coercion" and she soon resigned from the authority, seeing that "it won't work if America is to remain a free country." That seems to be the point at which she started a slow journey to conservatism.

She resigned from *Vanity Fair* in early 1934 and took off to Europe as a journalist for *Life* magazine, but not before finally meeting Henry Luce twice. At their first meeting he is reported to have all but totally ignored her, then left rudely; at the second he said he was going to obtain a divorce and marry her. He pursued her to Europe and his feelings for her were soon reciprocated. However, she insisted they must not meet again until his divorce was final.

Her marriage to Henry Luce in 1935 cemented her position in society, but Clare Boothe Luce's origins were humble, even colorful. She was born on April 10, 1903, in New York City. Her father was divorcé William Franklin Boothe, an itinerant violinist in a theater orchestra, and her mother was Anna Clara Snyder, a chorus line singer and dancer who went by the stage name of Ann Clare, names the couple gave to their daughter. Neither side — hers were Catholic, his fundamentalist Baptists — was remotely happy about the union or the births of their two children, David Franklin and his little sister Ann Clare.

They had little formal education in their early years as the family flitted from place to place. Clare enjoyed brief spells of schooling in Nashville and Chicago but was largely home educated — partly by her father, who worked mostly at night. She started Gibbon's *Decline and Fall of the Roman Empire* before she turned nine.

But while they were in Chicago Clare's father ran off to Los Angeles with another woman. Her mother told the children he was dead, and they all returned to her family in Hoboken, New Jersey. Clare later discovered her mom's lie when bumping into her dad on a train.

Mrs. Boothe was no victim. She networked extensively in the theater through her ex-husband's old friends and managed to arrange for Clare to be hired as the understudy to the actress Mary Pickford in a stage play. When Anna Clara Boothe's father died and left her a bequest, it was enhanced by a Wall Street friend who steered her to a stock that rose quickly. With that and some support from the children's father, she put David into a boarding school and took Clare to London and Paris, returning prematurely when war broke out in Europe in 1914.

Clare was enrolled as a scholarship student in eighth grade at the Episcopalian Cathedral School of St. Mary in Garden City, Long Island. She excelled, was an honor student, and was confirmed as an Episcopalian. Two years later her mother moved her to tenth grade at the Castle School in Tarrytown-on-Hudson, where Clare performed so brilliantly she skipped eleventh grade. She was head of her class, editor of the student paper and such a good swimmer that she was considered a potential Olympian. Clare graduated top of her class in June 1919 and, at 16 years and two months, was her school's youngest ever graduate.

But their lives were to change almost beyond recognition in 1922 when Mrs. Boothe married a Greenwich, Connecticut, surgeon and bank president, Dr. Albert E. Austin. Almost immediately he took his new bride, plus Clare and a mature female companion, on a tour of Europe. Returning to New York on the *Majestic,* Clare met and mingled with people who were to play a significant role in her future, including suffragette leader Alva Belmont and a wealthy childless older couple, Mr. and Mrs. James Cushman.

Back in the US, Clare threw herself into working for Mrs. Belmont on women's rights. With the help of a pilot, she took an old plane up dressed in goggles and helmet to drop leaflets. She also delivered flyers and posters around Washington, DC, and lobbied senators and congressmen in connection with the Equal Rights Amendment, which proposed equal rights for men and women. Meanwhile, it was through the Cushmans that she met her first husband. George T. Brokaw was co-heir with his sister and two brothers to a major clothing fortune. He was in his forties, nearly as old as Clare's stepfather, and, indeed, older than her mother. They disapproved but, ever her own woman, Clare married Brokaw in the Episcopal Church in Greenwich, Connecticut, on August 10, 1923. There were 150 guests but not, conspicuously, Brokaw's three siblings or the Austins. The couple set up home in New York City and the new Mrs. Clare Boothe Brokaw announced she was pregnant. Ann Clare Brokaw was born in April 1924.

With an estate on Long Island next door to Mrs. Belmont's, and a New York house, Clare was launched into society. Her photo appeared regularly in the press, and *Harper's Bazaar* soon chose her as one of its top four American women. But George had a drink problem and now he started to consume large quantities of gin which he hid in his golf trophies. This fueled his violent tendencies and Clare reportedly had three or four miscarriages brought on by his blows. She defied her mother, who begged Clare to stay with her husband, and went to Reno, Nevada, where she established legal residence by staying in a hotel for six weeks. In late May 1929, she was divorced from Brokaw. He quickly remarried but his new wife equally quickly dispatched him to a sanatorium, where he drowned in the pool. His widow then married actor Henry Fonda and became the mother of Jane and Peter Fonda.

Clare began writing plays, completing her first, *Abide With Me,* in 1935. Drawing on her journalistic instincts, which could spot a story in the most mundane situation or exchange, she penned the clearly autobiographical story of a young woman married to a violent old drunk. It opened in New York just before her wedding to Luce and the reviewers, including Luce's own critic at *Time,* crucified it. It closed after 36 performances.

While the newly-weds were finding their feet in this second marriage for both, Henry threw himself into the rebirth of *Life,* while Clare wrote her second play, *The Women*, in 1936. It featured a cast of 38 women and no men, and so frightened was she by the possible criticism that Broadway's first ever female-only production might receive that she sat out the opening night atop the Empire State Building thinking about life. However, it was a huge success. The play was rarely off the stage, was produced around the world, twice made for TV and twice made into a movie. The 1939 version starred Norma Shearer, Joan Crawford and Rosalind Russell. The opening titles boast that the play appeared on Broadway over 650 times. The 2008 version starred Meg Ryan, Annette Bening, Eva Mendes, Debra Messing, Jada Pinkett Smith, Carrie Fisher, Cloris Leachman, Debi Mazar, Bette Midler and Candice Bergen.

More plays followed, *Kiss the Boys Goodbye*, a comedy based on the casting of Scarlett O'Hara in *Gone with the Wind*, and *Margin for Error*, which was also made into a movie. Clare traveled extensively as Henry built his magazine empire. The more she read and saw and heard, the more she became anti-communist and anti-fascist. She noted how communism leaned heavily on violence and how the basis of fascism was compulsion, and she rejected them both.

But her conservatism became much more rounded when she returned to Europe in the spring of 1940 as a fully accredited reporter for *Life*. Her book, *Europe in the Spring* (dedicated to Henry), came out in the summer of 1940 and was reprinted many times, getting to number two on the New York Times bestseller list. In it Clare Boothe Luce tells how her visit, in which she witnessed bombing raids and house arrests, had led her to a deeper understanding of American democracy, especially the Declaration of Independence. She and Henry, who joined her briefly, returned to the US and used every connection they had to press for support for the UK and for opposition to Hitler at a time when over 70% of Americans were solidly isolationist.

With Franklin D. Roosevelt seeking an unprecedented third term in 1940 she, like Ayn Rand (Chapter 20) and Isabel Paterson (Chapter 15), threw herself behind the candidacy of Republican Wendell Willkie. Her friend Bernard Baruch had convinced her that the New Deal with its emphasis on relief, recovery and reform was doing much more bad than good by jeopardizing growth. Clare and Henry's meeting at the White House with Roosevelt on her return from Europe had not given her any cause for hope. The couple pressed the President to offer immediate aid to the UK but felt that he seemed to care more for his popularity than for principles. Clare made scores of appearances and speeches ripping into the New Deal, even directing personal comments at supporters such as fellow journalist Dorothy Thompson. "New Deal policies make some very strange bedbugs," she scoffed at one meeting. "Dorothy will have plenty of time to scratch herself after election day." Her passionate journalism translated perfectly to the spoken word — she was a great wordsmith and public speaker.

Much of 1941 was spent touring the hot spots of the Far East including a visit arranged by Chiang Kai-Shek to the Yellow River front in the Sino–Japanese war. A woman on the war front in the early 1940s was an unusual sight. She and Henry became convinced that Japan was a serious threat in the region, so much so that on their return to the US, Henry even went to Washington, DC, to warn senior generals, but to no avail. The Japanese bombed Pearl Harbor and Manila on Sunday, December 7, 1941. The following day *Life* hit the stands, its cover story a major interview with the US commander in the Far East, General Douglas MacArthur.

Clare Boothe Luce's journalism became ever more prolific in the opening months of 1942 as she traveled 75,000 miles from the USA to Cairo, Karachi, Delhi, Calcutta, and Burma. From Kunming she filed a story on the Flying Tigers who took out 497 enemy aircraft for the loss of only 13 lives, an astonishing ratio. She went on to Chungking, Delhi and Cairo, to Lagos and finally into trouble in Trinidad.

On leaving Cairo, the British authorities had sealed her papers in an envelope but once in Lagos, where she was held over for a day or two, she had impatiently broken the seal and started to review her notes in order to write a private report for her husband on everything she had uncovered or suspected in Africa, India and the Far East. Unfortunately for Clare, a British customs officer in Trinidad asked to see this great wad of paper. When officials realized their sensitivity, she was put under house arrest for five days. She was later escorted to New York and her papers handed to Lord Halifax, the British Ambassador. Halifax called for her to reprimand her. Had the documents fallen into the wrong hands, it could have affected the outcome of the war. However, he told her that her draft paper had been widely circulated and that Winston Churchill, whom she had befriended on earlier European trips, had read it and sent his very best wishes. Halifax nonetheless made Clare promise never again to visit a war zone and write one word of analysis before reaching home soil. She readily agreed and was later debriefed before the Joint Chiefs of Staff.

In November 1938, Clare's stepfather Dr. Austin had been elected as a Republican to the House of Representatives from Fairfield County, Connecticut. He served but one term before being defeated by a Democrat and then died in 1942. On Clare's return from her spring 1942 trip, Albert Morano, her late stepfather's right hand political operative, urged her to run for the seat.

She asked him to test the waters. He did so by briefing local and statewide newspaper editors. A furor erupted. One of those most opposed to Clare was local manufacturer Vivien Kellems (Chapter 17), who clearly wanted the seat for herself. But in mid-September the 86 delegates voted 84 for Clare and two for Vivien. Two months later Clare ousted the man who had beaten her stepfather, becoming the first woman to be elected to Congress from Connecticut. She had campaigned almost exclusively on the war and foreign affairs, drawing on her first-hand experience of five war fronts and bombing raids in Europe and Asia.

Her four years in Congress saw her soar to national recognition as she played to her foreign affairs experience, attacking FDR and simply asking "What will happen when the war ends?" However, the death of her only child, Ann Clare Brokaw, dominated everything. She was killed in a freak accident in Palo Alto, California, as she returned in a friend's automobile to complete her senior year at Stanford University.

Just the day before, a Sunday in early January 1944, Clare and Ann had been walking in San Francisco when Ann suddenly suggested they attend mass at a small Catholic church they were passing. This simple act, one of the very last things they did together, had a profound effect on the Congresswoman. By early 1946 she was ready to enter the Catholic Church. Many of her constituents were Catholics and she knew her political enemies would besmirch her conversion as mere political opportunism. She decided to stand down and rejoin Henry in New York.

But she was not to retire and disappear from public view. Her first venture was to pen an apologia on her conversion; the magazine fee went to charity while the publisher was inundated with requests for reprints. Her second was to go to Hollywood to turn British writer, academic and theologian C. S. Lewis's *The Screwtape Letters* into a movie, but it did not work out and in a long letter to C. S. Lewis she blamed the producer. Her third project was the screenplay for *Come to the Stable*, a movie about two nuns in Connecticut raising money to fund a children's hospital. Again the fee went to charity.

The Republican Party and the Catholic Church were now her twin foci. She even counseled General Eisenhower about his lack of religious affiliation. Ike was deeply religious but his family was Mennonite and there were no such churches in Denison, Texas, where he was born or Abilene, Kansas, where he grew up — indeed his family home served as the meeting place. He had a faith but not a church. Clare advised him to start going to church with his wife Mamie, a Presbyterian, and simply tell reporters interested in his presidential prospects that he was not a full member but enjoyed accompanying his wife to her church, as did many men. It worked and Ike ended up becoming a full member.

She worked hard for Eisenhower and he was duly elected President with Richard Nixon as Vice President. Ike offered her the post of Labor Secretary in his Cabinet and when she refused, he made another offer — ambassador to Rome. Henry already had an office there and was keen for her to take the job. Clare Boothe Luce became the first woman to hold such a senior diplomatic post.

Macho Italy was outraged — her appointment was clearly a slap in the face, a deliberate put-down.

Italian politics was a seething mass of fascists, communists, royalists and a Heinz 57 of other factions. When Clare's boat the *Doria* docked at Naples, the streets were clogged with people wanting to see her. A thousand police failed to control the crowds, and questions were screamed by some 200 journalists. A month later a newspaper revealed that 50% of Italians knew her name, whereas her predecessors had never scored above 2%.

She was quickly immersed in many tricky issues. At the top of the list was the future of Trieste, then occupied by the US and British armies while Italy and Yugoslavia disputed ownership. Her proposal was to have a secret four-way meeting between the Italians, Yugoslavs, British and Americans in London to hammer out a compromise. She also brokered a deal to ship hundreds of thousands of tons of wheat to Yugoslavia's General Tito. The London meeting was a success and the world awoke to a peaceful settlement with Italy inheriting most of the people (over 75%) as well as Trieste itself, and Yugoslavia obtaining most of the land (about 70%).

In the early 1950s, Communists dominated the leadership of Italian trades unions. At the same time the single biggest source of work for Italian factories was the US government's purchase program for NATO. To Clare this was fundamentally wrong. Not only was it bad politics to support your enemies — and communists were indisputably Eisenhower's enemy as the world entered the Cold War — it was also plainly illegal as the congressional bill authorizing the program was quite clear on the issue.

Clare flew to DC and confronted the President and the Secretary of State, John Foster Dulles. She was adamant that all such contracts where communists were in charge should be canceled. The President prevaricated; Dulles was hostile. Clare threatened to resign and they let her have her way. However, they warned her that if it went sour she would be given no support and would shoulder all responsibility. She returned to Rome and began to implement a pincer movement. At one end she started to cancel smaller contracts of a few million dollars each to demonstrate that she had the power and the will to do so. Then, at the other end of the scale, she targeted Fiat, which received enormous funds to develop and build jet fighter aircraft. She held many lengthy meetings with its senior management. At the final meeting, she told them she would accompany the Italian premier on his upcoming state visit to Washington and do all in her power to help him explain to the US taxpayer why its funds were being used illegally to bolster communist trades unions. The trip had barely started when the Fiat union in Turin held new elections. The communist vote, previously based more often on expediency than principle, crashed from over 70% to less than 40% as members stared the prospect of unemployment in the face. Luce had won.

After 18 months in Rome, she fell ill. Her appetite was low, she looked sick and her hair was falling out. Medical tests showed that for some time she had been ingesting tiny amounts of arsenic. The CIA was informed and she was interviewed. A team went to Rome and spent weeks looking into every aspect of food preparation at both the embassy and her house. Finally, a sharp-eyed officer spotted a film of white dust on a black disk (phonograph record) sitting on the music system in the room where she often worked late into the night. The cleaner came through and the dust disappeared, but the next morning it was back again. The agent this time brushed it up and sent it for tests — it was arsenic and its source was the old paint on the ceiling.

Nobody else had been affected because she was the only person to spend long hours with food and drink laid out on the table in that room. Her health was never 100% again, and in 1956 she resigned as ambassador to Rome after three years. Only the communist press did not mourn her departure. Elsewhere, "La Signora" received a wonderful send-off and she was awarded the Grand Cross of the Order of Merit of the Italian Republic. She went back to Rome in 1958 as the President's official representative at the funeral of Pope Pius XII and then just days later at the coronation of Pope John XXII.

Her final decade was active. After a period of recuperation at a Phoenix clinic following the arsenic poisoning episode, she and Henry purchased a large home there and made it their base. Henry continued to lead his media empire until 1964, while Clare learnt to paint, make mosaics, and scuba dive, continuing all the while to write and give lectures.

Nor did the couple retire from politics. They sat out the 1960 general election because of their personal friendship with John F. Kennedy but fought hard for Goldwater in 1964. Henry died after a very brief illness in 1967. Despite his passing, Clare built their long-planned home in Hawaii, which was to become her final base, with regular forays to Washington and New York. It was in Hawaii that she wrote her final play, *Slam the Door Softly* in 1970.

She continued to network and give advice through everything from the Dames of Malta to the President's Foreign Intelligence Advisory Board, receiving the Medal of Freedom from her much-admired Ronald Reagan in 1983. Other awards from honorary degrees to medals were heaped on her and when the US Chamber of Commerce named the nine greatest living Americans, she was the only woman represented. In 1979, she was also the first woman to receive the Sylvanus Thayer Award, given by the US Military Academy to acknowledge outstanding accomplishments in the national interest.

She died on October 9, 1987, and is buried with Henry and Ann at Mepkin Abbey, South Carolina, which they had frequented since the 1930s and where they had established a botanical garden.

Her legacy lives on. Beyond her plays and movies, there is the Clare Boothe Luce Award administered by The Heritage Foundation in Washington, DC and presented for dedication to conservatism. In 1993, the Clare Boothe Luce Policy Institute was founded to encourage the role of American women in developing and promoting conservative ideas. Clare Boothe Luce was not its benefactor but its role model. Its founder, Michelle Easton, expressly sought permission to use her heroine's name because it sends the message to young women "that if they work very hard and focus on personal and professional goals, they will have successful lives."

Finally, there is the lasting bequest Clare Boothe Luce made to the Henry Luce Foundation. The Clare Boothe Luce Program has over the past two plus decades become the single biggest supporter of women in engineering, science and math. By 2010 it had supported 1,500 young women.

CHAPTER 20. AYN RAND

"I swear by my life and my love of it that I will never live for the sake of another man, nor ask another man to live for mine." — Ayn Rand writing in *Atlas Shrugged*

Writer and Philosopher
February 2, 1905–March 6, 1982

NEW YORK CITY, NEW YORK

When America recently faced economic collapse followed by a raft of regulations and taxes under President Obama, what did its citizens do? Dig out the old college economics text book by Paul Samuelson? Rush for an injection of J. K. Galbraith? No! They turned their backs on Keynesian theories and rediscovered instead the novels and philosophical essays of AYN RAND, a Jewish immigrant from Russia who had died nearly 30 years earlier. Sales of her two biggest novels, *The Fountainhead*, published in 1943, and *Atlas Shrugged*, which came out in 1957, simply rocketed. Sales of *Atlas Shrugged* leapt from an already stellar 200,000 in 2008 to a stratospheric 500,000 in 2009. What was going on? And when and where did it all start?

Ayn (rhymes with "mine") Rand was born Alisa Zinovyevna Rosenbaum in St. Petersburg, Russia's city of gracious palaces and romantic canals, on February 2, 1905. Communist revolution was very much in the air. Her parents had fought their way out of the Pale of Settlement, originally established as a Jewish territory in order to keep Jews out of the rest of Russia. Her father Zinovy Zacharovich, a chemist, had built a pharmacy business, while her mother Anna Borisovna was the well-educated daughter of a businessman. She was keen that Alisa and her equally talented younger sisters Natasha and Nora should also apply themselves to their studies and Alisa's interest in literature was soon being encouraged.

Her happy, affluent upbringing with servants and tutors came to a screaming halt when Germany declared war on Russia in 1914. The family was on holiday in Switzerland and the only way back to Russia was via London, England, where the Rosenbaums waited for a ship. It was in London, where the big city sights and sounds set her imagination alight, that Alisa first conceived the idea of heroic fictional individuals who were bold enough to follow their own paths. The journey home to the newly named Petrograd through the North Sea where German war boats patrolled was full of excitement for Alisa as she reflected on her decision to become a writer.

Back home, grade school was a huge disappointment. She paid little attention to lessons and scribbled dramatic stories instead. By 1917, she was devouring the daily newspapers and following public affairs closely. The Russian Revolution of that year made a huge impact on the 12-year-old when Zinovy's business and home were taken over by the state.

The whole family fled south to Yevpatoria in the Crimea, surviving on assets cleverly hidden from the Communists. Zinovy again built a pharmacy, a difficult task at a time when control of the area fluctuated between the counter-revolutionary White Army and the communist Red Army.

Alisa attended high school where she discovered Aristotle, adding the Greek philosopher to her list of favorite writers and thinkers, which would eventually include Victor Hugo, Nietzsche, Dostoyevsky and Schiller. But the Crimea became impossible when her father's pharmacy was confiscated by the Communists, and the family headed back to Petrograd, where they were allowed just one room in the building they once owned in its entirety. It was grim; there was little food and millions died in Russia between 1921 and 1922 during the Great Famine.

Zinovy found work as a chemist, while Anna worked as a teacher and translator. Alisa studied history at Petrograd State University, where she discovered films and operettas. But it was a tense time; students such as Alisa who were not active Communists were expelled until pressure from the West saw them reinstated. She still succeeded in graduating with high honors from the newly renamed Leningrad State University in 1924. But when, following her dream to make movies, she moved on to film school, she was far from happy. Her fellow students worried that her scripts were too anti-Soviet. She later said: "I would probably have been dead within a year."

Her mother, too, was concerned that she would get into trouble. So when that same year Anna received a letter from a cousin in Chicago who owned a movie theater, it became the starting point for an elaborate plan to relocate Alisa to the United States. Anna sold her last remaining jewels; Alisa applied for a passport and a US visa to study American movies and to return (though she had no intention of doing so); and family members enrolled in all kinds of proletarian activities to prove their worth and establish good credentials with the Communists. Her mother, for example, joined the Communist Union of Educational Workers. The scheme took time but it worked.

Following five weeks on trains and a steamship to New York City, Alisa reached her cousins in Chicago in late February 1926. She immediately dropped the name Alisa Rosenbaum and reinvented herself as Ayn Rand. She watched movies by day and resolutely hammered out scripts by night, the clacking of her typewriter in the early hours soon exhausting the patience of her relatives.

On the renewal of her visa, her family in Chicago gave her $100 (worth about $1,200 today) to go to Hollywood with a letter of introduction to Cecil B. DeMille's production company from a local Chicago film distributor. Alisa registered at a hostel and traveled to the Culver City studios for a perfunctory meeting. No job. But on leaving, she bumped into the great movie maker himself sitting in his open-top car. They fell into conversation and he drove her to the set of *The King of Kings*, where he employed her for the next three months as an extra. It was there that she first met her future husband of 50 years, Frank O'Connor, who was also employed as a movie extra.

She went on to research story ideas for DeMille and then to head the wardrobe department at RKO Pictures. She married Frank in 1929 and became a US citizen in 1931, all the while spending long hours honing her English and trying to tone down her heavy Russian accent. The same year Universal Pictures bought her screenplay, *Red Pawn*, which was never filmed but the money allowed her to focus on finishing her first novel, *We the Living*. The backgrounds of both the film script and the novel are clearly autobiographical and the plots almost identical: a young woman named Kira is held prisoner in a statist society and feigns love with a Communist Party official to protect or seek the release of the man she really loves.

While Ayn's agent in New York promoted *We the Living* to a very cool and often pro-Soviet market, she wrote her romance murder mystery play *Night of January 16th*. The play is set entirely in a courtroom where an Ayn Rand-like character (Karen Andre) is on trial for the murder of Bjorn Faulkner, her employer and lover of the past decade. The innovative feature of the play was that each night 12 people were randomly selected from the audience and sat on stage as the jury. The evidence presented was evenly balanced and the result of guilty or not guilty hinged totally on the philosophical underpinnings of the 12 jurors. Ayn wrote two endings, one for each verdict. If you are a self-confident, assertive, bold, independent type of person who wants to advance in life, you will vote not-guilty. If you lack confidence, are envious of the success of others and want conformity of some central power controlling society, you will vote guilty.

Night of January 16th had a good run in Hollywood, and Broadway beckoned, so in late November 1943 Ayn and Frank relocated to New York City. But money became tight. Ayn switched agents, Frank was unemployed and the Broadway plans were scotched. Ayn took to freelance script reading for RKO and MGM. Eventually, though, the couple's gamble paid off when *Night of January 16*[th] enjoyed a 29-week run on Broadway. Ex-boxing champ Jack Dempsey was a celebrity juror on the opening night with 11 other stars of the era and later Helen Keller was the foreman of the jury when it was performed for a blind audience. It was performed on the radio, twice on TV and once as a movie that Ayn despised.

Ayn had voted for the first time in 1932 and like so many, including Clare Boothe Luce (Chapter 19) and Isabel Paterson (Chapter 15), she had cast her ballot for Franklin D. Roosevelt simply because of his opposition to prohibition. By the time she moved to New York, however, she had realized how deeply anti-capitalist her President really was and was becoming more and more upset at the inability of her fellow citizens to understand freedom which she conceived of as individual freedom rather than government intervention in such matters as the economy and people's personal affairs. It angered her how deeply America appeared to be in love with Russian communism during the 1930s and 1940s.

Britain proved more receptive to her anti-communist sentiments, however, and the publisher Macmillan agreed a print run of 3,000 hardcover copies of *We the Living*, though not before a ferocious debate in the New York boardroom. It came out in 1936 and was widely reviewed, though notices were largely negative. The books were slow to leave the shelves until word of mouth recommendations boosted sales and quickly exhausted the print run. Unfortunately Macmillan had not expected this and the printer's type had been melted down. *We the Living* was not to reappear in the US until 1959.

The *Night of January 16*[th] royalties had allowed Ayn to build up a nest egg and she now began to plot her next novel, *The Fountainhead*. Published in 1943, it had by 2011 sold more than seven million copies.

The Fountainhead's main theme is individualism and its main protagonist architect Howard Roark, who refuses to compromise his personal and artistic principles. He embodies personal integrity and independence while all around him people compromise and feed off others and the past.

Progress on the novel was slow and Ayn's fervent anti-communism led to her being blacklisted in certain Hollywood circles. But she managed to find some work, thanks to her command of several languages, reading books in French, German and Russian for studios, with a view to their adaptation for the big screen. She also worked as an architect's clerk in order to gain insights for her new novel, and read round the subject extensively at her local library.

Ayn took a break during the summer of 1937 and swiftly penned *Anthem*, her shortest novel. *Anthem* is a futuristic dystopian novella in which man has entered a collectivist dark age. Individualism has been eliminated and the word "I" has disappeared. Equality 7-2521 (a street sweeper) stumbles across evidence of the Unmentionable Times and discovers long-forgotten aspects of the past, such as electricity and freedom. It is the least known of all of her books, which is a great shame because it is so well written and contains many of the seeds of her later door-stoppers.

Again American publishers rejected it but the British came to her rescue. Cassell and Co. brought it out to some acclaim in the UK in 1938. It was not published in the US until 1946.

The 1940 election loomed and by now Ayn was so bitter about FDR that she volunteered to work full time for the Republican candidate Wendell Willkie. She was soon in charge of writing bullet points on behalf of the candidate and his supporters exposing the failure of the New Deal measures aimed at preventing a future depression, and she was a feisty and quick-witted public speaker.

"I chose to be an American. What did you ever do, except for having been born?" she retorted when heckled about her Russian accent during the campaign.

However, politics was not her real passion and in the end FDR trounced Willkie.

By now the opening chapters of *The Fountainhead* had been rejected by 11 publishers and Ayn sacked her agent. A twelfth rejection soon followed and she threw in the towel, but her husband begged her to continue. Following a tense night of arguing, she agreed to carry on with the book.

This decision was soon vindicated when Archibald Ogden, a very young newly hired editor at Bobbs-Merrill, agreed to consider it for publication. Within a week he was sending his boss the legendary telegram: "If this is not the book for you, then I am not the editor for you." As with *We The Living*, her work divided the board of the publishing house but Ogden prevailed and Ayn signed a contract to complete by December 31, 1942.

She was still freelancing to make ends meet and had also written around her New York contacts trying to scurry up the numbers to form a club of intellectuals. "Our side has no ideology," she complained. Her gripe was echoed across the Atlantic a generation later when Margaret Thatcher said, "We must have an ideology. The other side has an ideology. We must have one too."

Ayn fell under the spell of Isabel Paterson (Chapter 15), author of the weekly *Herald Tribune* column, *Turns with a Bookworm*. Paterson was at that time furiously penning her own epic treatise on individualism, *The God of the Machine*.

The Fountainhead was delivered by Ayn with only hours to spare and it was published on May 8, 1943. She hoped for six-figure sales; Isabel Paterson, herself a bestselling writer of novels, cautioned against such high expectations.

Early reviews and even her publisher's adverts skipped the philosophical battle between the individual and the state and instead focused on Howard Roark, the female protagonist Dominique Francon, and the sex. Then the liberal *New York Times* saved Ayn Rand's sanity with a glowing review. The critic, Lorine Pruette, had understood perfectly that this book was not about sex but about individualism and how one viewed the world. "Good novels of ideas are rare at any time. This is the only novel of ideas written by an American woman that I can recall. [Ayn Rand] has written a hymn in praise of the individual... you will not be able to read this masterful book without thinking through some of the basic concepts of our times."

Meanwhile, unbeknownst to Ayn, the Italian fascists had allowed a movie company to make *We The Living* into a two-part film, *Noi Vivi* (We the Living) and *Addio Kira* (Farewell Kira), believing the portrayal of their Communist Russian enemies would help their cause. However, the movie theaters were mobbed and the penny dropped — this movie was against all totalitarians, fascist or communist, and it was quickly pulled. When in the 1960s Rand mentioned *en passant* to her attorneys Erika and Henry Mark Holzer that the Italians had made two movies of *We the Living*, they were intrigued. The Holzers began a two-year search and in 1968 discovered the original negatives in a store in Rome. Rand worked on an "author's cut" of the movies on and off and, four years after her death, the movie version of *We the Living* premiered in the US to positive reviews.

Letters from readers flooded in to her publisher. She answered all of them. And an article for *Reader's Digest*, "The Only Road To Tomorrow," in January 1944, condensed her philosophy and brought her even more attention among the general public.

Six months after publication in June 1944 *The Fountainhead* was stuck at under 20,000 sales. While this was more than respectable, it was still far from her hoped-for six figures. However, Warner Brothers offered her $50,000 (or the equivalent of $615,000 today) for the movie rights and Ayn and Frank headed back to Hollywood in late 1943. As well as writing the movie script for *The Fountainhead*, Ayn was signed up to write other screenplays, a lucrative line of work that resulted in two other movies, *Love Letters*, adapted from a Christopher Massie novel, and the World War II romance, *You Came Along*. A comic book version of *The Fountainhead* appeared. Hayek's soon-to-be-published *The Road to*

Serfdom was given similar treatment. In both cases it helped to bring their ideas to a popular audience.

Isabel Paterson was responsible for a big increase in sales of *The Fountainhead*. Thanks to Paterson's 14 mentions in her weekly column, sales of Ayn Rand's novel reached 150,000 by summer 1945. Some 65 years later it is still right up there, reaching number one on Amazon's bestseller list in May 2009 and still managing a creditable eleventh place more than a year later in June 2010.

While the release of the 1949 movie, starring Gary Cooper, Patricia Neal and Raymond Massey, succeeded in further boosting sales of the book, the production process was a nightmare for Ayn. Even a trip to Washington, DC, to testify to the House Un-American Activities Committee as an expert on totalitarian propaganda and author of the monograph *A Screen Guide for Americans* did not cheer her up.

With the movie of *The Fountainhead* out and the book selling well, Ayn and her husband returned to New York in 1951. It was very much her city, the one she loved above all others, and it was now to be the setting for *Atlas Shrugged* in which she developed objectivism, a philosophy she had introduced in *The Fountainhead*. As she later wrote in *Capitalism: The Unknown Ideal* "Government 'help' to business is just as disastrous as government persecution... the only way a government can be of service to national prosperity is by keeping its hands off."

As with *The Fountainhead*, *Atlas Shrugged* is devoid of any references that can date it. This idea came from Isabel Paterson and it undoubtedly helps to keep both books fresh even two generations later. What she wrote transcended time, movements and trends. She summed it all up in one resounding sentence: "My philosophy in essence, is the concept of man as a heroic being, with his own happiness as the moral purpose of his life, with productive achievement as his noblest activity, and reason as his only absolute."

Atlas Shrugged is another dystopian novel and her magnum opus. In an increasingly government-controlled society, its heroine Dagny Taggart, a senior railroad executive, sees the world collapse around her as all the best and brightest minds, led by a character named John Galt, go on strike and disappear to a secret place high in the mountains protected from aerial observation by Galt's latest invention. Ayn Rand's advocacy of egoism and a society of voluntary associations among individuals for mutual benefit (referred to as the 'trader principle') is stated by John Galt in the novel: "I swear by my life and my love of it that I will never live for the sake of another man, nor ask another man to live for mine."

With *The Fountainhead* behind her, the search for a publisher was much easier and she quickly settled on Random House, which published *Atlas Shrugged* on October 10, 1957. However, the vitriol of the reviews stunned all associated with it. Once again word of mouth was to thank for it becoming a top-ten bestseller.

After the publication of *Atlas Shrugged*, Ayn became an American icon. In 1962 she debated on CBS's *The Great Challenge* with eminent conservative Russell Kirk, Pulitzer prize-winning writer Harry Ashmore, controversial businessman and writer David Lilienthal and presidential biographer James MacGregor Burns; in 1963 Johnny Carson had her on *The Tonight Show* three times in five months, so popular were her appearances; the March 1964 issue of *Playboy* magazine carried an interview with her; and in 1965 Paul Simon sang of her in his song "A Simple Desultory Philippic" that he had been branded a Communist by Ayn just because he was left-handed!

Ayn Rand was never to write another play, novel or film script. Instead she was to refine her philosophy and develop a theory she called objectivism, the central political tenet of which is that government should not hinder or intrude on the rights of the individual. And like that other major "ism" of the twentieth century generated by a woman, "Thatcherism," they both run counter to many of the other political philosophies of the times in being freedom-oriented.

From the publication of *Atlas Shrugged* in 1957 to her death in 1982, she spent 25 years promoting through every available medium the ideas advanced in *We the Living*, *Anthem*, *The Fountainhead* and *Atlas Shrugged*. As well as her television and magazine appearances, she gave an annual lecture at Boston's Ford Hall Forum and was also in demand as a lecturer at West Point and top universities, including Yale, Columbia, Princeton, Harvard, Massachusetts Institute of Technology and Johns Hopkins. Some philosophers (but not enough, to her chagrin) began to take note as her essays started coming out in collections such as *The Virtue of Selfishness*, *Capitalism: The Unknown Ideal*, *The Romantic Manifesto*, and *Return of the Primitive*. They sold in their hundreds of thousands.

A Library of Congress survey ranked *Atlas Shrugged* as second only to the Bible in its influence on people. Nearly 10% of all Americans have read her work. Ayn Rand's face appeared on the 33-cent stamp in 1999 and among those who owe her an intellectual debt are presidential hopeful Congressman Ron Paul, radio talk show host Rush Limbaugh, former chairman of the Federal Reserve Bank Alan Greenspan and Supreme Court Justice Clarence Thomas. While Milton Friedman is generally acknowledged to be the father of the all-volunteer army, being against compulsory military service, it was Rand's ideas and her disciples in the Nixon administration that drove the idea forward. She has even appeared in two episodes of *The Simpsons*. Today driving south on Interstate 95 one still sees billboards asking WHO IS JOHN GALT?, the opening line of *Atlas Shrugged*. This is the legacy of Ted Turner, who as a young businessman in the 1960s paid for nearly 250 advertising sites with that message.

While Ayn Rand had reservations about President Reagan and the emerging Libertarian Party, she did openly admire the UK's Margaret Thatcher and the

Australian politician Malcolm Fraser. When Fraser visited the US in 1976, Ayn and Frank were invited to the White House state dinner.

However, both she and Frank were facing serious health problems, and he died soon after their fiftieth wedding anniversary in 1979.

Ayn Rand's remaining two years were dominated by her efforts to turn *Atlas Shrugged* into a nine-hour television mini-series. It was one third complete when she died at home in March 1982 from pulmonary failure caused by a lifetime smoking two packs of cigarettes a day. Nearly a thousand people attended her funeral and she was buried next to her husband as Kipling's poem "If" was read. On April 15, 2011, (appropriately, tax filing day) the first of a three-part movie of *Atlas Shrugged* premiered starring Taylor Schilling as Dagny Taggart and Paul Johannson as John Galt. Hollywood had finally solved the problem of bringing *Atlas Shrugged* to the big screen.

Like many of the women who contributed to the cause of liberty in the US, Ayn Rand's life was not without major conflicts. In fact, she fell out spectacularly with her mentor Isabel Paterson and with psychotherapist Nathaniel Branden, whom she had earlier mentored. But to escape communism as she did, write bestselling philosophical novels and screenplays in a language that wasn't her mother tongue, and create a political philosophy, requires an uncompromising and determined character. Jerome Tucille wrote a glorious account of free-market circles in New York City in the 1960s entitled, "*It Usually Begins With Ayn Rand*," and even today the name of Ayn Rand is still constantly invoked in conversations with conservatives, classical liberals and libertarians. This and her political legacy — the belief that individuals should be free of government interference — are the reasons Americans reached for the works of Ayn Rand during the economic crisis of the early 2000s.

Chapter 21. Rose Friedman

> "Tolerance is the secret of a successful family life, as it is of a successful society." — Rose Friedman

Economist, Author, Political Activist
December 1911–April 18, 2009

CHICAGO, ILLINOIS

It was a chance meeting but it really changed the world of economics. When graduate economics student Rose Director joined a class in basic price theory at the University of Chicago in 1932, her teacher Professor Jacob Viner sat his students alphabetically by second name. Rose found herself placed next to a brilliant Rutgers graduate, Milton Friedman, and so began a relationship that was to lead not only to their marriage six years later but also to one of the greatest intellectual collaborations of the twentieth century.

ROSE DIRECTOR FRIEDMAN was the major driving force behind many of her husband's books, including the jointly written seminal work *Free to Choose* (1980) and co-producer with him of the ten-part television series of the same name. The book was an international bestseller and, with the TV series broadcast in every major western country except France, she helped popularize free-market ideas just as its most high-profile exponents, Ronald Reagan and Margaret Thatcher, were coming to power.

But *Free to Choose* did more than underpin the more libertarian acts of these two leaders. According to Ed Crane, co-founder and president of Washington, DC's libertarian Cato Institute, "It was the book that really kick-started the classical liberal movement in the United States." He saw it as being about "the dynamics of a free and open society," responsible for inspiring many of the people who, three decades after publication, support the concept of limited government today.

Rose managed to persuade her initially reluctant husband to take part in the television series, bringing to a much wider audience their ideas on public policy. But her contribution was far greater than that. While Milton Friedman was rightly seen as a towering giant in the history of economics and honored with a Nobel Prize in 1976, Rose was always the more policy focused and more forthrightly pro-liberty of the pair. She was fiercer and much more passionate than her more scholarly husband about free markets, private property rights and the rule of law all set in the context of individual freedom and responsibility. I once heard President George W Bush joke that the only person Milton Friedman ever lost an argument with was his wife.

The 1992 economics Nobel Laureate Gary Becker said: "It was an extremely close intellectual fellowship, and she was not someone who got credit for things she didn't do. They discussed ideas constantly. Her feelings about the importance of private markets and opposition to big government were even stronger than his. Her lasting influence will be as a collaborator, but she was a major contributor to the collaboration, and that's a significant legacy."

Of that she herself was in no doubt. Once asked if she felt overshadowed by her husband, Rose replied: "No, I've always felt that I'm responsible for at least half of what he's gotten... I feel that I have much of the responsibility for his success."

Rose Director left the region of Russia that is now the Ukraine when she was only two or three years old, just before the outbreak of World War I. With her mother and four older siblings, Anne (15), Aaron (12), Becky (9) and Lewis (6), she joined her father who was busy working his way up from peddler to general store owner in Portland, Oregon. In Russia he had worked for his father, a local miller, and they had lived with her grandfather in a home with no electricity or plumbing. As part of the local Jewish community, the family spoke Yiddish and had little contact with the majority Christian or Russian population. As soon as they stepped off the train in Portland, having traveled by railroad and boat from Europe, Rose and her brothers and sisters were in a world of running hot water, gas lighting and later central heating and a telephone.

The children had a strict Orthodox upbringing and were educated at local public schools. Being a decade older than Rose, the highly academic Aaron was a father figure and mentor to his younger sister. After Yale, a year in Europe and a job or two, he went to the University of Chicago as a graduate student. He wanted Rose to finish high school quickly and do her undergraduate degree in Chicago at the same time as he did his PhD. But their mother flatly refused to allow her 16-year-old daughter to head 2,000 miles east and Rose was enrolled at the local private liberal arts school, Reed College. She finally transferred to Chicago two years later. Aaron was now on the faculty and went on to found the *Journal of Law and Economics* in 1958 together with 1991 economics Nobel laureate Ronald Coase.

Rose quickly advanced from the Chicago undergraduate program to graduate work, meeting her future husband, Milton Friedman, in the process. The Chicago Economics Department was already star-studded and she took History of Economic Thought with the eminent economist and scholar Frank H. Knight, becoming his research assistant from 1934 to 1936. On completing the coursework for her PhD, Rose consulted Knight at length and decided to write her thesis on the history of capital theory. But in spite of writing two early chapters and a further two while on her honeymoon in 1938, she never completed her dissertation and so never earned a doctorate.

Over the next eight years the couple moved around as Milton did a range of jobs, including statistical work for the military, before settling back in Chicago for more than 30 years. This time also saw the arrival of daughter Janet and son David, who would later become a force for liberty in academia.

While Rose became famous in later years for popularizing free-market limited government ideals, her Chicago training made her an indispensable sounding board and a source of ideas and insights for Milton. While he is best known for his work on money and in particular the quantity theory of money, to many economists — and to Milton himself — his 1957 book *A Theory of the Consumption Function* is his biggest single contribution to advancing economic theory. Indeed, he later called it "my best purely scientific contribution."

It drove a coach and horses through the British economist John Maynard Keynes's explanations of the determinants of consumption and savings at a time when the Keynesian revolution in economics was in full swing. This challenge to Keynes had developed over a number of years, fueled by conversations between Milton and Rose, often held in front of a big log fire. He also drew on her earlier work in the field of household consumption with fellow economists Dorothy Brady and Margaret Reid. In the Preface to *A Theory of the Consumption Function*, Milton refers to the book as "in its essential respects a joint product of the group, each member of which not only participated in its development but read and criticized the manuscript in its various stages."

In his famous 1936 book *The General Theory of Employment, Interest, and Money*, Keynes had written out an equation for "the propensity to consume" as part of his algebraic model of the overall economy's level of income.

From this he derived what he called the "multiplier," which Milton wrote "professes to tell how many dollars will be added to the total income by an extra dollar of investment or government deficit spending." He added, "The multiplier was happily welcomed by governments as a scientific justification for what they were eager to do anyway, namely spend more without raising taxes."

In the Keynesian model, how much people spend in a given month depends on how much income they earn that month. For a totally destitute beggar this might be true, but from Rose's work, and that of Brady and Reid, Milton knew that people typically take a much longer lifetime view. As George Mason University economist Don Boudreaux has written: "Young workers today understand that their future incomes are likely to be higher than their current incomes, so they rationally transfer some of that future income into the present by borrowing. Today's spending is higher than today's income; tomorrow's spending is lower. The result is that spending is spread over many years to reflect reasonable expectations about the pattern of receiving income over the years or even over a lifetime."

It follows that a temporary spike or dip in this month's income has almost no effect on what you spend this month. You will save almost all of a sudden windfall, and correspondingly keep consumption up in a month of surprisingly low income by borrowing or by drawing down savings. The key to your current level of consumption spending is your real wealth or expected lifetime income, not your current-period income. Real wealth includes lots of things from savings to property to the earning capacity provided by education and relevant work experience. As with so many great new insights this is not at first glance particularly startling — and Milton later called it "embarrassingly obvious" in *Two Lucky People*, the 1998 memoir he wrote jointly with Rose. However, its long-term implications for economics and government were profound. Rose had been one the key players in uncovering the idea.

Another example of her behind-the-scenes work was the classic *Capitalism and Freedom* published by the University of Chicago Press in 1962. Rose took a set of Milton's lectures sponsored by the free-market Volker Fund and delivered at Wabash College, a men's liberal arts college in Indiana, and turned them into a bestselling book. Milton wrote in the preface: "She pieced together the scraps of the various lectures, coalesced different versions, translated lectures into something approaching written English, and has throughout been the driving force in getting the book finished."

Capitalism and Freedom is ostensibly by Milton Friedman, but in reality both he and Rose are staking out the case for economic liberalism and then applying it to a series of problems. The themes covered include the need for economic freedom in order to have political freedom; the all-volunteer army, putting an end to conscription; freely floating exchange rates; the abolition of economic licensing which, it is argued, does nothing but keep out competition; the benefits of a flat tax (the rich simply avoid progressive taxes); the benefits of school vouchers to encourage competition; a constant money supply growth rate of 3% to 5%; free trade; the reform of social security and the use of a negative income tax to alleviate poverty.

Capitalism and Freedom was largely considered too extreme, not worthy of general review and certainly not to be mentioned in polite circles by discerning people. Yet it went on to sell well over 500,000 copies, be translated into 18 languages, be published underground in Poland and Russia and inspire many to discover liberty. It played an especially important role behind the Iron Curtain.

"We are much impressed by numerous letters from residents in the former Soviet Union and Soviet satellites maintaining that *Capitalism and Freedom*, along with books and writings by Ludwig von Mises and Friedrich Hayek, played a major role in spreading and keeping alive an understanding of the meaning of a free society," wrote Rose in 1998.

But Rose was not without her own separate intellectual pursuits. She took issue with President Lyndon Johnson's 1964 State of the Union Message which declared "unconditional war on poverty." She was unhappy with the way in which Johnson's economists defined poverty as current money income of $3,000 or less per annum per family. To Rose with her background in consumption data this was crude beyond belief. If you rely on current money income, she argued, you probably double the number of the poor by overlooking non-monetary sources of income ranging from the benefit of owning your home to a fringe benefit. The American Enterprise Institute published her report as *Poverty: Definition and Perspective* in early 1965.

With the award of the Nobel Prize in Economics in the fall of 1976, Milton Friedman became without doubt the most famous, notorious, loved, hated, admired and decried social scientist of the twentieth century. He had just retired from the University of Chicago and the couple had settled in a co-op apartment block at 1750 Taylor Street in San Francisco, an hour's drive north of Palo Alto's Hoover Institution, where he joined the permanent staff on the Stanford University campus.

The Taylor Street building was very tall, over twenty floors, with two apartments per floor, one small with mediocre views and one much bigger with glorious views from the Golden Gate Bridge to the Bay Bridge. Initially Rose and

Milton had a smaller apartment lower down. However, higher up the building with a large apartment was their friend Dorian Crocker (Chapter 24) who was widowed and about to marry the British free-market intellectual entrepreneur and founder of London's Institute of Economic Affairs (IEA), Antony G A Fisher. When the media came to film the Friedmans, the couple would borrow Dorian's much larger lounge with its stunning views. In their turn, Milton and Rose were readily available to inspire the stream of would-be think tank entrepreneurs coming from all over the world to seek Fisher's input and help. Later Rose and Milton were able to move higher up 1750 Taylor and into a larger apartment.

Within weeks of settling at 1750 Taylor, the Friedmans were approached by PBS television station WQLN of Erie, Pennsylvania. Would they be interested in making a major television series, with spin-offs such as a book, to bring to a wider audience their ideas about the benefits of free markets and the dangers of overarching government?

Milton was not at all sure. He believed in the power of the written word over television and, with others such as F. A. Hayek, felt it was his job to reach opinion leaders, not the masses. Rose, on the other hand, was very excited about the project and much more optimistic about the benefits of mass outreach. By the summer of 1977, after four long meetings with the principals, Rose had prevailed and Milton was ready to sign up. They thought the resulting product would dominate their lives for around 18 months — it turned out to be nearly four years.

But Rose and Milton were opposed to taxpayer funding of television and they wanted total editorial independence. They suggested a few names of potential donors and the equivalent of $10.5 million in today's money was raised, a large sum for one project.

The project quickly outgrew the capability of WQLN and the hunt was on for a major league producer who was also sympathetic to the Friedman world view. Through Ralph Harris, then director of Antony Fisher's London based IEA — Margaret Thatcher's favorite think tank — the name of Antony Jay came up. He was an ex-BBC man who had set up a private production company. He was also a Friedman fan. Jay knew his economics, including the writings of 1986 economics Nobel Laureate Professor James M. Buchanan, most recently with Virginia's George Mason University, which offered a close analysis of the incentives faced by "disinterested" public servants. This later led him to write the BBC comedy series *Yes, Minister* and its sequel *Yes, Prime Minister*, which ran in the 1980s and still run today; they were great favorites in the Thatcher and Hayek households.

Jay now moved into top gear, appointing the younger Michael Latham as the on-site producer. It was Jay who suggested a 30-minute documentary followed by 30 minutes of Milton in discussion with both allies and enemies. He felt strongly that such a format would display the debating skills of Milton much better than a documentary could. It was bold and it would also be less expensive.

Rose was deeply involved, steeped in the ideological and logistical aspects of the whole project as well as the psychology of building a team that could be open and honest yet constructive as they struggled to bring complex ideas to the television screen. It was, after all, to be presented by somebody who, while an old hand at televised interviews and debates, had to date never experienced the unnerving sensation of looking directly into a camera. In an early exchange with Jay, would-be presenter Milton set out his stall thus:

> "Perhaps I can indicate the source of my uneasiness best by stating what seem to me four essential requirements for the series:
>
> 1. No gimmicks.
> 2. This is an intellectual program, openly and unashamedly so.
> 3. There shall be no talking down to the audience. More than willing to sacrifice numbers for thoughtfulness.
> 4. I am going to speak my own words and no one else's."

Outlines for the themes and content of the ten programs were quickly agreed and a pilot *Who Protects the Consumer?* was made to show to investors, to iron out kinks in the format and to educate Milton and Rose as to what input was needed from them.

As the pilot progressed, history began to repeat itself. A decade earlier a group of six graduate students had filmed the R. W. Grant book, *The Incredible Bread Machine: A Study of Capitalism, Freedom and the State.* Most of the film concerns the students arguing with the producer and his staff about the ideas they are trying to film. Ten years later Rose watched fascinated as something similar happened off camera on the Friedman project. Every scene, which had been developed by Milton and Rose, evolved into a seminar between Milton and the crew.

With filming finished in nine days — three in California and six in Washington, DC — everybody involved met to hammer out the next nine episodes. The production schedule now called on Rose and Milton to travel the world filming in scores of locations.

It was hard work but lots of fun. They piled up books of Acts from the 1930s onward in the Library of Congress to show the growth of regulation. They filmed Milton in the Bureau of Engraving and Printing hitting a button to stop the printing presses churning out yet more money. Milton talked from the vaults of the Federal Reserve perched on a bench of gold bars. And they had lecture hall shots contrasting alert students at private Dartmouth College with sleeping students at tax-funded UCLA.

As well as extensive filming in the US, they went to Hong Kong, Japan, India, Greece, West Germany and the UK.

Rose was ever present. "*Free to Choose* was billed as 'A Personal Statement', Milton's views by Milton," recalled Briton Eben Wilson, who was head of research on the production. "In fact the views were those of Milton adjusted by Rose and edited by both. When Milton spoke to camera what you heard was the result of a fascinating brainstorming session involving both of them. Logic, language and ideas were battered into shape on location and without a script."

Milton refused to be scripted but would try out a few lines on Eben and the producer and ask what they thought. He would rehearse a few more times after hearing their comments, at which point Rose, who would be sitting nearby, would say:

"Well, you know. I'm not so sure!"

At this Milton would often stop mid-sentence with the camera running and say, "Wait a minute, wait a minute, what was that, Rose?"

Eben and the rest of the crew would turn to see her looking perplexed or a little irritated, and then she would offer her own views. This led to one or more of four things: a technical discussion between husband and wife on the relevant economic theory; a reworking of the words; a complete new start; or a good argument, at the end of which they'd agree to disagree. In the case of the last of these outcomes, Milton would go back to delivering the lines his way. "Inevitably he would be terrible so Rose always won," laughed Eben Wilson.

Milton Friedman himself backed up this account of Rose's involvement in *Free to Choose* when he later wrote: "Her title as associate producer was far more than a formality. She played an indispensable role: she participated in every planning session and every editing session; she was on every shoot and involved in every discussion about the content of my statements to the camera; she was the best critic of my performance, and perhaps more important, the only one willing to be blunt in criticizing me, and the most helpful in setting me on the right track."

After the documentary section came the issue of the location for the discussion segments and the choice of moderator and debate participants. A large reading room at the University of Chicago was quickly chosen for the discussions. Canadian Bob McKenzie was the choice for moderator. He had studied at the London School of Economics (LSE) and then taught sociology there from 1949 to his death in 1981. He had relevant experience with the BBC and was famous in the UK for the televised operation of his "swingometer" on election nights to show how many seats were likely to be won by the major parties.

The idea was to have Milton Friedman and four others in the debate, two who agreed with him and the very best two opponents that could be found.

The names of the ten programs and their order were not decided until July 1979, some two years after the project started. Over that summer Rose took the transcripts of each program and turned them into corresponding chapters for the *Free to Choose* book, which they wanted to have in the bookstores by Christmas 1979. They made it and the book was the non-fiction number one bestseller of 1980. It sold 400,000 in hardback and probably more than a million in paperback in the US alone, with 17 translations. In Japan alone an astonishing 200,000 copies sold in hardback. As with *Capitalism and Freedom*, samizdat translations circulated behind the Iron Curtain.

The PBS broadcasts started in early 1980 and it became a TV phenomenon with viewer numbers exceeding the much-loved prime-time drama series, *Masterpiece Theatre*. Friedman was beating adaptations of classics, such as the novels of Charles Dickens!

Jay's company, Video Arts, marketed the series around the world and, in the case of the UK and Japan, separate discussion segments with local experts were filmed. A set of the ten one-hour tapes was marketed to schools and colleges.

Such was the reach of *Free to Choose* that when Milton and Rose were invited aboard Queen Elizabeth II's yacht *Britannia*, moored in San Francisco harbor, for dinner in March 1983, she greeted the economist enthusiastically with a reference to his television series. "I know you," she said. "Philip [her husband the Duke of Edinburgh] is always watching you on the telly [television]."

Rose and Milton quickly followed up on *Free to Choose* with another book and television combination, *Tyranny of the Status Quo*. It was a low-budget affair focused on discussions Milton holds with a small group of students about a range of topics with the overarching theme of how to defeat the "iron triangle" represented by bureaucrats, politicians and other vested interests. It was shown on far fewer stations but the book is still relevant today.

Interestingly, Rose's model of social change seemed to alter with the making of the two television series and their accompanying books. She came to view the television broadcast merely as the bait to hook the inquiring mind in order to lead it to the book and more thoughtful reflection.

Heading into their eighties and nineties, both Friedmans remained active and took up an issue Milton had first studied in 1955 — school vouchers. In his eyes, government performs three roles in education: it mandates you to have to go to school; it taxes to pay for schools; and it operates the vast majority of schools. Milton and Rose Friedman accepted the notion of mandatory education funded by taxpayers. But they flatly refused to accept that governments should operate the schools using a system that allocated a school primarily on the basis of the family's address.

Time and again throughout a 60-year period, and particularly in their last 15 years, they advocated school choice through vouchers — offering freedom to choose your school. The idea was a simple one: if you want to subsidize education then subsidize the customers (the parents and children) not the producers (the schools) which are captured by special interests in the shape of teacher unions.

Responsibility for education was a parental matter and parents should be free to choose, they believed. In its simplest and purest form, the entire education budget would be divided by the number of pupils each year, giving a figure equal to the average cost of a year's education for one pupil. Then that amount of money would be given to parents in the form of a voucher redeemable only at accredited schools, whether private or public. Such a system would turn grade school education on its head.

Together Rose and Milton Friedman founded the Milton and Rose D. Friedman Foundation in 1996. Its aim was to promote freedom of choice in education and the use of school vouchers.

They were a long-lived couple. Milton Friedman died in 2006 at the age of 94, while Rose passed on just shy of a century in 2009. For over 70 years she had been a strong advocate for liberty and an original thinker in her own right, while doing all she could to promote the career of her husband. She was a rare individual.

Chapter 22. Rosa Parks

"We were taught to be ambitious and to believe we could do what we wanted in life." — Rosa Parks

Civil Rights Activist
February 4, 1913–October 24, 2005

MONTGOMERY, ALABAMA

In 1971 an old bus was retired from service on the Cleveland Avenue route in Montgomery, Alabama. Senior managers in those not very environmentally conscious times ordered employees to dump the old vehicle in a nearby river. However, a state police officer, Roy H. Summerford, with a need for cheap storage space on his smallholding let it be known that he was always in the market for an old bus to park and use for such a purpose. For the next 30 years bus number 2857 rusted away in his field with all the seats, engine and anything else he could use or sell ripped out. He died in 2001 and his family put the bus up for auction. After fierce bidding the Henry Ford Museum in the metro-Detroit suburb of Dearborn, Michigan, acquired the piece of junk metal for close to half a million dollars. Today, fully restored, it is a major tourist attraction.

Why so much for an old rusty bus and why Detroit? Read on and you will find out.

Rosa Louise McCauley — later to become ROSA LOUISE McCAULEY PARKS or plain Rosa Parks — was born in Tuskegee, Alabama, home to the Normal and Industrial Institute for Negro girls, founded by civil rights leader Booker T. Washington and so admired and supported by Madam C. J. Walker (Chapter 12). Rosa's mother Leona had earned enough college credits to qualify as a teacher, while her father James was a carpenter. Leona's dream was for James to teach at the college, for them to qualify for faculty housing, and for their family to grow up on campus in a well-educated and cultured environment.

James had other ideas, preferring an itinerant life wandering from job to job. After just two years Leona, Rosa and her new brother Sylvester settled in Pine Level, Alabama with Leona's parents. After that, Rosa saw her father just twice more, once as a child and again in her twenties.

It is hard to judge Rosa's circumstances. On the one hand her father was gone, her mother worked as a schoolteacher eight miles distant so was away from Monday to Friday, and Rosa was a black girl in Alabama where, 50 years after the abolition of slavery, she was banned from traveling, worshipping, eating or studying with whites. Her school year was shorter than that of white children, starting later and ending earlier, and she walked to school whereas white children were bussed. Once there, she sat in a wooden structure (white youngsters sat in brick buildings) which had no heating or windows and there was one teacher to teach a class of 50 or 60 children of all abilities and ages. From age six Rosa also worked as a field hand.

On the other hand her mother was employed, her grandparents owned and farmed 18 acres, the family never went hungry, and there was an overarching commitment to education and personal betterment.

The end of World War I saw the return of black regiments to Alabama. This in turn sparked an explosion of violence by the Ku Klux Klan, white supremacists determined to eradicate any "false" notions of equality such veterans and their kin might have. Rosa's grandfather slept at night in a rocking chair, well-armed and with a good line of sight on their front door, Rosa asleep by his side on the floor.

Repeatedly and from a young age, Rosa witnessed people standing up against "bad treatment" and was prepared to defend herself too. When a white boy threatened to punch her, she offered him a brick in the face should he dare to do so.

Determined that Rosa should get ahead in life, Leona sent her 11-year-old daughter to relatives in the capital city of Montgomery. The contrast with her previous life was stark. Not only was urban life very different from her rural existence on a farm, but the insulting though comparatively small-scale segregation she was aware of in Pine Level gave way to the full Jim Crow treatment in Montgomery. Blacks could not even be buried near whites.

At that time, in 1924, Montgomery had just re-segregated its buses. An earlier 1900 boycott by blacks had led to such large revenue losses that the operating company had quickly folded. But the post-World War I rise of the Ku Klux Klan turned back the clock on the integration of black people in society.

Leona, however, felt the oppressiveness of full-fledged Jim Crow rules was worth enduring for Rosa's ongoing education at Miss White's Montgomery Industrial School for Girls. Alice White and other white northern women braved bombs, mobs, repeated arson attacks, verbal abuse, and close to total social ostracism in order to teach some 300 young black women in a city which had had no public high schools for black girls until she opened her school after the Civil War.

Rosa's curriculum ranged from the traditional three Rs through science to domestic skills. These included nursing, because blacks were not allowed in the predominantly white hospitals. This made it highly probable that any young black woman would put these skills into practice. Above all, Miss White taught self-confidence and discipline, self-respect, and high goals.

After over 60 years, however, a now very elderly Alice White gave up and returned North. Fortunately for Rosa, the Booker T. Washington Junior High had just opened. From there she moved to the laboratory school at the Alabama State Teacher's College for Negroes where trainee teachers earned credits for tutoring higher grade students. But before she could graduate, Rosa had to put familial duty first; she was obliged to move back home to care for a dying grandmother and a sick mother. The former soon departed, though Rosa's mother lived several more decades.

But the move home had an upside. Rosa was introduced to Raymond Parks, a 28-year-old barber who was very taken with her, now 18. As a member the NAACP (National Association for the Advancement of Colored People), he was the first fully-fledged civil rights activist she had met. Raymond opened her eyes to a range of authors, newspapers, and organizations. The couple married and Raymond encouraged Rosa to finish her high-school diploma but, even armed with this, all the available jobs were menial.

Over the next 20 years Rosa immersed herself in the issues of the day and served as the unpaid secretary of the Montgomery NAACP at a time when very few women were involved at all. Her commitment to the NAACP grew as Raymond's faded. He felt it too representative of the professional class and too unrepresentative of working men such as himself.

For Rosa the key tactical issues were the right to vote and bus desegregation. She saw the former as the route to economic opportunity and achievement and the latter as the most frequently experienced of many injustices.

Even though the right of black people to vote was enshrined in Constitutional amendments, they had to jump through hoops to register that were never put in the way of whites. As a result, only 31 out of around 50,000 black people in Montgomery were indeed enfranchised — and Rosa discovered at least some of the 31 were dead. So Rosa decided to try to register herself. The authorities put extraordinary hurdles in her way. The registration office opened intermittently, without advertised times, and always during regular work hours when she was hard at work as a seamstress. Then she would have to read aloud a passage of the Constitution and answer oral questions — whites were exempt from this. Finally there was a written test of 21 tough questions.[1] Rosa tried three times. She was told she had failed the first two, so on the third try she copied down her answers on a separate sheet in order to challenge the decision, but to her surprise she was told she had passed.

There was one last hurdle — a poll tax of $1.50 a year after turning 21, the age of majority. By 1945, when Rosa's registration was accepted, this presented her with a bill of $16.50 (today $210). She paid it and promptly voted for the new governor.

This year also saw the return to Alabama of Rosa's brother Sylvester McCauley from active duty in both Europe and the Pacific. But Sylvester and his wife and children soon packed and left for Detroit, feeling obliged to escape white supremacists' efforts to squash any notion of liberty or equality of opportunity.

Rosa continued working, sometimes as a seamstress, sometimes doing secretarial and other jobs which were open to black women, but she also carried on volunteering long hours for the NAACP. She ran its Youth Council and with her students daily asking to take out books from white libraries — something they were not allowed to do — she selected the integration of Montgomery's public libraries as a suitable campaign target.

But the buses were another challenge entirely. Unlike libraries, you pretty much had to use them. The white drivers were armed and insulting; worse, they were backed up by the police. It was a daily lesson in humiliation for non-whites.

The front ten of the 36 seats were reserved for whites and the back ten set aside for blacks. What happened in between varied, as drivers had some latitude.

---

1 Typical questions were: If a person charged with treason denies his guilt, how many persons must testify against him before he can be convicted? (Answer: two); If the President does not wish to sign a bill, how many days is he allowed in which to return it to Congress for reconsideration? (Ten); Which area of authority over state militia is reserved exclusively to the states? (The appointment of officers).

However, when large numbers of white people got on, black passengers were forced further and further back in those middle four rows of four seats each.

The flashpoint would come when, say, 19 white and 18 black customers boarded the bus, because four blacks (a whole row to stop different races mingling) would have to stand and move back to accommodate one white passenger. There would then be three adjoining empty seats.

One of the most vigilant drivers was a man called James Blake, who drove Rosa's Cleveland Avenue route. Rosa first crossed swords with him in 1943 when she was a secretary at the desegregated local air force base where she enjoyed eating and sharing transport with whites. But public transport was a very different proposition. Boarding Blake's bus one evening, Rosa had paid her fare only to be told to exit the bus and re-enter the back door. She could see the stairwell already packed full and knew the driver might well drive off the second she exited. A furious row had ensued, especially when she insisted on sitting down on an empty "white" seat to retrieve her purse that had somehow ended up on the floor. Although she had finally alighted and waited for the next bus, for the next 12 years she made sure never to enter a bus driven by James Blake again.

On 17 May 1954, the Supreme Court ruled unanimously that "separate but equal" was unconstitutional on the basis of a case called Brown vs Board of Education in which a black family from Topeka, Kansas, were told their daughters could not attend a new local "white" school but had to make the long trip to the "colored" school.

But that victory did not mean that tens of thousands of schools, transport companies, and other bodies were to change their rules overnight.

Bus companies were among the most intransigent. For some years a handful of black women had been sitting in "white" seats, and the NAACP had been looking for a good transportation test case to take to the Supreme Court while local activists had been in search of the perfect moment to begin a boycott.

At age 42 Rosa had an ailing mother and a husband who brought home a low wage. She was highly respected for her work ethic and her contributions to both the civil rights movement and church life, and had a large circle of black and white friends. It was at this point that she met a very young, newly appointed minister at Montgomery's top black church, Dexter Avenue Baptist. His name was Martin Luther King Jr. Rosa was very impressed by this charismatic and articulate preacher. She didn't know it at the time, but an enormous collision of individuals, talents, interests, social trends, and the law was about to take place.

On Thursday, December 1, 1955, Rosa left work with her mind full of volunteer tasks she had to attend to that evening. Her bus pulled up and for once she failed to look at the driver. She had paid her fare and sat down before she realized that the driver was James Blake, whom she had successfully avoided since

1943. Rosa was in the front row of the so-called colored seats. There was plenty of space; in all probability there would be no trouble. But more and more white people entered the bus until the presence of one white man meant four black people had to move.

Blake bellowed back at Rosa's row to make it "light or easy" on themselves by moving. Two women and one man in Rosa's row capitulated. Rosa did not. The bus grew silent around her. Sensing trouble, passengers began to disembark. They wanted to be off the bus and to find other ways home.

Historians argue: had the NAACP asked her to do it? Was she just tired? Or did she just snap? There is likely to have been an element of all three. She knew the NAACP needed better plaintiffs and she was tired of it all. But seeing her old bully Blake from 12 years earlier, she did dig her heels in, replying to his: "Are you going to stand up?" with a flat "No."

"Well, I'm going to have you arrested," he snarled.

"You may do that," was her curt reply.

Not "can" but rather "may."

This was the history-altering moment that led Nelson Mandela to comment many years later that "Before [Martin Luther] King there was Rosa Parks." Police officers Day and Mixon took her to City Hall, booked, and fingerprinted her. Water and a phone call were initially denied but both eventually were forthcoming. Word of her arrest spread, and a small army descended on the police station to protest. Her trial was set for Monday, December 5, and local NAACP president Edgar Nixon posted $100 bail (today worth over $1,200). Some 150 minutes later Rosa was free.

A feverish debate about strategy and leadership exploded that evening and immediately made Raymond worry about their safety. Rosa was more concerned about her mother's health.

But they were under pressure to make decisions. It was by now early Thursday evening. Professors and students at Alabama State College crafted a handout with a short message and printed 35,000 copies; by Friday afternoon every black person in Montgomery had been asked to boycott the entire bus system from dawn on Monday, December 5.

As these flyers were going out on every corner in the city, some 70 black ministers met in the basement of Martin Luther King Jr.'s church where, urged by King and Rosa Parks, they agreed to preach in support of the Bus Boycott from every pulpit on the Sunday.

On Monday morning the buses were totally empty of black people. Rosa was supported in court by 500 folk and pled guilty. She was fined $14 (today about $175), a decision she appealed. That night a mass rally voted unanimously to continue the boycott.

And so it all unfolded: the birth of the modern civil rights movement with Rosa as its founding mother.

The boycott never faltered. The media flew in from all over the world as did packages of clothes, particularly shoes, for the "Walking City." Rosa was made redundant from her job undertaking alterations at a store called Montgomery Fair on January 7, 1956, and took sewing work at home. At the same time she was often doing 18-hour shifts as a volunteer dispatcher for NAACP, which organized alternatives to the City buses. To the disgust of Montgomery's mayor many white women drove to pick up their black maids. There was car-pooling, black taxis pitching in with bus-level fares, and of course politically directed police brutality.

From the very start it was suggested that Rosa be used to challenge bus desegregation all the way to the Supreme Court. This strategy had been discussed before but all previous candidates had for different reasons not been the ideal test case. Rosa was ideal from a PR perspective, though one of her attorneys, Clifford Durr, a close white personal friend, feared that because the bus had been full when she refused to move the City could formulate a counter argument under which the word segregation might not even appear.

The ongoing day-by-day success of the Bus Boycott led the rapidly emerging Martin Luther King Jr. and his Montgomery Improvement Association (MIA) to launch a legal appeal under which four other Montgomery women — Aurelia Browder, Claudette Colvin, Susie McDonald, and Mary Louise Smith — sued Mayor W. A. Gayle for permitting the now outlawed "separate but equal" treatment on buses. The two actions went forward not hand in hand but rather simultaneously, with the Bus Boycott not ending until the Supreme Court ruled 381 days later in favor of desegregation.

It was an astonishing turn of events. Within a year of her December 1, 1955, protest, 42 other pro-desegregation movements had begun in the South. A quiet, hard-working female activist had prompted a movement which led to a case in the Supreme Court. Better still she had prevailed. Her great inspirations had been Sojourner Truth (Chapter 6), Harriet Tubman (Chapter 10) and Elizabeth Cady Stanton (Chapter 8). Rosa Parks, like Elizabeth Cady Stanton, was stubborn, refusing to bend when she believed in the justice of a cause.

When Rosa's colleagues presented petitions to the city council asking, for example, for the drivers to be polite to black passengers, she would attend as NAACP secretary to record the spoken words but she would not sign it herself. She wanted full-blown reform, not a plea for change that would fall on deaf ears.

The year 1956 saw a bloody ideological battle. There were bombings of black ministers' homes and an all-white grand jury indicted 89 black leaders, including Rosa, for violating a law that made boycotts illegal. Only Martin Luther King

Jr. was finally sentenced, which hugely enhanced his popularity. He was given 386 days' jail or $500. He chose the latter, a fine that would today be equivalent to $7,000. Alice Paul (Chapter 14) would have counseled, do the time, don't pay the fine.

Rosa never really capitalized on her fame. Over the decades she spoke regularly in public and was interviewed by the world's media, but her speeches were almost exclusively for her church and the NAACP. She even went to New York City and met Eleanor Roosevelt, who wrote a very enthusiastic column about her which was syndicated nationally.

In June 1956, the Federal District Court ruled in favor of the King's MIA and against the city, which appealed immediately to the Supreme Court. In November the Supreme Court again found for King. The Bus Boycott, however, continued until civil rights leaders were in possession of official court papers — they arrived December 20, 1956. The boycott ended at 5:45am the next day, as King and Edgar Nixon symbolically boarded the first bus of a new era.

Look magazine tracked down Rosa at home and persuaded her to get on a Cleveland Avenue bus for its photographers. The resulting image was seen around the world. It is one of the most famous photographs of all time.

The fight was by no means over. Newly integrated buses were hit by sniper fire, black churches and ministers were bombed, and Rosa's hate mail and phone calls reached astonishing proportions. Friends began to call her at home every evening for long hours just to stop the tsunami of vitriol.

By the summer of 1957, it became too much for her. Her brother wanted her in Detroit; her husband and mother were both ailing; and she was weary of it all. King and others had emerged to national and international roles, but Rosa just wanted to head north. The MIA gave her $800 (today over $11,000) to help her prosper.

Detroit was her home until her death in 2005. She threw herself into her church, rising to be a deaconess. She saw John F. Kennedy and Robert F. Kennedy assassinated, and when Martin Luther King Jr. was murdered, she and her mother wept and prayed together on hearing this news.

She worked for over 20 years until September 1988 as an assistant to John Conyers, the Representative for Michigan's first congressional district. In that role she continued to perform the same unstinting voluntary work she had undertaken for Edgar Nixon for so long, helping, advising, and counseling constituents.

Her new boss good naturedly pointed out that more people dropped by his office to see her than to see him. After all, she had succeeded in persuading Martin Luther King Jr. to support him and King rarely endorsed a politician so openly.

Her legacy would be immense. In 1965, Cleveland Avenue was renamed Rosa Parks Avenue and a museum in Montgomery was named after her, too. In 1987, she began a foundation called the Rosa and Raymond Parks Institute for Self Development with her friend and former tailor Elaine Eason Steele. This foundation funded "Pathways to Freedom" bus trips for students to discover their heritage, particularly along the Underground Rail routes used by nineteenth century slaves to escape to free states (see Chapter 10 on Harriet Tubman).

Honor after honor came her way. She received the Presidential Medal of Freedom from Bill Clinton, the Congressional Gold Medal from Al Gore, and a Time nomination as one of the 20 most influential people of the twentieth century.

She wrote three books: *Rosa Parks: My Story* (1992), *Quiet Strength* (1994), and *Dear Mrs. Parks — A Dialogue with Today's Youth* (1996).

Rosa Parks died aged 92 and her coffin was displayed in the Capitol Rotunda for public viewing for two days so that her many admirers could pay their respects. She was the first and to date only woman so honored. Some 4,000 attended her Detroit funeral on November 2, 2005.

On December 1, 2005, exactly 50 years after her refusal to renounce her seat, President George W. Bush signed a bill for a statue of Rosa to stand next to that of Confederate president Jefferson Davis in the National Statuary Hall. He said: "What had begun as a simple act of civil disobedience ended up galvanizing the modern movement for civil rights."

That very day bus systems all over the United States kept the seat behind the driver empty and above it placed a poster of the famous photograph Look had used at the end of the 381-day boycott. On it was printed: "It all started on a bus on December 1, 1955. Rosa Parks changed the course of history and inspired us all." It is that bus which stands on show at the Henry Ford Museum in Detroit, the modest symbol of a whole struggle for justice, recognition, and dignity.

CHAPTER 23. JANE JACOBS

"I believe in control from below and support from above." — Jane Jacobs

Writer and Urban Activist
May 4, 1916–April 25, 2006

NEW YORK, NEW YORK and TORONTO, CANADA

It was the mid-1930s and New York City was languishing deep in the Great Depression. Jobs were few and far between, but young secretary Jane Butzner dreamed of being a journalist. At weekends she could often be found walking and cycling all over the city, getting to know different neighborhoods. She discovered and fell in love with Greenwich Village, and moved there with her older sister Betty.

Jane was fascinated by the everyday life of New York and she started writing articles about it. She sold stories to *Vogue* about the fur, flower and diamond districts, and even learned how to read the numbers and letters on manhole covers so as to know what exactly was going on beneath the sidewalks. She wrote about that too in an article published in *Cue*, a listings magazine.

This was the start of a career in writing and activism that was to change forever and for better the way we view our cities. As JANE JACOBS, her married name, she took on the notion that cities are best served by bureaucrats, planners and elected officials with deep taxpayer-funded purses, wide powers of eminent domain, and large-scale grandiose projects. And neither did she have much time for the private-sector architects and companies who rode on the tails of such efforts. When they were awarded contracts to tear down old communities and replace them with tower blocks, they became responsible for creating ugly, dysfunctional paradises for graffiti artists, drug addicts, muggers, rapists, and worse. Jane stood up to the federal bulldozer that offered cities 90% funding to destroy old neighborhoods; she stood up to the local bureaucrats and elected politicians. And she won. She won the intellectual argument and along the way she won notable political battles too.

To Jane Jacobs, the best cities are the result of human action not human design; they are built on diversity and dense mixed use, not zoning and attempts by government to impose order and fit people into neat little boxes. They are spontaneous and no two should be alike. They should not have monopoly public transit systems but rather private competition among many types of vehicle and operator and good, solid, easily enforced rights that make it hard for public authorities to ride roughshod over private property owners.

Her first and most famous book, *The Death and Life of Great American Cities* (1961), was detested by big government representatives of all parties but embraced by the conservative and libertarian right, especially *National Review* founder William F. Buckley and novelist Ayn Rand (Chapter 20), and economist and future Nixon adviser Martin Anderson, whose own book on the subject, *The Federal Bulldozer: A Critical Analysis of Urban Renewal 1949–1962*, came out in 1964. To this day free-market litigators such as Washington's Institute for Justice sing Jane Jacobs' praises, and her book is now required reading in universities the world over.

And yet she had no university education or professional training herself. She was born Jane Isabel Butzner in Scranton, the coal mining capital of Northeastern Pennsylvania, the third child of four of a doctor, John Butzner, and his wife Bess, a nurse. Her ancestors came from all over northern Europe and had fought both times on the winning side in the Revolutionary and Civil Wars.

As she grew up, her parents taught her to question everything. She loved the city of Scranton and preferred making trips downtown to heading out to the countryside. However, when she reached her teens the bottom fell out of the local market as coal reserves ran out and the car replaced the steam train. This economic revolution sparked in her an early interest in what makes a city tick.

The conformity of grade school grated on a child encouraged to think for herself. By third grade she was reputedly a voracious reader but showed little interest in what her teachers were trying to instill, preferring to devour books hidden in her lap. Her parents gave her a good grounding in the ideals and spirit that drove the heroes of the Revolutionary War, which helped develop her personal ideology. She was distrustful of the state and understood, in Thomas Jefferson's words, that "the price of freedom is eternal vigilance" against trends or laws, however innocuous, that might lead to its loss.

She graduated high school in 1933 but eschewed college (which her parents could afford), spending most of the next two years working on local papers in Scranton and North Carolina, where she lived with a maternal aunt. In 1935, she joined older sister Betty in New York City, which became her home for the next three decades.

After surviving on a series of secretarial jobs and freelance writing about the working districts of New York, she took a job with a magazine called *Iron Age*. This led to an opportunity to give something back to Scranton. Jane wrote about the decline of the coal and iron and steel industries in Northeastern Pennsylvania and how this meant that there were many skilled unemployed men available to help in the war effort. A condensed version of her article appeared in the *New York Herald Tribune* and came to the attention of a company which made parts for the B29 bomber. It soon opened a factory in Scranton and back home Jane was hailed a heroine.

She moved to the Office of War Information to be a feature writer and then became a reporter at the State Department's overseas magazine, *America Illustrated*. It was while working for the Office of War Information that she met Robert Hyde Jacobs Jr., a Columbia-trained architect. Before two months were up, the couple was engaged. They wed at her childhood home in Scranton in late May 1944, and their marriage lasted for 52 years until Robert's death in 1996.

They made their home at 555 Hudson Street in Greenwich Village, taking on a small rundown three-storey building that had been a candy store. They invested a great deal of sweat turning it into a family home to which they welcomed James in 1948, Ned in 1950, and May in 1955.

Jane's big professional break came in the spring of 1952 when she walked into the office of Douglas Haskell, editor of *Architectural Forum*, to which her husband subscribed, and talked her way into a freelance assignment. This led to her becoming an associate editor. She was given the brief to cover schools and hospitals and every night biked home from the Rockefeller Center with armloads of blueprints that Robert would patiently work through with her. Robert went on to design 22 hospitals himself in the space of 14 years. Haskell was so pleased with her work in this area that in 1954 he added city planning to her list of responsibilities.

The previous 25 years in American history had been tumultuous. From the Crash of 1929 through the Great Depression and World War II to the baby boom and the post-war economic good times, it had been a roller coaster ride. Black people had moved to cities in the North; Puerto Ricans had immigrated in their thousands; and white people had fled on new roads to the new suburbs in their new cars, enjoying their federally backed mortgages. The flipside was that public transport was neglected and became the preserve of the poor and the criminal classes.

Meanwhile the 1949 Federal Housing Act gave cities 90% of the cost of building new public housing. But the mayor only received his money once the bulldozers had already started demolishing whole blocks of "slums" to make way for the orderliness but utter soullessness of high-rise buildings and civic centers. There were master plans, planning tsars and talk of wiping out hundreds of blocks in New York City alone. Any hint that a block might be a target for demolition became a self-fulfilling prophesy; no one wanted to invest in or maintain a building that was about to be condemned.

Jane Jacobs came to the issue with her self-confidence, her faith in the vision of the Founding Fathers, her love of cities and two decades of walking and biking around New York City. She had as yet no great political or philosophical opinion, just a love of neighborhoods with a rich diversity of people, architecture and activities. It was on this foundation that communities and local economies were built. Her first city planning assignment was to go to Philadelphia to study changes being made there. Within hours of stepping off the train from New York, her eyes were opened to the tragedy unfolding as a result of contemporary urban planning. There in Philadelphia, she saw the "before" — a bustling, lively but obviously poor street slated for demolition — and the "after" — a bleak, empty scene with little to commend it but a great sight line.

Closer to home, Jane was alerted to an urban disaster in East Harlem. Far from improving residents' lives, so-called renewal had torn them apart. The streets were now dangerous; hundreds of small businesses had been forcibly closed down, creating unemployment; there was vandalism and more opportunity for crime; children could not play outside because their parents might now be ten or twenty floors above them and unable to supervise from their home. The glue of society, the churches and clubs, had gone too. What she saw in East Harlem led Jane to a thorough study of Title I of the 1949 Housing Act and she rapidly came to the conclusion that it was destroying whole neighborhoods, increasing segregation and white middle-class flight, and benefiting a mere handful of people — the wealthy who could afford to move into the luxury apartments that sprang up. But space-hungry institutions such as New York and Fordham Universities were also using it to expand significantly, brushing whole communities aside.

A key moment for Jane occurred in the spring of 1956 when she represented the *Architectural Forum* at a conference at Harvard. As she outlined her basic theme that the way people use space is messy and cannot be planned, she was — much to her surprise — warmly applauded. She met leading public intellectuals such as Lewis Mumford, who was among many things a writer on architecture for the *New Yorker*. Her speech was reprinted as an article in *Architectural Forum* together with photographs and drew a very large and approving mail bag.

Also in the audience was William H. Whyte, an editor at *Fortune*, part of the same Henry Luce empire (Chapter 19) and author of the bestselling *The Organization Man*, which described how men paid the price of climbing the corporate ladder with a long commute into the city and long hours away from their wives and families. Whyte, like Jane, was concerned about the decline of the city as the suburbs exploded and recognized in her a fellow individualist and tilter at windmills. He commissioned her to write "Downtown is for People" for *Fortune*. The article caused a ruckus among the staff, who considered her a "most inappropriate choice," but when it was published it garnered one of the biggest and most positive reader responses in the history of the magazine. It came to the attention of the Rockefeller Foundation which offered Jane a grant to turn it into a book. Lunch with an editor at Random House followed, which produced an advance and a contract. Jane was soon taking leave from *Architectural Forum* to start on her seminal work, *The Death and Life of Great American Cities*.

It took just over two years to write and three years to be published but it was worth the wait. This astonishing work, public policy as English literature, is comparable in recent years only with *The Beautiful Tree* by James Tooley, which gives a radical insight into the success of private education for the poorest people in the poorest countries. In the case of Jane Jacobs' book, it gave the reader a new set of eye glasses for looking at the urban world. Jane did not beat about the bush. She used the word "attack" three times in the first paragraph. Her book was to be an "attack on current city planning and rebuilding"; but it was not an "attack" based on "hair-splitting"; instead it was an "attack" on the "principles and aims that have shaped modern, orthodox city planning and rebuilding."

She set out her stall in paragraph two: "In setting forth different principles, I shall mainly be writing about common, ordinary things: for instance, what kinds of city streets are safe and what kinds are not; why some city parks are marvelous and others are vice traps and death traps; why some slums stay slums and other slums regenerate themselves even against financial and official opposition; what makes downtowns shift their centers; what, if anything, is a city neighborhood, and what jobs, if any, neighborhoods in great cities do. In short I shall be writing about how cities work in real life, because this is the only way to learn what principles of planning and what practices in rebuilding can promote social and economic vitality in cities, and what practices and principles will deaden these attributes."

It was serialized, heavily advertised, positioned for the Christmas gift market and widely critiqued. Her book polarized opinion. Some reviewers loved it but formally educated male planners asked what a woman from Scranton without even an undergraduate degree could possibly teach them. She must have felt a little like British prime minister Margaret Thatcher two decades later when the latter said: "I always cheer up immensely if an attack is particularly wounding because I think, well, if they attack one personally, it means they have not a single political argument left."

While Jane Jacobs denounces the planners and their all too willing private-sector architects and developers, she also shows us what works as well as what fails so miserably both in the short and the long term. She warned against tsunamis of federal cash; she embraced high population densities, pointing out they were not the same as overcrowding; she exposed for a falsehood the notion that more roads relieve congestion; and she doubted that suburbs were better or safer for children. At the heart of what works is the haphazard, untidy, densely populated small block with its mix of buildings of different conditions, sizes, ages, ownership and use. It is mostly market driven and it is most definitely not neat, large-scale, single-use zoning with clear sight lines.

The Death and Life of Great American Cities was a widely discussed book and over the last five decades it has influenced generations of students. While not a bestseller, it has over the long run sold several hundred thousand copies and appeared in at least six languages. It was a book that was pivotal in recasting our cultural mindset, a book as likely to be read for a general studies degree as one in urban planning. In fact, it can be argued that *Death and Life* was one of a trio of influential books by women in the early 1960s that succeeded in questioning — rightly or wrongly — received ideas, the other two being Rachel Carson's *Silent Spring*, which sounded alarm bells on the environment, and Betty Friedan's *The Feminine Mystique*, which is credited with launching the modern women's movement.

Even before publication, Jane had already been a prominent local activist. She had helped to stop a highway being run through Washington Square Park and to halt plans to widen her own street by some ten feet by carving five feet off each sidewalk. However, these were mere preludes to two huge battles she was to fight. The first campaign was to prevent her very own neighborhood from being condemned, cleared and rebuilt, and the second was to kill off plans for a Lower Manhattan Expressway.

The battle to Save the West Village began in February 1961 with news in *The New York Times* of a $350,000 study of a 14-block area. Jane immediately noted that the fee for such studies was normally a fixed percentage of the total cost of the job. The very fact that there was an agreed fee implied to her that a backroom deal had already been done. She suspected that the deal involved tearing down all 14 blocks and replacing them with higher rent — meaning a bigger tax base — buildings such as apartments for the middle classes.

The fight was long, arduous and acrimonious. The government did its utmost to bypass, ban or ride roughshod over consultation. There were even rumors that community leaders were bribed with the offer of free housing.

But Jane and her neighbors fought a brilliant campaign. They researched the relevant law, and they conducted a survey of every building to prove their blocks failed the "slum" test. Crucially, they received advice from an insider who warned them that if asked, "What do you want?" they should answer only: "Please remove the designation of 'slum'." Any helpful suggestion, such as proposing that the authorities plant a tree in a particular corner, would immediately reclassify the individual or group that put in the request as being no longer an enemy but on the side of the city as they would now be participating positively in the process. Jane Jacobs had no desire to side with the city authorities or participate positively. She simply wanted to stop the soul being torn out of her community.

It was a classic fight, citizen against the state, David versus Goliath. There were court appeals, demonstrations, arrests at civil meetings, moles inside City Hall, and endless news stories as the saga gained traction. In the middle of all this Jane's book came out, adding fuel to the campaign. A year later in January 1962 she had won, but immediately a battle to defeat the Lower Manhattan Expressway loomed. This ten-lane, two-and-a-half-mile federally funded freeway would necessitate the removal of 2,000 family homes, eight churches and 800 businesses employing 10,000 people. The opponents' battle cry was that this would "Los Angelize" the city of New York; they used many of the same tactics as in the earlier fight and again they won.

But it was a long, hard campaign. There were three attempts to build the Expressway first in the summer of 1962; then the idea resurfaced in 1965, but the mayor who supported it was beaten. It came up yet again in 1968, only to be officially killed off by the Mayor in 1969. As Jane Jacobs quipped, "The rule of thumb is that you have to kill expressways three times before they die."

Jane showed up to every picket or demonstration in her trademark long white gloves. *The New York Times* ran a piece entitled "Mrs. Jacobs' Protest Results in Riot Charge" in its April 10, 1968, issue. "Jane Jacobs, a nationally known writer on urban problems, was arraigned in Criminal Court yesterday and charged with second-degree riot, inciting to riot and criminal mischief," it reported. "The police had originally charged that Mrs. Jacobs tried to disrupt a public meeting on the controversial Lower Manhattan Expressway. 'The inference seems to be,' Mrs. Jacobs said, 'that anybody who criticizes a state program is going to get it in the neck.'"

She had become notorious but was unrepentant. She also opposed the Vietnam War and the same year as the Expressway riot, the entire family moved to Toronto, Canada, where her husband had been offered a position as a hospital architect. It suited her well; Jane herself wanted to escape the demands of endless campaigning in New York City and refocus on writing, and her sons were approaching draft age.

Once in Toronto, Jane started to write increasingly about economics — another area in which she had ideas but no training. She produced *The Economy of Cities* in 1969 and *Cities and the Wealth of Nations* in 1984, which influenced 1995 economics Nobel laureate Robert Lucas and his work on economic development. He acknowledged his debt to her in both his writing and his speeches. She began to doubt the efficacy of welfare and its international cousin, third world aid. Her mistrust of officialdom led to her doubting the need for public-sector involvement in energy, transport and the delivery of letters and packages. *Systems of Survival* (1992), *The Nature of Economies* (2000) and *Dark Age Ahead* (2004) dealt with some of these issues and completed her main output.

She became more and more reclusive and seemed to shun the attention she received. "I do not know who this celebrity named Jane Jacobs is — it's not me," she once said. "You either do your work or you are a celebrity; I'd rather do my work." She spurned honorary doctorates, of which many were offered. She was an arch individualist who was highly suspicious of big government yet refused to be pigeonholed politically. She was a public intellectual who spurned — despised even — the rules of academia. But her legacy is all around us, from the way we all now think about eminent domain and zoning to successful urban schemes such as the St Lawrence neighborhood of Toronto, Canada, which adopted her ideas on land use and population density.

CHAPTER 24. DORIAN FISHER

"I had already learned a great deal about market economics from my first husband, and so I didn't need to be converted. But after I married Antony I believed in them even more strongly! The whole purpose of Antony's life was to get others to believe in them too. I was extremely proud to help him in any way I could." — Dorian Fisher in *Antony Fisher: Champion of Liberty* by Gerald Frost.

Strategic Philanthropist
September 14, 1919–April 3, 2007

SAN FRANCISCO, CALIFORNIA

It was September 1975 and Dorian Crocker was a wealthy widow in her fifties. Her investment adviser, Samuel H. Husbands at DeanWitter Reynolds had invited her as his official guest to a regional meeting of the classical liberal-oriented Mont Pelerin Society (MPS) at the private Hillsdale College in Michigan. The Society had been founded by the celebrated economist F. A. Hayek after World War II and Dorian had often been to its meetings with her late husband. At the last moment Sam had to cancel but said to Dorian, "Say hello to my pal Tony Fisher for me." She approached entrepreneur and think tank founder Antony Fisher who was speaking at the meeting and did as her investment adviser suggested. The pair talked for a long time and he was very smitten. They exchanged addresses and so began a partnership that brought the message of liberty and free-market principles to a worldwide audience.

DORIAN FISHER, as she was to become when she married Antony, was privately, quietly, without any fuss or fanfare, one of the most important ladies for liberty of the past generation. For 25 years she helped her second husband create a network of liberty-minded organizations and think tanks around the world and when she passed on she left her fortune to four of them. She was fun, smart, witty, beautiful, generous, and tough, but she was principled, and reasonable with it. She successfully brought people together using her charm and her incredibly positive attitude to life.

Dorian was born Dorian Dodge in Wisconsin in 1919 but grew up in Illinois. Her family tree stretched back to a Tristram Dodge of Taunton, in the county of Somerset in south-west England, who migrated in 1661 to settle on Block Island, Rhode Island. On another line, the Yeamans, she was a Daughter of the American Revolution. Her father was a prolific inventor of improvements for automobiles but not a member of the famous automobile family of the same name, a coincidence to be repeated. Dorian, a bright child, enjoyed the private co-educational Laboratory Schools, an integral part of the University of Chicago. Founded in 1896 by John Dewey, today it is ranked in the top five by the *Wall Street Journal* as a feeder to the Ivy League universities. Malia and Sasha Obama attended until late 2008 when their father became President.

From Chicago she moved in 1936 to California, entering the elite private Mills College, Oakland, the first women's college west of the Rockies and another top-five institution today, rated fourth in the west by *US News and World Report* in 2011. Whether she graduated and the topic of her major is not known, but it seems probable that she did not graduate. She married the first of her three husbands, George N. Crocker, in a big wedding ceremony in San Francisco in 1941. He was 13 years her senior and an attorney, newspaper columnist, businessman, author and US Army major. In spite of his name, he was not a scion of the Crocker banking family, just as Dorian's father was no relation to the Dodge brothers who founded an auto empire. However, Dorian impishly opened an account at the Crocker Bank and never mentioned her lack of family connections or later changes of name.

Her husband George went on to be one of the judges in the longest court martial of World War II, described in *On American Soil* by Jack Hamman. He was a vociferous critic of the New Deal and in the 1950s wrote *Roosevelt's Road to Russia*, which claimed that Franklin D. Roosevelt was a secret supporter of Stalin. With Dorian he toured the world, often attending meetings of the MPS. Dorian understood the free-market principles espoused by the MPS, and her exposure to them laid the foundation for her later work with Antony Fisher. George N. Crocker was a wealthy man and the couple moved in 1964 to a brand-new building at 1750 Taylor Street, San Francisco, where they lived until George died in

1970. His 51-year-old widow, who was well provided for, continued to occupy their fabulous apartment.

Earlier, when they had been trying to decide which floor to buy on, the building was nothing but a steel framework with a small elevator cage. The very glamorous Dorian rode that cage many times, stopping at every level. Eventually, in her typically analytical way, she figured out that the top floors were less desirable than ones six to ten floors lower down. The heat in California's Central Valley sucked in the fog from the Pacific through the nearby Golden Gate Bridge, shrouding the top floors in impenetrable mist on a regular basis and ruining the panorama that stretched from the Golden Gate to the Bay Bridge. Rose and Milton Friedman, who were to move to the same building (Chapter 21), listened to her advice when later upgrading their original small apartment to a larger one.

She helped them in another practical way before that, lending them her own lovely apartment for televised interviews after Milton Friedman won the Nobel Prize for economics in 1976.

Meanwhile Antony George Anson Fisher had been born in England in 1915 to well-off parents. He attended Eton, the elite private school, and Cambridge University and was a fighter pilot in World War II. In April 1945 he was still in the Royal Air Force working in Whitehall in the center of London when he read the condensed version of Hayek's classic anti-socialist, pro-liberty book, *The Road to Serfdom* in the April 1945 edition of *Reader's Digest*. It changed his life.

Hayek advised him that rather than going into politics, he should set up an institute that would make the case for liberty to society's intellectuals. Antony Fisher did little about this advice for a decade. Instead he became a successful entrepreneur, bringing from the US to the UK the concept of factory farming of chickens.

Then finally in the summer of 1955 he founded the London-based Institute of Economic Affairs (IEA), publishing a little book by George Winder on why pre-World War II exchange controls should be abolished. It was a hit, persuading him to take on a young economist named Ralph Harris as the IEA's part-time director starting January 1, 1957.

Antony Fisher became Chair of the Board and for close to two decades the IEA launched a barrage of pamphlets against the post-World War II consensus of centralism and dirigisme and in favor of markets. The arguments coming out of the IEA began to resonate around the world and a group of businessmen from Vancouver decided to set up their own version in Canada.

Meanwhile Antony Fisher had sold his chicken business, started a dairy farm and a turtle farm in the Cayman Islands and lost almost everything, including his first wife. He started to help the new IEA, named the Fraser Institute, in Vancouver.

It was at this difficult point in his life that he first met Dorian at the MPS meeting in Hillsdale College in Michigan.

Dorian and Antony met for a second time at an international meeting of the MPS in St Andrews, Scotland in 1976 to mark the bi-centenary of the publication of the Scottish economist Adam Smith's *The Wealth of Nations*. Not long after, he proposed, first in San Francisco and then, when she said no, on a cruise down the west coast of South America ("Separate cabins of course. We're conservatives!" she is reported to have said). She accepted and they married in October 1977 in Pebble Beach, California, with Antony moving into 1750 Taylor Street.

Dorian not only made it possible financially for Antony to build an international network of free-market oriented think tanks, but also actively worked with him on a daily basis. Dorian helped to organize her husband, taking detailed notes of meetings and typing them up, providing useful cuttings from magazines and newspapers for him to read in the evenings, arranging travel for him and giving dinner parties for people in the think tank world. A consummate hostess, she charmed everyone. It is highly unlikely he would have been so successful without her.

By 1981 there was a network of six institutes: the IEA in London, Fraser in Vancouver, the Manhattan Institute in New York City, the Centre for Independent Studies in Sydney, Australia, the Pacific Research Institute in San Francisco, California and back in London, UK, the Adam Smith Institute. In that year Antony incorporated the Atlas Economic Research Foundation in Delaware with offices in San Francisco to act as a focal point for the growing hordes who wanted to know how to copy the IEA, which had become known as "Margaret Thatcher's favorite think tank."

The President of Atlas, Alex Chafuen, recalls Dorian Fisher's intellectual contribution. "When Antony was working on a long manuscript he would almost always show it to Dorian. She would have pointed suggestions. Sometimes I saw manuscripts go back and forth almost endlessly, until both Antony and Dorian were satisfied."

Antony and Dorian's eleven years together saw that list of think tanks grow to about 30 in more than 20 countries. With homes in San Francisco, New York City and London, the couple ceaselessly wooed donors and potential trustees; they counseled the intellectual think tank entrepreneurs; and they traveled the world together scouting for talented, pro-liberty people. They were a highly effective team — those from Anglophile cultures responded better to Antony's British reserve, while those who preferred American openness warmed to Dorian.

As the 1983 regional meeting of the MPS in Vancouver neared, a young Fraser staff member named Sally C. Pipes phoned Antony and pointed out that nearly all of the think tanks with which he was associated were sending a representative and suggested bringing them together for a day before the main meeting with others who might be thinking of setting up an institute. This was the first of many workshops to be run by Atlas over the ensuing three decades. From this first workshop, Dorian produced a manual showing what worked and what failed in the think tank world. It was used for many years by start-up groups.

When Antony passed on in the summer of 1988, knighted only four weeks earlier by Britain's Queen Elizabeth II, Dorian took his seat on the Board of Trustees of Atlas. She served on the Board from August 1988 to January 1997. When she joined, Atlas listed some 40 groups or institutes in 20 countries. By the time she stepped down, there was a network of over 100 institutes in 60 countries and today, 30 years after its inception, there are over 250 in 100 countries. This is a considerable achievement for an organization that started out as two tiny offices in downtown San Francisco staffed by Antony Fisher and one secretary.

Dorian's third marriage was to Canadian entrepreneur John Adams, whom she met a few months after Antony's death. They married in 1989 and settled in Bermuda, with Dorian selling off her properties. She drew her new husband into the network she and Antony had created and this new alliance did not dint her efforts for freedom and liberty. When John Adams died in 1999, she returned aged 80 to her much-loved San Francisco.

She died in 2007, leaving her fortune to the Atlas Economic Research Foundation and three think tanks — London's IEA, Dallas's National Center for Policy Analysis and San Francisco's Pacific Research Institute.

It is hard to think of another American woman who did more internationally for liberty than Dorian Fisher in the last quarter of the twentieth century. She and her second husband planted acorns that are today young trees. A network of free-market think tanks was Hayek's vision applied by Antony Fisher, but Dorian Fisher made it happen.

Chapter 25. Mildred Loving

"I believe all Americans, no matter their race, no matter their sex, no matter their sexual orientation, should have that same freedom to marry." — Mildred Loving, in a speech to mark the fortieth anniversary of her Supreme Court Case, June 12, 2007.

Legal Activist
July 22, 1939–May 2, 2008

CENTRAL POINT, VIRGINIA

It was two o'clock in the morning on the night of July 13, 1958, when Sheriff Garnett Brooks arrived with two other sworn officers at the home of a newly-married interracial couple in Central Point, Caroline County, Virginia. Mildred and Richard Loving were living in the downstairs bedroom of Mildred's parents' residence while her husband built their own house. A tiny rural community, Central Point was the kind of place where nobody locked their home, even at night. The Lovings were no exception and the officers using flashlights quickly and easily entered, found the downstairs bedroom, woke the couple, and arrested them.

The Lovings were charged with a felony punishable by one to five years in prison. They were accused of contravening Section 20-59 of the Virginia Code which forbade miscegenation — interracial marriage and sex — and of breaking Section 20-58 which prohibited interracial couples from that state going elsewhere to marry and then returning home which was called the "evasion" statute. Section 20-57, on the other hand, declared interracial marriages to be null and void. The Lovings were being confronted with the full force of the law.

Virginia had had such laws since 1691 and 12 other southern states had similar statutes, as did Texas, Delaware, and West Virginia for 16 in total. The definition in Virginia of what was colored changed: in 1866 it was a quarter or more black heritage but in 1910 it had moved to a sixteenth. But the Virginia law of 1924, the Racial Integrity Act, proceeded to ban marriages unless both parties were 100 per cent white.

However, things were different in Central Point, Caroline County, Virginia. It was known as the Passing Capital of America, because it was relatively easy for people of mixed heritage who were born there to pass themselves off as white when they moved elsewhere. People of different races — white, black, and Native American — that made up Central Point's community had been coexisting harmoniously since anyone could remember and there were many residents of mixed race in the area. This made for successful integration and a relaxed social structure. For example, Richard's father had for 25 years driven a truck for a wealthy black farmer, not the other way around. When questions about skin color were asked of a person from Central Point, a bit of black heritage could easily be explained as Native American, which didn't necessarily preclude marriage to a white person.

Richard Perry Loving (October 29, 1933–June 29, 1975) was a white bricklayer and stonemason, and a racing car enthusiast. MILDRED DOLORES JETER LOVING was six years his junior. Tall and elegant, she was part Native American (Rappahannock) and part black. Both from Central Point, they had attended different schools and churches but their families had socialized extensively. This meant that the couple had known each other since childhood. At age 18 Mildred became pregnant by Richard Loving following a long courtship.

At Richard's suggestion they drove north to Washington, DC which allowed interracial marriages. They picked a minister from the local phone book, married with her father and one of her brothers as witnesses, and returned home the same day to Virginia. It was later claimed that Richard knew of the ban on marriage but was ignorant of the "evasion" statute. Mildred, it was said, thought they were just avoiding red tape such as the blood tests each party needed in order to marry — this was required by Virginia but not by the District of Columbia.

But the authorities received an anonymous tip-off just five weeks after Mr. and Mrs. Loving had returned from DC. County Prosecutor Bernard Mahon asked local Justice Robert W Farmer to issue arrest warrants. Thus Sheriff Brooks and his officers turned up at the couple's home. "What are you doing in bed with that woman?" the Sheriff demanded of Richard as he burst in on the sleeping couple.

Before he could fully awaken and answer, Mildred sat up and pointed to their framed marriage license hanging on the wall.

"I'm his wife!" she retorted.

"That piece of paper is no good here," the Sheriff answered, tearing it from the wall. However, it was very good for one thing. It was clear evidence that the laws of Virginia had been broken, in particular the law against "evasion." He took it with him as Richard and Mildred were taken away for questioning.

Richard, as a white man, was held for one night only but Mildred, as a "Negress," spent another four nights locked up in a rat-infested cell, despite his best efforts to free her.

They promised to separate for the time being and a bond of $1,000 (today costing $8,000) was demanded to assure the Court that they would turn up for their hearing.

Bewildered, the couple decided that they would need a talented attorney to fight their case. They took on Frank Beazely, the very best in the county, and while their judge Leon M Bazile was extraordinarily hostile, he did have a high opinion of Beazely.

The facts of the case were not in dispute so the Lovings pled guilty and waived their right to trial by jury, placing all matters in the hands of Judge Bazile.

On January 6, 1959, Bazile accepted the guilty pleas and made his views quite plain in his sentencing. He sentenced Mildred and Richard to one year each in jail and finally suspended that sentence for 25 years, provided they both left the state immediately and did not return "together or at the same time" for 25 years. He said: "Almighty God created the races white, black, yellow, malay [brown] and red, and he placed them on separate continents. And but for the interference with his arrangement there would be no cause for such marriages. The fact that he separated the races shows that he did not intend for the races to mix."

The judge asked if the couple wanted to say anything. Mildred refused. On the one hand a 25-year suspended sentence was an astonishingly long one; on the other they might instead have been required to serve a jail sentence of up to five years. They each paid costs of $36.29 (today a total of $600), packed up, and headed north to Mildred's cousin in Washington, DC.

Richard crossed the Potomac into Virginia every day to work. Mildred returned alone to Central Point so that Richard's mother, a midwife, could attend the births of Sidney (1958), Donald (1959), and Peggy (1960). It was often commented — and family photos bear this out — that Sidney took after his black antecedents while Donald was more Native American-looking and Peggy was more white.

At Easter 1959 the couple returned together to Central Point, though they slept in separate homes. Attorney Beazely had advised them that this was possible, but they were rearrested as such a visit clearly violated the conditions of their parole. The attorney rushed before the judge and took 100 per cent of the blame for misinterpreting the court's order. As a result, the Lovings escaped the year in jail that they might have received and were free to head back to Washington, DC, a place of exile they hated.

And it might well have ended there, with Mildred raising their children and Richard making good money as a stonemason in a seemingly recession-proof city.

They were a quiet couple and neither was a member of any political organization or civil rights pressure group. They were shy, even described as "painfully" so by civil rights lawyer Phil Hirschkop, and they were not motivated by broad political principles so much as a simple desire to live as man and wife and bring up their three children in Caroline County, Virginia, rather than in Washington, DC, or anywhere else.

While they struggled to adapt to life in the big city, the issue of bans on interracial marriages was fermenting at the state level. It expanded to include a host of other legal matters from child custodianship to inheritance. The states can be broken down into four groups, namely those that had never had such bans[1]; those that had tried them but abandoned them before the Loving case blew up in 1958[2]; those that repealed them after 1958 but before Loving vs. Virginia was finally decided by a Supreme Court ruling in 1967[3]; and 16 states that still enforced them at that point.[4]

It was a legal minefield as not only did different states have different definitions of the different races but also different rules as to what was legal and what was not. A handful of states just counted Negroes as non-white, while Georgia, for example, prohibited marriage with anyone of "ascertainable blood" from a whole list of races.

There were also different enforcement policies in different states. A lenient interpretation of the same ban in one state could easily be strictly enforced elsewhere. Penalties varied from a fine of a few hundred dollars to up to ten years in prison.

Mildred was better educated than her husband, having finished eleventh grade to Richard's ninth grade. She also followed politics, the dominant industry in her new hometown, quite closely. As the Civil Rights Bill was being debated

---

1 Alaska, Hawaii, Wisconsin, Minnesota, New York, New Jersey, Connecticut, New Hampshire and Vermont.
2 Maine, Massachusetts, Rhode Island, Pennsylvania, Ohio, Michigan, Illinois, Iowa, the Dakotas, Montana, Kansas, Colorado, New Mexico, California, Oregon and Washington.
3 Maryland, Indiana, Nebraska, Wyoming, Idaho, Nevada, Utah and Arizona.
4 West Virginia, Maryland, Missouri, Kentucky, Texas, Virginia and ten other southern states.

she wrote from their home in Washington DC to Attorney General Robert F. Kennedy in the late spring of 1963, asking if the new legislation, which would the following year become the Civil Rights Act, might at least allow the Lovings to visit family in Virginia together or, ideally, permit them to go back home permanently. He replied that the Bill would not cover their circumstances and referred her to the American Civil Liberties Union (ACLU).

On June 20, 1963, Mildred followed Kennedy's advice and wrote a letter to the ACLU. She laid out the facts of her marriage in DC as a "part Negro and part Indian" to a "white," the couple's return to Virginia, the threat of prison and their banishment. She explained simply that she accepted the need for them to be in exile but expressed a wish to visit friends and family as a family. She also detailed their lack of funds to pay attorneys.

Interestingly, in the letter she asks only for the right to "go back once and awhile [sic] to visit our families and friends" rather than for the total overhaul of the ban on interracial marriages. Her letter was immediately referred to local attorney Bernie Cohen, a volunteer ACLU lawyer, and the journey along the road to the Supreme Court had started.

Cohen was not a civil rights specialist and doubted his ability to succeed, but he could see how important the case was and took it on. He needed to find a way to get the Loving case back to court. After several months he hit on the solution. Because the Lovings' 25-year suspended sentence was still ongoing, the case was not governed by the usual 120-day rule for appeals against criminal conviction. Rather the case was still "in the breast of the court." On November 6, 1963, he kicked off with an appeal against the Loving verdict, claiming that the sentence was cruel and unusual punishment because it exceeded a reasonable period of time. But as well as causing undue hardship to Mildred and Richard, banishment also affected interstate commerce. Crucially, he also argued that banishment was a violation of the due process of law and was clearly improper because it was based on a statute that broke the Fourteenth Amendment. It must therefore be unconstitutional, he maintained.

The Fourteenth Amendment to the Constitution was one of the Reconstruction or Civil War Amendments adopted between 1865 and 1870. It gave citizenship to black people and overturned the Dred Scott ruling of 1857 that had deprived them of such rights. Its due process clause protected private contracts and outlawed some social and economic regulation. Its equal protection clause did some good by laying down that no state could deny people equal protection under its laws before metamorphosing into "the separate but equal" doctrine. This was used by segregationists to justify keeping whites and blacks apart provided the latter were treated equally in a public context, for example school funding resources.

Section 1 of the Fourteenth Amendment reads as follows:

[all] persons born... in the United States... are citizens of the United States and of the State wherein they reside. No State shall make or enforce any law which shall abridge the privileges or immunities of citizens of the United States; nor shall any State deprive any person of life, liberty, or property, without due process of law; nor deny to any person within its jurisdiction the equal protection of the laws.

Bazile took the case under advisement but the months dragged by. Every time Cohen called he was fobbed off by a court official who would tell him that the judge was still thinking through the issues. He was clearly obfuscating.

By the first anniversary of her letters to Kennedy and the ACLU, Mildred Loving penned a letter to Cohen. "Hope that you remember us," she wrote. "You took our case. We haven't heard anything from you for so long we had given up hope."

Cohen knew he had to try a different tack. Stonewalled by Bazile, he decided to consult his former Georgetown professor Chester Antieu. At the very same time as he went to see Antieu, another former pupil and civil rights lawyer, Phil Hirschkop, had also dropped by. It was a fortuitous meeting. Cohen laid out his problem on the faculty lounge coffee table and Hirschkop solved it. He told Cohen to file a "2283 motion" asking for a panel of three federal judges to review why his request was stuck in Bazile's lower court. Cohen did so and the pair went on to work on the case in tandem. (Unfortunately, the 1996 movie *Mr. and Mrs. Loving* featured Cohen but made no mention of Hirschkop, which led to an irrevocable split.)

So Cohen and Hirschkop sought federal intervention. At the same time the Commonwealth of Virginia became involved, asking that Cohen's appeal be reviewed by the Virginia Appellate Court. Cohen and Hirschkop countered this by claiming that such a move was a waste of time as that court had made its position known many times.

In the fall of 1964, Hirschkop and Virginia Attorney General Robert McIlwaine agreed an off-the-record truce regarding the place of residence for the Loving family. The Lovings were to be allowed to move back to Virginia, to King and Queen County just a few miles south-east of Caroline county. The Attorney General agreed to leave them in peace there so long as no political pressure to rearrest them grew; and if such pressure did begin to surface he promised the Lovings a grace period of seven days to flee north again. Clearly, senior attorneys now knew which way the wind was blowing.

Initially, there were some small commotions and a cross-burning but the Lovings soon immersed themselves back in rural Virginia. The closest they came to a legal confrontation was when their eldest child Sidney started school in neighboring Essex County. The prosecutor there knew exactly who Sidney was and threatened to arrest Mildred and Richard should they ever cross into his jurisdiction.

Mildred was delighted to be out of the city and in the country where there was lots of land for her children to play. She made sure to keep her DC address just in case they had to flee, and Richard commuted back north to the DC metropolitan area daily for his $5-an-hour (today equivalent to $40) job. But the legal establishment could sense the likely route of the case and the final outcome. It was suddenly agreed that if any prosecutor went after the Lovings, then a reasonable bail would be set immediately as long as the matter was before the state courts "and in the Supreme Court, if and when the case should be carried there."

The three-judge panel now gave the state 90 days to decide on Cohen's appeal or, in the absence of such a decision, the matter would move to the federal courts. On the one hand there was lingering sensitivity to the rights of states to decide such matters; on the other there was concern about the 25-year-long threat of prison hanging over the Lovings and their right to a speedy decision on their appeal.

On the eighty-ninth day Bazile ruled against all of Cohen's claims. Cohen and Hirschkop immediately appealed on the grounds that the Judge had erred on the Fourteenth Amendment, had erred on due process and had erred on reasonableness. They both knew that the appeal to the Virginia Supreme Court was purely academic. They would lose, but that would keep them on the road to the highest court in the land, the Supreme Court. And they did lose; but all the while the Lovings could lead the quiet undisturbed life they craved. In rural Virginia, with no telephone, they were almost immune from attack. Their attorneys, however, received hate mail, vindictive late night calls, vilification in the white supremacist press, and sugar in their autos' gas tanks.

Cohen and Hirschkop appealed to the Supreme Court on May 31, 1966. The story began to make the news and other attorneys emerged to join and strengthen their team. The main basis for appeal was the Fourteenth Amendment, and when one of their team delivered the appeal to a clerk of the Supreme Court (quite possibly Benno C. Schmidt Jr., later President of Yale and more recently an important figure in education reform), he was greeted with the words: "We have been waiting for this one." Just over six months later the Supreme Court voted unanimously that it had probable jurisdiction in the matter.

With the Cohen and Hirschkop team strengthened and the case now at the Supreme Court, the ACLU nationally began to fund it. And amicus briefs — legal arguments from ethnic groups such as Jews and Native Americans not directly involved in the action — began to appear. The Presbyterians, Catholics, and Unitarians all took a pro-Loving stand.

The brief to the Supreme Court ends with a passionate plea: "The time has come to strike down these laws; they are legalized racial prejudice, unsupported by reason or morals, and should not exist in a good society."

The case was argued before the Justices on April 10, 1967, and on June 12, 1967, they found unanimously in favor of the Lovings and against Virginia. Chief Justice Earl Warren had assigned the case to himself (although Benno did all the hard work) and based his judgment mostly on the Fourteenth Amendment, finishing with these words:

> To deny this fundamental freedom on so unsupportable basis as the racial classifications embodied in these statutes, classifications so directly subversive of the principle of equality at the heart of the Fourteenth Amendment, is surely to deprive all the State's citizens of liberty without due process of law. The Fourteenth Amendment requires that the freedom of choice to marry not be restricted by invidious racial discriminations. Under our Constitution, the freedom to marry, or not marry, a person of another race resides with the individual and cannot be infringed by the State.

Mildred and Richard declined their right to public seats in the Supreme Court and it is said they never read the entire judgment. They did however attend the post-judgment press conference; Mildred was well aware that, in initiating an action that had turned into a cause célèbre, interracial couples would never again be subject to the senseless persecution that she and her husband had endured.

"I feel free now," Mildred said. She added: "This has been a great burden to us but I was always sure the Supreme Court would go our way." Richard declared: "If they had not gone our way then we would have waited for five years and tried again."

In the end the whole matter had unfolded very rapidly. Founder and President/CEO of the Institute for Justice, William H. Mellor comments: "The speed of judicial review can sometimes reflect what the Justices believe to be the social urgency of a case."

After June 12, 1967, some states such as West Virginia moved very quickly to comply with Loving vs. Virginia while others in the deep South dragged their heels and it often took repeated threats by attorneys to force petty bureaucrats to comply. Within the US Army a Judge Advocate General (JAG) officer flew around the South confronting local officials when interracial couples were refused permission to marry. It was not until the year 2000 that Alabama repealed its long unenforceable law by a referendum. Sixty per cent of the voting public came out in favor of repeal.

Mildred and Richard finally moved back into Caroline County, building a house close to both sets of parents on, of all places, Passing Road. Richard was killed in 1975 by a drunk driver in an accident that cost Mildred her right eye. He was laid to rest in a mostly black burial ground and his son Donald was buried next to him when he died unexpectedly in 1994. Mildred lived a further 33 years after her husband, before passing on from pneumonia on May 2, 2008.

To some, Mildred simply caught the wave of the times. To others she is as important and as brave as Rosa Parks. Her shyness and humility have led history almost to overlook or to downplay her key role in making such a huge difference. But, crucially, she refused to accept the law as it stood, contacting the ACLU and sticking with her plan of attack for four long years. She once said she felt that she and Richard had been put on Earth to marry and change the law.

A recent HBO documentary *The Loving Story* makes it more than clear that Mildred and Richard knew exactly what this was all about. The contemporary footage shown of them discussing the issues and principle involved is inspiring and undermines even dispels the myths perpetuated about them heretofore.

Not long before she died she commented: "We weren't bothering anyone, and if we hurt some people's feelings that was just too bad. All we ever wanted to do was get married because we loved one another. Some people will never change, but that's their problem, not mine. I married the only man I ever loved, and I'm happy for the time we had together. For me, that was enough."

Mildred Loving is a true lady for liberty — one of the best.

Afterword

As I finished writing the stories of my "Ladies for Liberty," word about this book spread and I began to receive speaking invitations to address this theme. Typically, I spoke a little about all of them; then I explored three to five in depth, and finally drew out some lessons.

Here are the ten lessons I gave to the staff of the Liberty Fund on September 8, 2010, at its headquarters in Indianapolis, Indiana.

1. I am puzzled by the temperance movement, which hardly ever appears in my text (my choice); but all the ladies of the mid to late 19th century are pro-temperance while all the ladies of the mid 20th century such as Paterson, Luce and Rand voted for FDR in 1932 solely because he pledged to end Prohibition. I think the answer is rooted in property rights. The married ladies circa 1850 had no such rights and could not stop a wayward husband from drinking away their shared fortune; the ladies of circa 1930 had far more rights and were appalled by the crimes induced by Prohibition.

2. The pattern of education of these women is very erratic, to put it mildly, and the word "bored" appeared repeatedly in my research. In the Revolutionary era, the tutors of the brothers did the job to some extent. Truth and Tubman were illiterate while Madam CJ Walker made great strides at self improvement as an adult. Cady Stanton benefited from family libraries and interface with the men in her father's law office before several years of school. Beecher Stowe's much older sister ran a school, so she benefited there. Bina West was one of a very few to enjoy a stable straightforward education with a large home library. Rose Wilder Lane's education was erratic and she was bored. Isabel Paterson attended for a month, aged seven, and two years, aged say

0875868649

bar

11 and 12, but hid in a corner and pursued her own reading. Lila Bell Wallace survived regular family moves and graduated college. Vivien Kellems was on course for a PhD but never finished; likewise Rose Friedman. Taylor Caldwell was bored and wrote stories, leaving school at 15 to work while going to night school. Clare Boothe Luce was largely home schooled until 8th grade when her dad left home. Rand was another bored student, as was Jane Jacobs; the former scribbled stories while the latter read books hidden in her lap. Jane refused college while Dorian went but never graduated. Two thoughts occur to me: one is the old adage that the hardest pupil to keep engaged in class is the brightest, and the other is the quote from Southern California newspaper entrepreneur R C Hoiles, who said to Isabel Paterson, "You were lucky not to get a public school education."

3. It is interesting to note how often upstate New York appears in these stories. Harriet Tubman, Sojourner Truth and Elizabeth Cady Stanton were all there at times; so were other ladies such as Lucretia Mott, Harriet Bloomer and Susan B Anthony. On the male side, William H. Seward who lost the Republican nomination to Lincoln, Gerritt Smith of the Secret Six, and Theodore Weld who married Angelina Grimké, were there too. In *Going Rogue — An American Life*, Sarah Palin details how she was invited in the summer of 2009 to go to the Finger Lakes region to join a celebration of Seward's life (it was he, of course, who purchased Alaska from Russia when he was Secretary of State, hence the sobriquet of "Seward's Folly"). Palin notes, "It was inspiring to see the historically rich region, home to heroic figures I had read so much about, including Elizabeth Cady Stanton, Susan B Anthony, and Harriet Tubman."

4. Likewise, the Quakers pop up in key roles in several stories, from the Grimké sisters through Harriet Tubman to Sojourner Truth.

5. And there were personal and family connections galore, from Mercy and Abigail to Martha and Abigail; Mercy and Rose Wilder Lane were distant cousins, as were Abigail and husband John; Cady Stanton and Gerritt Smith were close first cousins; John Adams claimed (not proven) that his wife Abigail (née Smith) was a cousin of Theodore Weld's wife's mother Mary Grimké (née Smith); Harriet Beecher Stowe's father, Lyman Beecher, taught the husbands of both Elizabeth Cady and Angelina Grimké; and Rose Wilder Lane, Isabel, Clare and Ayn lunched together.

6. There is a surprising amount of violence in these stories, in particular in the build up to the Civil War. I came to the conclusion that a lot of this violence was engendered not by the topic of abolition as such but because some men were disturbed at the sight of women speaking in public and to audiences that were of mixed gender and mixed race too. This, much more than the topic itself, agitated them greatly.

7. These ladies both advocated and practiced what they preached. Isabel Paterson (not at all well off) refused social security because it was a "Ponzi" scheme. She also stopped voting in 1940. Harriet Tubman

would not go with Sojourner Truth to visit with Lincoln while Negro regiments got half the pay of their white counterparts. They were mostly plumb line ladies.

8. They were often great strategists, too. The Grimké sisters were terrific at segmenting their market and tailoring their message accordingly. The patriots ran great boycotts of British goods and the abolitionists likewise with slave produced goods. The Kansas Aid movement to persuade New Englanders to relocate to that mid-west state is another example.

9. As in all life, there were extraordinary cases of serendipity. Two stand out for me. The first is that Elizabeth Cady Stanton ended up living close to Lucretia Mott, with Harriet Bloomer down the road, who then brought in her friend Susan B Anthony. The second is the marriage of Jane Jacobs to an architect whose subscription to *Architectural Forum* went to their home, not his office, thus setting off a huge domino effect.

10. Finally there are the huge amounts of raw courage shown again and again. Mercy was guilty of sedition and Martha risked her life running the winter camps for George. Abigail's letters to her husband could have led to charges of spying and the Grimké sisters were mobbed at times. Tubman's journeys on the railroad and Truth's facing down mobs, eggs and stone throwers are inspiring. Stowe's hate mail; Stanton's, West Miller's, and C J Walker's travels in quite hostile areas at times for women alone; the childhoods of Laura, Rose Wilder Lane and Isabel; Lila Bell's determination; Vivien's battle with the IRS; Taylor's five years in the backwoods of Kentucky; Clare's war reporting and later facing down Italian communists; Ayn and Rose Friedman escaping Russia; Jane's fights with huge NYC vested interests and Dorian's think tanks, at least two of which were bombed... There's a phenomenal amount of courage and determination in these women.

Ten Matters for Discussion

1. In Chapters 2 through 4, the attitudes of Mercy Otis Warren, Martha Washington and Abigail Adams towards their husbands and their careers differ sharply. Discuss.

2. Chapters 5 through 8 and 10 all focused in different ways on the abolition of slavery. Discuss how the women involved set about their common mission. What would they do today if faced with similar injustice?

3. Bina West Miller and Madam C J Walker both tried to empower women in the economic sphere. Of the two, which teaches us more for today?

4. Would Vivien Kellems and Dorian Fisher have wholeheartedly agreed or totally disagreed over strategy for social change?

5. If you could go back in history and observe just one event mentioned in this book, which one would you choose and why?

6. The formal education of these women ranges from close to zero to PhD level, and many of them reported being thoroughly bored in grade school. Does this surprise you, or is the old adage true namely that the hardest child to keep engaged in class is the brightest?

7. All of the characters in *Ladies for Liberty* have passed on; their achievements are complete. If you were to write a book on such women who are alive today, who would you list and why, in the USA and elsewhere?

8. Is there a distinction to be made between the stories of the women who were married to famous men (e.g., Martha Washington and Rose Friedman) and those who were single, long divorced or married to less well-known men? If so, what kind of distinction can be drawn?

9. To what extent would these women approve of the modern concept of feminism?

10. Imagine Mercy Otis Warren, Martha Washington and Abigail Adams met for lunch. Also imagine Clare Boothe Luce, Ayn Rand, Isabel Paterson and Rose Wilder Lane met for lunch. The former could easily have happened — the latter definitely did happen. At which lunch would you prefer to be a guest and why?

Further Reading

I am not a scholar, although I am very careful about every word I write. I am more a distiller, an ideologue, and one who popularizes; and I hope you all share my unabashed and uncritical (mostly) enthusiasm for my Ladies for Liberty and their friends, colleagues and associates. I have not by any means read every book by and about them, but below I mention several works which I think are of particular merit. We range from feast to famine here, as in some cases — such as Martha Washington, Abigail Adams and Ayn Rand — there is a vast literature, whereas in other cases such as Bina West Miller, Vivien Kellems and Taylor Caldwell, not very much at all comes to hand. All three would make great subjects for future researchers.

If you want to learn more about these 20 women who made such a difference in American history here is what I suggest.

For the Revolutionary era, I particularly recommend two books by Cokie Roberts: *Founding Mothers: The Women Who Raised Our Nation* (2004), and *Ladies of Liberty: The Women Who Shaped Our Nation* (2008).

Mercy Otis Warren's *History of the Rise, Progress and Termination of the American Revolution*, edited and annotated by Lester H. Cohen, is available in a splendidly produced set from Liberty Press of Indianapolis, Indiana; her plays, pretty hard going for a modern audience, are published by Dodo Press; biographies include *The Muse of the Revolution: The Secret Pen of Mercy Otis Warren and The Founding of a Nation* by Nancy Rubin Stuart; *A Woman's Dilemma: Mercy Otis Warren and the American Revolution* by Rosemarie Zagarri; and *Mercy Otis Warren* by Jeffrey H. Richards.

For information on Martha Washington, it is hard to beat *Martha Washington an American Life* by Patricia Brady. For Abigail Adams, Woody Holton's *Abigail Adams* along with David McCullough's *John Adams* and Robert V. Remini's *John Quincy Adams* are excellent.

There are many books on the Grimkés, from *The Grimké Sisters* by Catherine H. Birney (1885) through the short but entertaining 1972 novel, *Turning the World Upside Down* by William and Patricia Willimon, and *Lift Up Thy Voice: The Grimké Family's Journey from Slaveholders to Civil Rights Leaders* by Mark Perry (2001).

Sojourner Truth's own *Narrative* is a good place to start but not easy going; *Sojourner Truth: Slave, Prophet, Legend* by Carleton Mabee with Susan Mabee Newhouse is a much easier read.

Elizabeth Cady Stanton wrote an autobiography, *Eighty Years & More: Reminiscences 1815–1897*, and Elisabeth Griffith has provided a useful biography, *In Her Own Right: The Life of Elizabeth Cady Stanton*.

On Harriet Tubman, there are two recent books: the serious, scholarly, but accessible *Harriet Tubman: The Life and the Life Stories* by Jean M. Humez (2003) and the even more readable and nicely illustrated *Harriet Tubman: Imagining a Life* (2007) by Beverly Lowry.

For Harriet Beecher Stowe, the starting point has to be one of the many editions of *Uncle Tom's Cabin*, some of which come with excellent notes and introductions. For background see *The Beecher Sisters* by Barbara A. White, published by Yale University Press in 2003 which covers the whole family for over a century.

Bina West Miller has yet to find her biographer but the company she founded published a centennial corporate history in 1992 entitled *An Enduring Heritage*, by Keith L. Yates, which is still available. While lavishly illustrated, it is a pedestrian read.

A'Lelia Bundles wrote an excellent biography of her great, great grandmother Madam C.J. Walker. Published in 2001, it is called *On her Own Ground: The Life and Times of Madam C.J. Walker*.

For Laura Ingalls Wilder and Rose Wilder Lane, you cannot beat *The Ghost in the Little House: A Life of Rose Wilder Lane* by William Holtz; and there are of course all of the "Little House" novels, Rose's own novels, as well as her *The Discovery of Freedom: Man's Struggle Against Authority* and the separately printed *Islam and the Discovery of Freedom*.

Isabel Paterson's *The God of the Machine* is available from Transactions Publishers with an introduction by Stephen Cox which he later developed into a very well-done biography, *The Woman and the Dynamo: Isabel Paterson and the Idea of America*. I do not recommend any of her novels to today's readers.

John Heidenry's *Theirs Was the Kingdom: Lila and de Witt Wallace & The Story of the Reader's Digest* is a good critical account while Vivien Kellems retells her battle with the IRS in *Toil, Taxes and Trouble*.

My favorite Taylor Caldwell novels are all mentioned in her chapter but there are, of course, many, many more. She too, like Bina West Miller and Vivien Kellems, has yet to attract a full-blown biography, but her co-author in her later years, Jess Stearn, wrote a short book entitled *In Search of Taylor Caldwell* based on a series of conversations with her. The closest Caldwell came to writing an autobiography was a little collection of essays *On Growing Up Tough*, the best part of which is the truly haunting painting of her on the cover, aged 20 and holding her first-born on her right hip, standing next to her oil-prospecting husband in front of their tent in the wilds of Kentucky.

In 1997 Random House, New York, published a fabulous biography *Rage for Fame: The Ascent of Clare Boothe Luce* by Sylvia Jukes Morris — unfortunately it stops halfway through her life! For a full account see *Clare Boothe Luce* by Stephen Shadegg.

When people ask me about Ayn Rand's books, I always suggest a start with the too often overlooked novella *Anthem* and the play *Night of January 16th*, before moving on to her big novels in chronological order from *We the Living*, through *The Fountainhead* to *Atlas Shrugged*; likewise her philosophical works are best read in chronological order. On the biography front, Jeff Britting's 2004 *Ayn Rand* is a beautifully illustrated and meticulous piece of work — he was also associate producer of the documentary film *Ayn Rand: A Sense of Life* which received a nomination for an Academy Award. In 2009, we saw the publication of two very serious biographies, namely, *Goddess of the Market: Ayn Rand and the American Right* by Jennifer Burns and *Ayn Rand and the World She Made* by Anne C. Heller.

For Rose Friedman, I suggest *Capitalism and Freedom* followed by *Free to Choose* and *Tyranny of the Status Quo*. There is also *Two Lucky People: Memoirs*, by Milton and Rose; it's a door stopper of mega proportions, but packed with informative personal anecdotes.

In addition to Jane Jacobs' oeuvre, all of which is mentioned in her chapter, there have been two recent biographies, *Jane Jacobs: Urban Visionary* by Alice Sparberg Alexion and *Wrestling with Moses: How Jane Jacobs Took On New York's Master Builder and Transformed the American City* by Anthony Flint. Recently a volume of 35 essays was published entitled *What We See: Advancing the Observations of Jane Jacobs*, edited by Stephen A Goldsmith and Lynne Elizabeth — see the third chapter in section 1, *The Mirage of the Efficient City*, by Sanford Ikeda, which is very insightful and particularly well done. There is also *The Power Broker: Robert Moses and the Fall of New York* by Robert A Caro.

Finally, for Dorian Fisher, see *The Woman Who Made Atlas Possible* by Linda Whetstone, elder daughter of Sir Antony Fisher, published as an appendix to the condensed version of *Antony Fisher: Champion of Liberty* from NCPA in Dallas, Texas.

FURTHER READING FOR ADDITIONAL CHAPTERS

By far the best book on Anne Hutchinson is *American Jezebel: The Uncommon Life of the Woman Who Defied the Puritans* (2004) by Eve LaPlante who is descended from her subject. Also see *The Times and Trials of Anne Hutchinson: Puritans Divided* (2005) by Michael P. Winship and his *The Trial of Anne Hutchinson: Liberty, Law, and Intolerance in Puritan New England* (2005) co-authored with Mark C Carnes.

Clara Barton: Professional Angel (1987) by Elizabeth Brown Pryor is excellent, as is a much shorter profile by Martin Morse Wooster in his *By Their Bootstraps: The Lives of Twelve Gilded-Age Social Entrepreneurs* (2002).

For Alice Paul you cannot do better than to read *A Woman's Crusade: Alice Paul and the Battle for the Ballot* (2010) by Mary Walton, along with *Alice Paul and the American Suffrage Campaign* (2008) by Katherine H. Adams and Michael L Keene.

Hilary Swank played Alice Paul in the 2004 movie *Iron Jawed Angels* with Frances O'Connor, Julia Ormond, and Angelica Huston also starring. It is a movie, not a documentary, but captures a lot of the atmosphere of those times.

With Jim Haskins, Rosa Parks wrote *Rosa Parks: My Story* (1992) which is brief and well-illustrated. *Rosa Parks: A Life* (2000) by Douglas Brinkley is authoritative and scholarly yet well-written and accessible. Finally, for younger and older readers, *Rosa Parks: Courageous Citizen* (2008) by Ruth Ashby is a full color production packed with photos and illustrations. In 2002, Angela Bassett played Rosa in *The Rosa Parks Story*. Again, it is a movie, but it does stick very closely to the actual story with only the occasional departure for dramatic purposes. However, it ends halfway, while the boycott is still on and the Supreme Court has yet to decide.

Mildred Loving has also attracted film makers with the movie *Mr. and Mrs. Loving*, starring Lela Rochon and Timothy Hutton (1996), while HBO produced a stunning documentary, *The Loving Story* (2012). The former takes a few liberties for dramatic purposes while the latter uses a lot of original material to superb effect. Phyl Newbeck's *Virginia Hasn't Always Been for Lovers — Interracial Marriage Bans and the Case of Richard and Mildred Loving* (2004) is a must read while *Loving v. Virginia: Interracial Marriage* (2000) by Karen Alonso is a quick read.

Acknowledgements

When I read books, I always check the acknowledgements carefully and I am often surprised at how many names are listed. But writing a book is very much a team effort and even with this comparatively short volume, many people helped.

First, a very big thank-you goes to James Lowry Blundell, younger son, for prompting the original idea for this book; and to Colleen Dyble and Yiqiao Xu, then both at the Atlas Economic Research Foundation, for their early enthusiasm when I tested the theme on them.

As the work progressed, I received many forms of support and assistance. I thank the following:

Professor David T. Beito (University of Alabama); David Boaz (Cato Institute); Dr Tom G. Palmer (Atlas Economic Research Foundation); and Marty Zupan (Institute for Humane Studies at George Mason University), for early advice;

Christine V Blundell, Ellen B. Corman, and Susannah M. Hickling for research and editorial help;

Meg and Maria Allen and Dan and Pete Peters for enthusiastic support. Pete in particular encouraged my inclusion of Abigail Adams but passed on in late 2010 before publication;

Whitney Ball (Donors Trust), Dr. Ingrid Ann Gregg (Earhart Foundation), Andrea M. Rich (Center for Independent Thought); and Dr. Sarah Skwire and Amy Willis (both at Liberty Fund), modern-day "ladies for liberty" who cheered on the whole project;

Professor Leonard P. Liggio of George Mason University for reading the entire manuscript and for making many helpful and always highly nuanced suggestions. Leonard has been my number one mentor for 37 years now. Thanks also to Walter E. Grinder, in particular for deepening my understanding of Taylor Caldwell's contribution, but also for many other very valuable suggestions;

Professor Don Boudreaux (George Mason University); William H. Mellor Esquire (Institute for Justice); Kira M. Newman (American Enterprise Institute); Professor Lawrence H. White (George Mason University); Eben Wilson (Main Communications); and Professor Todd Zywicki (George Mason University), for answering questions and/or reading individual chapters;

Christie Russell of Paris, Illinois for solving several genealogical problems; and finally

The Heritage Foundation in Washington, DC, under whose umbrella I wrote this book. In particular I thank Dr Edwin J. Feulner Jr. (President); Dr Matthew Spalding (Vice President and Director, B. Kenneth Simon Center for American Studies); and Phillip N. Truluck (Executive Vice President).

Obviously, the usual disclaimer applies.

FURTHER ACKNOWLEDGEMENTS FOR SECOND EXPANDED EDITION

I thank Christie Russell of Paris, Illinois for unfailing enthusiasm for this project.

Professor David Beito (University of Alabama), David Boaz (Cato Institute), Dr Tom G Palmer (Atlas Economic Research Foundation), Andrea Rich (Center for Independent Thought), and Professor Lawrence H. White (George Mason University) all helped me with the selection of these outstanding characters.

Christine V Blundell and Susannah M. Hickling again provided research and editorial help and both Professor Leonard P. Liggio (George Mason University) and Walter E. Grinder again read early drafts of all five new chapters and provided valuable input.

Maria Allen, Meg Allen, Dan Peters, and James Whitaker have been great supporters as have the senior officers of The Heritage Foundation, Washington, DC listed above under whose rubric I wrote both editions as a Visiting Fellow.

Finally, I thank the staff of Algora Publishing, New York for their help with both this book and my earlier book Margaret Thatcher: A Portrait of the Iron Lady (2008).

Again, the usual disclaimer applies.

INDEX

A

Acheson, Barclay, 130-131
Acheson, Lila Bell (see Lila Acheson Wallace)
Adams, Abigail, 2, 5, 16, 19, 22, 28, 31-37, 61, 64, 216, 219-222, 227
Adams, John (Entrepreneur), 15-22, 26, 28, 31-37, 47, 61, 84, 203, 216, 222
Adams, John (President), 15-22, 26, 28, 31-37, 47, 61, 84, 203, 216, 222
Adams, John Quincy, 22, 31, 33, 35-37, 47, 61, 222
Adams, Samuel, 16, 18-21, 34
Adams Charles Francis Sr., 35, 61
Agnew, Spiro, 107
Ahmad, Imad-ad-Dean Dr., 106
Anderson, Martin, 192
Anderson, Terry, 119
Andre, Karen, 163
Andrew, John, 83
Anthony, Susan Brownell, 5, 66-68, 110, 116, 216-217
Antieu, Chester, 210
Arden, Elizabeth, 98
Arnold, Colonel Benedict, 64
Arthur, Vice-President Chester A, 76
Ashmore, Harry, 168
Austin, Albert E, 154

B

Barton, Clara, 7, 71-73, 75-77, 225
Barton, Clarissa Harlowe, 71-72
Baruch, Bernard, 155
Baumfree, Isabella (see Sojourner Truth)
Bazile, Leon M, 207, 210-211
Beazely, Frank, 207-208
Becker, Gary, 172
Beecher, Catherine Esther, 59
Beecher, Harriet (see Harriet Beecher Stowe), 47, 54-55, 57-61, 82, 216, 222
Beecher, Lyman, 57-58, 216
Beito, David T, 106, 227, 229
Beito, Linda Royster, 106
Belmont, Alva, 154
Bening, Annette, 155
Bennett, RB, 120
Bergen, Candice, 155
Blake, James, 185-186
Boaz, David, 108, 227, 229
Boothe, William Franklin, 134, 153
Boudreaux, Don, 174, 228
Bowler, Francis, 119
Bowler, Isabel Mary (see Isabel Paterson)
Boynton, Major Nathan S, 89
Brady, Dorothy, 173
Branden, Nathaniel, 169
Breedlove, Lucy Crockett, 95
Breedlove, Sarah (see Madam CJ Walker)
Bright, John, 69
Broderick, Matthew, 73, 84
Brodess, Edward, 79-80